T0383694

# MOLDING
## the
# MEDIUM

## Studies on Contemporary China

THE POLITICAL ECONOMY OF CHINA'S
SPECIAL ECONOMIC ZONES
*George T. Crane*

WORLDS APART
RECENT CHINESE WRITING AND ITS AUDIENCES
*Howard Goldblatt, editor*

CHINESE URBAN REFORM
WHAT MODEL NOW?
*R. Yin-Wang Kwok, William L. Parish, and Anthony Gar-On Yeh
with Xu Xueqiang, editors*

REBELLION AND FACTIONALISM IN A CHINESE PROVINCE
ZHEJIANG, 1966–1976
*Keith Forster*

POLITICS AT MAO'S COURT
GAO GANG AND PARTY FACTIONALISM
IN THE EARLY 1950s
*Frederick C. Teiwes*

THE MAKING OF A SINO-MARXIST WORLD VIEW
PERCEPTIONS AND INTERPRETATIONS
OF WORLD HISTORY
IN THE PEOPLE'S REPUBLIC OF CHINA
*Dorothea A. L. Martin*

MOLDING THE MEDIUM
THE CHINESE COMMUNIST PARTY
AND THE *LIBERATION DAILY*
*Patricia Stranahan*

Studies on Contemporary China

# MOLDING
# the
# MEDIUM

## The
## Chinese Communist Party
## and the
## *Liberation Daily*

## PATRICIA STRANAHAN

Routledge
Taylor & Francis Group

LONDON AND NEW YORK

First published 1990 by M.E. Sharpe

Published 2015 by Routledge
2 Park Square, Milton Park, Abingdon, Oxon OX14 4RN
711 Third Avenue, New York, NY, 10017, USA

*Routledge is an imprint of the Taylor & Francis Group, an informa business*

Notices
No responsibility is assumed by the publisher for any injury and/or damage to
persons or property as a matter of products liability, negligence or otherwise,
or from any use of operation of any methods, products, instructions or ideas
contained in the material herein.

Practitioners and researchers must always rely on their own experience and
knowledge in evaluating and using any information, methods, compounds, or
experiments described herein. In using such information or methods they should
be mindful of their own safety and the safety of others, including parties for
whom they have a professional responsibility.

Product or corporate names may be trademarks or registered trademarks, and
are used only for identification and explanation without intent to infringe.

**Library of Congress Cataloging-in-Publication Data**

Stranahan, Patricia.
    Molding the medium: the Chinese Communist Party and the
Liberation daily / Patricia Stranahan.
        p.    cm.—(Studies on contemporary China)
    Includes bibliographical references.
    ISBN 0-87332-662-8
    1. Chieh fang jih pao (Yen-shih, China) 2. Chung-kuo kung ch'an
tang. 3. China—Politics and government—1976– 4. Government and
the press—China. I. Title. II. Series.
PN5369.Y463C488    1990
079′.5118—dc20                                                    90-8385
                                                                      CIP

ISBN 13: 9780873326629 (hbk)

The role and power of the newspapers consists in their ability to bring the Party program, the Party line, the Party's general and specific policies, its tasks and methods of work before the masses in the quickest and most extensive way.

Mao Zedong

# Contents

# Acknowledgments

I often think that I will be best remembered in the field as the historian who read every issue of the *Liberation Daily*. That is no mean feat because, for the most part, I did not have access to the originals at the Hoover Institution and worked from microfilm. Lest the reader pities me, I want it to be known that the years I have spent reading the *Liberation Daily* have been pure pleasure. In my mind, there is no better source of Communist Party history for the period than that four page newspaper from the Shaan-Gan-Ning Border Region. The articles in it opened a whole new world to me. They showed me how the Communist Party worked during its growth years and how it adapted to its environment. Moreover, more any other source I have ever read, it introduced me into the world of the Chinese peasant. I learned how they lived and how they viewed their world. Equally important, I understood better than ever before how these impoverished people fit into the Communist Party's scheme of things.

This study began as a research note intended to introduce other scholars to a rich and vital source. Like Topsy, it has grown. When I accumulated more materials than were reasonable for a journal article, I decided to write a short monograph on the *Liberation Daily* as a research tool. In 1986, however, while researching another project in Shanghai, I came across a series of analyses of the *Liberation Daily* in a Chinese journal that made me reevaluate my project and look at it from a political point of view. Although a survey of the newspaper's contents remained a crucial part of the study, I now turned to questions of inner-Party struggle and the role of propaganda in it. Influenced by research being done elsewhere in the field and my own interest in the evolution of Communist Party power, I rewrote my manuscript. What follows is an attempt not only to introduce the newspaper's contents to the researcher but also to examine the impact of this medium on the Communist Party from 1941 to 1947. In my opinion, it is an excellent example of the power of propaganda within a system.

Needless to say, the study has not evolved without considerable help. I received funding from the Naomi Lewis Fellowship, the College of Liberal Arts' Summer Research Stipend, and the International Enhancement Grant at Texas A&M University. Additional funding came from the National Endowment for the Humanities and the Stanford East Asia National Resource Center. The libraries of the University of Pennsylvania, Bryn Mawr College, Texas A&M University, Fudan University, the University of Washington, the Fairbank Center at Harvard University, and the Hoover Institute all opened their resources to me. Jill Houston provided invaluable help in word processing working valiantly through pages of romanization.

Most of all, I want to thank those who have taken time from their busy schedules to help me. Chris Gilmartin, always the loyal friend, provided her usual support throughout the project and took time from writing her own manuscript to interview a former *Liberation Daily* staff member. Peter Seybolt introduced me to new ideas and materials from his own extensive work on the Border Region. Jeff Wasserstrom came across a gold mine of materials for me in Shanghai while conducting his own research. Tim Cheek, in a flurry of letters between Colorado and Texas, debated issues of propaganda and power with me. It is to these colleagues—and good friends—that I dedicate this book with thanks.

# MOLDING
## the
# MEDIUM

# The Medium

News is any event that varies from what people view as normal. What readers believe about that event is shaped by those who control the news. By focusing on certain issues while ignoring others, these controllers are able to limit access to ideas and manipulate the truth to provoke action. In other words, they do more than paint a picture of reality—they construct it. Under their guidance, news becomes an ideology. And, because ideology is fundamental to social order, the bodies that create and promote it become essential social institutions.[1] No institution played a more important role in constructing the reality of the Chinese Communist Party during the 1940s than did the Central Committee's official newspaper, the *Liberation Daily* (*Jiefang ribao*). From its first edition on May 16, 1941, until its last on March 27, 1947, the newspaper served as the official mouthpiece of the Central Committee.

The 1940s were a critical time for the Communist Party. During those years, it devised and implemented the programs that would insure its ultimate victory in China. It was also the time when Mao Zedong and his faction asserted their dominance over Party and government. No publication reflected crucial issues and events and their impact better than the pages of the *Liberation Daily*.

It was the medium through which Party leaders gave direction to cadres who organized and implemented the Party's political line among the masses. Articles provided cadres with the information they needed to convince people that Party programs were not just feasible but were desirable. Only when the masses saw the value of trying something different would they accept the need for change. Part of the newspaper's responsibility, therefore, was to provide the guidelines for that acceptance. Through liberal use of examples, articles sought to prove that Party policies were attainable and that, when people followed them, those people prospered. Articles on labor heroes/heroines (beginning in the spring of 1942) and the Great Production Drive

(1943) provided such inspirational lessons. Through them, Party leaders believed the masses would come to accept the Communist Party as indispensable to achieving their true interests and adopt desired policies. In other words, they would become efficient and dedicated members of a Communist society.[2]

The *Liberation Daily* served in more than a "pedagogic-utilitarian" capacity, however.[3] It also constructed reality by reflecting the major concerns of a time when the Party was building its institutions and developing the body of economic and social programs that it would use throughout China after 1949. All major policy statements appeared in the newspaper, as did analysis of various campaigns and programs. Predominance was given to those issues of most concern to Party leaders. When they redefined their goals, so did the *Liberation Daily*. The best example of this is "rectification of styles" campaign, the study and reform movement beginning in early 1942, which formed part of a larger rectification movement. Like all units of the Party bureaucracy, the *Liberation Daily* underwent a thorough study of itself and made the requisite changes to conform to the new situation.[4] When the Maoists took control of the press, there was a clear change in content, style, and format.

More than simply a mouthpiece of the Central Committee, the *Liberation Daily* wielded power and influence in its own right. It shaped the events in its world as much as did its contemporary, Shanghai's powerful *L'Impartial* (*Dagong bao*), or today's *New York Times*. That power did not reside in a modern office building with a professionally trained staff of reporters and editors, however. Rather, the staff of the *Liberation Daily* was a diverse group of nonprofessional men and women. Primarily urban intellectuals, they might have been more at home on the moon than in the Shaan-Gan-Ning Border Region, that poverty-stricken area of Northwest China where the Central Committee had its headquarters between 1935 and 1947. Living in caves and facing such daunting problems as no paper, staff members managed to produce an invaluable record of the Chinese Communist Party for the 1940s.

## The *Liberation Daily* as a Major Newspaper

The adverse conditions under which the *Liberation Daily* was published did not mean that its structure and organization differed from that of major newspapers elsewhere. Consistency is essential in reporting the news. It comes about only when news organizations follow definite procedures to assess what is news, how it should be reported, and where it should be placed in the newspaper. The *Liberation Daily* followed such rules.

In any newspaper, editors meet daily to discuss events in order to determine what is newsworthy and what claims will be made on their resources. Even though those who control the press may determine its biases, editors of a newspaper "make news together."[5] The propaganda functions of the *Liberation Daily* are discussed below but it is important here to add that its editors were not as free to make news as their counterparts in today's American press, for example. News professionals in the United States claim to be independent of both ownership and management because they exercise the right to judge what the news is.[6] In the *Liberation Daily*, the editors exercised that right to a limited extent before the reform of 1942. After that, Communist Party leaders claimed the sole right to determine the news.

Bo Gu (the alias of Qin Bangxian) was the editor-in-chief of the *Liberation Daily* from 1941 until 1944.[7] Under his direction, the editors met daily to discuss the content of the day's edition. In the first year of its publication, *Liberation Daily* articles concentrated heavily on the war in Europe and only vaguely on Border Region affairs. Staff members and editors were part of the Party bureaucracy but received little guidance from above. That changed after the reform, when the Party tightened its control over the newspaper. Members of the Central Committee and Politburo took a more active role in the affairs of the *Liberation Daily*, with many contributing comments and editorials. All articles concerning the government and military were read by appropriate officials before publication. Articles focused less on international affairs and more on Border Region and local issues—areas where the Party had control. The new restrictions did not mean that the *Liberation Daily* lost its independence entirely. Although scattered, important articles appeared throughout the life of the newspaper that contradicted the accepted Party line.[8]

Like editors everywhere, the editors of the *Liberation Daily* had to know their audience in order to determine what was newsworthy. Who was that audience? The severe paper shortage in the Border Region and the high cost of publishing the newspaper prohibited individual subscriptions and limited its circulation. But even if paper had been plentiful, the *Liberation Daily* was never meant to be read by the general population. The Central Committee used the newspaper to communicate with people in official positions in all areas under its control. Through it, the leadership disseminated information to cadres who would, in turn, give that information to the masses. As a result, although information within the newspaper had to be sophisticated enough that top levels of the Party could exchange ideas and communicate complex viewpoints to lower levels, it could not be too sophisticated. Cadres came from all backgrounds. Some were revolutionaries of long standing; others were young intellectuals from urban areas joining forces with the Party not because of ideology but because it was fighting the Japanese; still others were peasants whose lives had never gone beyond their own villages.

Diversity of background and lack of ideological understanding aside, most cadres had a difficult time reading the *Liberation Daily* even with its limited vocabulary of 2,000–2,500 characters. Many of these men and women had only a rudimentary education, so directives from above had to be in language simple enough for them to comprehend and implement. Added to this restriction was a second and equally important problem: Cadres, whatever their education, worked with a backward and largely illiterate population. Nobody expected the mass of people to grasp the complexities of Marxism-Leninism, so Party leaders reduced policy goals to simple, easy-to-understand formulas that could be readily transmitted into action. One central task dominated each policy goal; realism counted, not dogmas and doctrines.

Once editors decided what was newsworthy, they dispersed their reporters. Before 1942, the limited staff of the newspaper rarely went out into the field and reported stories. Articles on international and national issues were copied verbatim from wire stories while Border Region news came from documents and reports. One of the principal criticisms of the newspapers made during the reform was that reporters were aloof from the masses. That ended as reporters were sent "down to the villages" to rid themselves of their elitist attitudes and, at the same time, to gather stories.

When making assignments to their reporters, the *Liberation Daily*'s editors considered readers' interest in events in specific localities, activities of specific organizations, and specific topics.[9] Naturally, all assignments were made with the view of promoting the Party line. By

1944, the staff had expanded from the original twenty-three to over six hundred and was large enough to maintain branch offices throughout the Border Region. Reporters now went out to cover the Great Production Drive, major meetings of the Border Region Assembly, mass campaigns, and battles, among other things. They were encouraged to develop personal friendships with the people they covered and to write in a livelier, less didactic style than what had been the norm prior to the reform.

Stories gathered by this coterie of reporters were positioned in the *Liberation Daily* according to well-established rules of layout. All newspapers are divided into sections and pages. The first pages contain factual general stories drawing from all segments of the news organization. Specialized topical subjects appear on clearly delineated pages or in special sections of their own in the back pages. Furthermore, all articles, with the exception of "soft news" feature stories, are presented within a framework of fact. Although certain pages may concentrate on particular subjects, the front page strives to achieve a balance among international, national, and local news.[10]

Throughout its life, the *Liberation Daily* followed these rules carefully. Editions generally ran four pages, with the major news story of the day in the upper right-hand corner of page 1. That might have been news of the European or Asian war, announcements of major policy decisions, or news of important Border Region meetings. Editorials or commentaries appeared along the left side. Prior to the 1942 reform, page 2 contained war news; page 3, national news; and page 4, regular columns and features. After the focus shifted to more news of the Border Region, page 2 contained news of the liberated areas; page 3, national news; and page 4, international news. Page 1 continued as it always had although Border Region news appeared more frequently than before as the major news story.

### The *Liberation Daily* as a Propaganda Organ

The structure and function of the *Liberation Daily* was similar to that of major newspapers elsewhere. Like them, it constructed reality and promoted the ideology of those who controlled it. The similarities ended there. The *Liberation Daily* was also the major propaganda organ of the Chinese Communist Party. When the newspaper shaped events, it did so within the framework of the accepted Party line.

Through the media, Party leaders educated and mobilized the people.[11]

For many Americans, the term "propaganda" brings to mind negative images of brainwashed masses being fed lies by oppressive governments for insidious purposes. In fact, in the course of our daily lives, we are all victims of propaganda. Advertising, for example, is a very effective means of propaganda.

Propaganda's aim is more than modifying ideas, however. It is "the deliberate and systematic attempt to shape perceptions, manipulate cognitions, and direct behavior to achieve a response that furthers the desired intent of the propagandist."[12] Its purpose is to promote a partisan cause and, while propaganda is always value and ideology laden, it can range from fact to fiction.[13] No one can criticize the intent of influencing others and, in fact, the Chinese word for propaganda— xuanchuan—is a relatively neutral term. It means "to publicize or to make known" and does not necessarily imply manipulation for a special purpose.[14]

Of course, as applied in the *Liberation Daily*, propaganda was intended to gather support for Party policies and programs. The best example of that is found during the rectification of styles campaign. As those who supported Mao Zedong consolidated their positions within the Party, they had to rally support among rank-and-file Party members and, through them, the masses. Propaganda gained special importance because not everyone supported the Maoists wholeheartedly.[15] Middle- and lower-level cadres went through a period of intense study and debate to eradicate elitism and ideological ignorance among the rank and file. This was all part of the increased emphasis on "mass line" that sought to make cadres more accessible to the masses and attuned to their lives. But the rectification of styles campaign was more than a study movement. Many cadres found themselves victims of intense criticism in a manner similar to that experienced during the Cultural Revolution.

The problems facing the leadership at this time extended beyond the Party itself. The war was not going well for the Communist army; neither was the Party's relationship with the Guomindang government, which tightened its blockade around the Border Region. When the leadership called for all men and women in the region to rally to overcome the crises, it found that many of the programs it believed to be working well were not. To survive there had to be a drastic revamping of policy so that the Shaan-Gan-Ning Border Region could function as an independent and economically self-sufficient unit.

It became doubly important, therefore, for both cadres and the masses to see the value of revised Party programs and the personal benefits of supporting them. Propaganda became an important tool to insure the acceptance of that idea. "Once the masses know the truth and have a common aim," said Mao Zedong, "they will work together with one heart."[16] Where better to learn the truth (or the accepted version of it) than the *Liberation Daily*, the Party's primary organ of communication? Mao supported that idea when he said: "How can everyone be expected to get moving and how can anything be done well? To solve this problem the basic thing is, of course, to carry out ideological education on the mass line, but at the same time we must teach these comrades many concrete methods of work. One such method is to make full use of the newspapers."[17] Mao, like Lenin, believed that the press functioned to carry out propaganda, agitation, organization, and self-criticism. In addition, and perhaps most important, he believed it functioned to mobilize the masses.[18]

There are two kinds of propaganda: agitation and integration. The *Liberation Daily* made ample use of both. Agitation propaganda seeks to induce people to make the extra effort necessary to achieve goals previously thought unattainable. Articles written during the Great Production Drive of 1943 are good examples of this. Each day, article after article highlighted progressive cooperatives like Nanniwan or interviewed model workers and labor heroes/heroines. They exhorted people to work hard and follow Party guidelines promising better lives for all as a result.[19]

Integration propaganda helps people to reshape their thinking so they can adapt their daily lives to new realities. Articles in the *Liberation Daily* illustrating this kind of propaganda occasionally mixed fact with fiction. That did not mean writers falsified data. Rather, these were propaganda stories printed in a manner like that used for factual reports. (These are stereotyped and easy to identify.) Articles contained fabricated examples to educate cadres about certain points of policy or to teach them how to do things. Two examples are the September 29, 1941, article "Zenyang zai funü yundong zhong zhankai diaocha yanjiu gongzuo" (How to expand research and investigative work in the women's movement) and the October 26, 1941, article "Bushi haoban" (Bad management). Although not literally true, they reveal the major concerns of the period.

The practice of mixing fact with fiction brings up an important question: What constituted responsible journalism in the Shaan-Gan-Ning Border Region? Party leaders took the Marxist view that journalism was a public service superior to the kind of "for-profit" journalism found in capitalist countries. The journalist served the public by faithfully transmitting the Party line. Such a system had its problems, however. It assumed that the Party was always public-spirited and always right. Furthermore, it assumed that the Party line was always in the interest of the people. As with most things, theory did not necessarily coincide with practice.

To implement responsible journalism, one central organization, the New China News Agency, directed the press, radio, and film in the Shaan-Gan-Ning Border Region. Until May 1944, Bo Gu served as both head of the news service and editor-in-chief of the *Liberation Daily*. In May he left the *Liberation Daily* but remained the head of the news agency. More will be said in chapter 2 of the relationship between the New China News Agency and the newspaper, but here it should be noted that the two had a history of strong cooperation. When the Central Committee tightened its control of the *Liberation Daily* during rectification, it established its own propaganda committee, chaired by Mao Zedong, to oversee operations in the newspaper. The Central Committee also named Lu Dingyi, former head of the propaganda bureau of the Eighth Route Army's political department, to be the newspaper's general editor. As Mao's representative at the *Liberation Daily*, Lu became its dominating force. During the Yan'an years, the Party did have an official propaganda bureau. Nevertheless, because all major decisions were announced in the name of the Central Committee, little information exists on the inner workings of the bureau.[20]

Such strict control of the press was not uncommon in China at that time; it was the regular practice of the Guomindang government.[21] An editorial in Shanghai's powerful *L'Impartial* once voiced the concern that such control in peacetime would make people lose confidence in newspapers. The editorial's fears fell on deaf ears, however. The position of the government was that Chiang Kai-shek alone knew what was best for China, and the people must trust him completely. Any critic who went against him had to be "Communist-inspired." That left the press little room for maneuvering. Those who chose to ignore government dictates were punished in several ways. One of the most effective was to order the Post Office to stop circulation of offensive writings. No newspaper lasted long if it could not circulate its papers.

The Guomindang government did finance several newspapers of its own. One was the *Central Daily News* (*Zhongyang ribao*). All news found in it came from either the government or Party organs and had to be approved first by the appropriate officials. Nothing unfavorable to the government was permitted, so no crime or sensational stories appeared; neither did news of depressions and business failures. Editorials rarely appeared. What resulted was an official gazette that simply recorded meeting resolutions and promulgations of laws and regulations. It was so dull that even the low subscription rate could not induce people to buy it.

From the earliest dynasties, the Chinese government has controlled the dissemination of information. During the 1930s, even the strongest advocates of freedom of the press believed in some form of restraint, with the government responsible for defining it. Unlike the constitutional guarantees enjoyed by the American press, no Chinese laws protected press freedom. Moreover, advertisements, which determine so much of what appears in the American press, never played a major role in Chinese newspapers. Nevertheless, what existed in Guomindang-controlled areas cannot be compared to what existed in the Shaan-Gan-Ning Border Region. Chiang's government lacked the organization and economic power that gave the Border Region government so much control. Since it did not own all the newspapers, the Guomindang government never exercised firm ideological control over the press. Instead, it had to rely on brute force.

As a result, large newspapers, fearful of potential repercussions, published only reports issued by the government-controlled Central News Agency and refrained from discussing any controversial issues in their editorials.[22] When the war with Japan began in 1937, everyone accepted without question strict censorship of the news. As a result of the Publication Law of 1937, the Ministry of the Interior along with local governments took responsibility for regulating all publications. Editors and reporters became scarcely more than copyists repeating dispatches from the Central News Agency which exaggerated victories and minimized defeats.[23]

To be fair to Chiang's government in Chongqing, it did allow an opposition press, unlike its Communist counterparts in Yan'an. According to Theodore White and Annalee Jacoby, when Guomindang officials argued as much, Communist Party leaders had an irrefutable answer. They write: "The printing press on which they [i.e., Communist Party] published their paper had been smuggled through from a Japanese-occupied city; the paper on which they printed was brought out of the occupied areas under the guns of the Japanese. If the [Guomindang] wished to publish in [Yan'an], they said publicly, let the [Guomindang] send a printing press and enough paper into their city; they would gladly allow it."[24]

Surprisingly, the freest of all newspapers in China was that opposition press. First in Hankou and then in Chongqing, the Communist Party published the *New China Daily* (*Xinhua ribao*). The newspaper was established as a condition of the agreement reached by the Guomindang and the Communists for a united front against Japan in 1937. Zhou Enlai, the head of the Party's delegation in Chongqing, supervised its publication. Because it existed to advance the Party's programs and to revile the Guomindang government, almost everything it did violated press controls instituted by the Chiang government. There was little anyone could do to stop it, however, since that would endanger the coalition.

Oddly enough, the Communist Party newspaper became the biggest advocate of freedom of the press in wartime China. Like all publications, the *New China Daily* was subject to official censorship. Instead of just printing the censored article, however, the newspaper indicated deletions by using such symbols as "ooo," or "xxx." Sometimes an edition had blank spaces where news had been deleted. Unwilling to risk their luck, the *New China Daily*'s editors meticulously followed the censors on minor issues. It continued to publish in full all Party documents and Central Committee announcements, however.

The newspaper owned its own (hidden) printing equipment and had its own clandestine source of paper from a mill in a small Sichuan town. As a result, the government had few alternatives if it wanted to halt publication without violating the united front agreement. Nevertheless, it was determined to thwart publication of the *New China Daily*. Attempts to block its distribution through the mail proved to be the most effective means, which led the newspaper to resort to all kinds of tricks, both legal and illegal, to distribute its copies. On one occasion after Guomindang forces attacked the New Fourth Army in January 1941, Zhou Enlai himself went out on the streets to hawk the paper. Because the government denied it access to the mails, the newspaper's editors established an elaborate distribution system. In the wartime capital of Chongqing, for example, it recruited more than a hundred poor boys aged eleven to sixteen, housed them, fed them, and trained them to deliver the paper. Sometimes these youths had to travel great distances by bus or foot and risk arrest by Guomindang agents to deliver their papers.

## The *Liberation Daily* as a Nation Builder

Although the *Liberation Daily* shared many characteristics with its contemporaries elsewhere in China and with newspapers everywhere, it was unique. It appeared without competition in a highly controlled environment. Moreover, the newspaper reflected the ideology and events of a government in the process of forming its own character. That nation-building process is reflected both on the pages of the *Liberation Daily* and in its history. In the 1940s, the Chinese Communist Party enjoyed the longest period of peace and stability since its founding. That may seem an odd statement given the fact that it was fighting a war with the Japanese, expanding territory under its control, engaging in both ideological and armed battles with the Guomindang, and experiencing dissension within its own ranks. Nevertheless, the Central Committee spent twelve years in one location, a luxury it had never enjoyed before. This period of stability allowed it to see the effects of its programs and to make revisions where necessary. During that time, it discovered that many of the social and economic policies employed in the earlier Jiangxi Soviet were too radical and needed to be modified in order to work effectively among the masses.[25] The Central Committee had the time and the organization available in the Shaan-Gan-Ning Border Region to go one step further and evaluate the effects of revised policy. One reason why the Communist Party assumed control of chaotic and war-torn China as quickly and efficiently as it did in 1949 was that it already had a core of workable programs and (although far too few) tested cadres to implement them. In other words, it had undergone the beginning stages of nation building.

The Yan'an period also gave the Communist Party a legitimacy it had not enjoyed before. Each time Western and Chinese journalists, American military observers, or dignitaries visited the Shaan-Gan-Ning Border, they acknowledged the Party government as a legitimate political entity in China. No longer was the Communist Party seen as a vagabond group of "Red bandits"; it was now an established government with recognized leaders. Many who visited the Border Region and talked with authorities there believed it was *the* force to be reckoned with in China.

Certainly, Party leaders were aware of their impact. Theodore White, who visited the Border Region in 1944 described their attitude well:

> They were smug. [Chongqing] had expected them to wither away when the blockade was imposed in 1941; instead they had survived and by 1944, when I visited [Yan'an], they were physically and mentally sounder than the [Chongqing] leaders. They were so completely sure that their way was perfect that they found it difficult to ascribe any valor or ability to the officials or the soldiers of [Chongqing]. They glowed with self-confidence; there was always a slight tinge of sanctimoniousness in their speech. You were reminded sometimes of the religious summer camps where people go about clapping each other on the back in rousing pious good-fellowship.[26]

Playing a key role in this nation-building process was the *Liberation Daily*. Mass persuasion is critical in determining the relationship between leaders and led, and the role of people in programs of national construction. More than any other medium, the *Liberation Daily* put what often appeared to be unrelated events into an ideological context. It helped to mold the masses into a disciplined, organized group ready to build a new society. The articles, short stories, poems, and songs that appeared in the pages of the newspaper all illustrate the role of the *Liberation Daily* in persuading the masses. Its most important strength lay in its capacity to mobilize people. Through the newspaper, Party leaders had access to every major social group and the means to advertise campaigns and Party policies. Another of its strengths was its ability to ignore, or even rid itself of, demoralizing opposition.[27] No place is that seen better than in the attacks on critical writers during the rectification of styles campaign, which will be discussed in chapter 2.

A third strength was its self-designated watchdog function. The American press assumes this duty on its own, determining alone who, what, when, and how to criticize. In theory, only owners and management have the power to restrain it.[28] In a country like China, however, a newspaper's social control function is institutionally assigned under the leadership and supervision of the Communist Party. Because the *Liberation Daily* was the primary medium in the Shaan-Gan-Ning Border, it was the only place where the masses could publicly participate in social control. When the newspaper exposed deviant behavior of Party or government cadres, it exerted public pressure on them to change. The campaign against critical writers, particularly Wang Shiwei, once again provides the best example of the newspaper's social control function. There is a flaw in this kind of social control, however, and that is also evident in the *Liberation Daily*. Being restricted ideologically and structurally means that there can be no spontaneous criticism and self-criticism of crucial matters.[29] Everything is orchestrated from above; editors and writers have little control over the positions taken in their newspaper.

### The *Liberation Daily* as an Instrument of Inner-Party Struggle

After 1942, Mao Zedong orchestrated the life of the *Liberation Daily*. Prior to that time, his chief rival for power was Wang Ming, leader of the Internationalists.[30] Bo Gu, a prominent member of the group, served as the *Liberation Daily*'s original editor-in-chief. His stamp and that of the Internationalists were clearly imprinted on the newspaper during its first year of publication. When Mao took control in the spring of 1942, he did not get rid of Bo Gu, who remained as editor-in-chief until 1944. He was no longer the newspaper's driving force, however. Lu Dingyi, a close associate of Mao's, replaced Bo in that capacity.

The struggle between Wang Ming and Mao for control of the Party is well documented so there is no need to reiterate the details here.[31] Nevertheless, because the last battle between Mao and the Internationalists took place in the newspaper, it is important to look at the *Liberation Daily*'s role in the struggle between the two groups.[32]

In any revolutionary movement, those who control the communications system—of which propaganda is the key element—gain access to enormous power over the movement itself. When contending groups exist, they must fight until one dominates the propaganda system and uses it effectively to defeat the other(s). Mao knew that all too well. Dominating the *Liberation Daily* became a crucial factor in his strategy to destroy the Internationalists' power and to gain undisputed control over the Communist Party. When he took control of the newspaper in 1942, he used propaganda to cement his own position. What Mao instituted in the *Liberation Daily* became the propaganda that successfully unified the Party's leadership and contributed to the revolution's ultimate victory. It defined propaganda and journalism for the Chinese Communist Party for the next thirty years.

Politically, Mao had much to gain from his ideological battle with Wang Ming. Although he was Stalin's man and therefore could not be ignored, Mao was determined to gain ideological leadership of the Party. That meant uniting theory with reality firmly based in the concrete tasks of leading a rural revolution. By mid-summer 1937, Mao was first among equals in the Party and had begun his rise to pre-eminence. There was evidence at that time of an emerging personality cult, and his collected essays were published in Shanghai.

Wang Ming recognized Mao's dominance in a speech entitled "Learn from Mao Zedong" delivered at the Zedong School for Young Cadre on May 3, 1940.[33] His public capitulation did not mean, however, that the Internationalists were dead. Until the rectification campaign, they retained a degree of power, which the *Liberation Daily* illustrates well. Nevertheless, they had lost the real prize: leadership of the Party. Mao pointedly suggested in a speech on May 5, 1941, that the Internationalists ought to return to the classroom to receive further instruction in Marxism-Leninism (their area of expertise), but they never became targets of the campaign as did Liu Shaoqi and his faction during the Cultural Revolution.[34] At the Seventh Party Congress in 1945, Mao cleared the air concerning his rivals when he referred to the "legality" of their leadership (1931–34). No matter how "mistaken" their policies might have been, their leadership had been legally established, and there was no question of criminal prosecution or physical punishment.[35]

Although the Internationalists' fate was all but sealed by the time the *Liberation Daily* began publication in May 1941, the newspaper, under the leadership of Bo Gu, remained a stronghold of their ideas. During its first year, it reflected the preferences of its editor-in-chief. International news, editorials, and essays dominated it. Articles on World War II took precedence over national and Border Region news. Important Party and Border Region matters received coverage, but the articles lacked the concrete examples cadres needed to help them implement policy. The problems of the *Liberation Daily*'s first year will be discussed in detail in the next chapter, but suffice it to say here that the newspaper was aloof from matters that most concerned its readers. It avoided the agitation propaganda role that was crucial to the revolution at this time. There are several explanations for that flaw, but one important one was the editor-in-chief. Bo Gu lacked experience in these areas and did not consider them the key issues for the newspaper.

Rectification changed all that. The newspaper published all documents and essays designated by the Central Committee for study. It became a Maoist textbook and a vital instrument in the final push of Mao's supporters to elevate their leader to a preeminent position and to guarantee the place of his thought in Party ideology. The potential power of the *Liberation Daily* was not lost on Mao. He knew that control over the principal propaganda organ would allow him to promote or ignore the programs and policies of his choice. Bo Gu may never have used the newspaper against his enemies, but Mao had other ideas. He was determined to dominate the publication and use it not only to consolidate his control over the Party but to destroy his rivals. Beginning in April 1942, Mao did precisely that. Under the guise of implementing a study movement for reform within the newspaper, he remade the *Liberation Daily* in his own image. Bo Gu was rendered powerless. Although he continued to serve as editor-in-chief until 1944, Internationalists' views no longer affected the course of the newspaper.

The ascension of the Maoists is clearly seen in the revised structure, format, and content of articles in the *Liberation Daily*. It became a truly political newspaper, performing both its agitation and integration propaganda roles well. Change occurred not only in the layout, as more Border Region news found its way to page 1, but also among the staff. No longer did they remain isolated in their cave on Qingliang Mountain. An expanded staff went "down to the villages" to experience real life and report it. Because articles focused on concrete programs of change, they reported more accurately on life in the Border Region than did prereform articles. The kinds of articles found, their manner of presentation, and weight given to them provide a rare glimpse into the inner workings of the Party, an unparalleled record of the events in the world of the Chinese Communist Party and how those events were interpreted.

What follows is an analysis of the *Liberation Daily* in two parts. The first examines the relationship between the Chinese Communist Party and the newspaper during the three stages of its life. In each of these, Party politics shaped not only the content but the format and occasionally even the staff. Never static, the *Liberation Daily* reflected the vast changes taking place within the Party and throughout Communist-controlled areas. The rectification of styles campaign illustrates those changes best and is examined separately.

The second part introduces the newspaper's contents through an annotated survey. It avoids listing articles page by page because indexing fails to provide information needed to use the newspaper to its best advantage. Such an index exists in the *Index to the "Jiefang ribao" ("Kaiho nippo" kiji mokuroku)*.[37] The survey here assesses the newspaper in such a way as to acquaint the researcher with the major trends in the *Liberation Daily*, important articles, columns, and editorials. It outlines the newspaper in a chronological survey of four-month segments that illustrate the important issues of the day. Citations concentrate primarily on issues of concern to the Border Region, other liberated areas, and China in general. A topical survey follows the chronology.

Examining a society through its communications process, according to Lucien Pye, "provides a common basis for analyzing both the manifest structural problems and the most subtle questions of attitudes and values in the total process of political change and nation building."[38] The goal of this work is to introduce the *Liberation Daily*—the principal means of communication in the Shaan-Gan-Ning Border Region—through its history, political role, and content so that the attitudes, values, and problems of the Communist Party during this critical period of nation building can be better understood.

# ONE

# The Medium and the Party

An official government newspaper was nothing new to China. The world's first newspaper, the *Di bao*, summarized court activity during the Han dynasty (206 B.C.–A.D. 220); similar publications presented court policy in later dynasties.[1] In like manner, the Communist Party supported numerous publications from the time of its founding in 1921. When Mao and his followers established the Jiangxi Soviet in 1931, newspapers and journals formed the core of their system to transmit information quickly. *Red China* (*Hongse Zhonghua*) published its first edition on December 11, 1931. Serving as the official organ of the soviet, it appeared first weekly and later every three days; by 1934, it had a circulation of fifty thousand. Other publications dating from the period include *Red Star* (*Hong xing*), published by the Red Army's General Political Department from 1931 until 1934 when the Long March began, and *Struggle* (*Douzheng*), a newspaper created from the 1935 merger of *Plain Talk* (Shihua) and *Party Communication* (Dangshi jianshe). *Struggle* later served as the official publication of the soviet area's Central Bureau.[2]

Beginning in 1930, Chiang Kai-shek's Guomindang forces mounted ''extermination'' campaigns against the Jiangxi Soviet. During the first four campaigns, the Red Army withstood the onslaught, but its position became untenable during the fifth campaign in late 1933. The Party abandoned the Soviet in August 1934. From Jiangxi, the Communist forces began their epic Long March to Northwest China, which ended in October 1935 when the first contingents reached the Party-controlled area of famine-ridden Shaanxi Province. Needless to say, the Party's communication system broke down during this time. Therefore, one of the Central Committee's first actions in Shaanxi was to set up an efficient system for disseminating information quickly. A variety of Party publications appeared: *Liberation Weekly* (*Jiefang zhoukan*), the Central Committee's official publication; *The Communist* (*Gongchandang ren*), the Central Committee's internal publication;

*Eighth Route Army's Political Magazine (Balujun junzheng zazhi)*, the publication for the general political section of the Eighth Route Army; and *New China Daily (Xin Zhonghua bao)*, the immediate predecessor of the *Liberation Daily*. First published on February 7, 1939, the *New China Daily* served as the major propaganda organ of the Central Committee. Under the direct leadership of the Party's newspaper committee, it appeared at three-day intervals.[3]

After the New Fourth Army Incident in January 1941 when the Guomindang attacked and decimated Communist forces in Anhui Province, the Central Committee reevaluated its publications. The United Front had ruptured. The times called for a strong separate Central Committee government with a publications system impervious to outside influences. They also demanded a well-disciplined Party communications system as Party leaders turned away from the policies of the united front to those of revolution. The Central Committee decided to combine the *New China Daily* and *Today's News (Jinri xinwen)* and establish a large-scale newspaper adaptable to current conditions and designed to expand the Party's work. On May 15, 1941, it issued a directive stating that "Beginning on May 16, [we will] combine the *New China Daily* and *Today's News* to publish the *Liberation Daily*. . . . All Party policies will be announced through the *Liberation Daily*. Its editorials will be written by comrades from the Central Committee and [other] important comrades."[4] To make this new official propaganda organ even stronger, the Central Committee stopped its other publications.[5] The *Liberation Daily* served as the official voice of the Central Committee until March 1947.

An editorial committee directed the *Liberation Daily*, but the New China News Agency (Xin Hua she, hereafter NCNA) managed its affairs.[6] The NCNA grew out of the first Communist Party news service, Red China News (Hongse Zhonghua she), which published a thousand-character summary of national and international news for the Red Army in the early 1930s. When the united front went into effect, the agency changed its name to New China News (Xin Zhonghua she) and supplied the *New China Daily* with translations from wire services. The second name change occurred after the New Fourth Army Incident when it became New China News Agency (Xin Hua she).[7] Occupying an office beside the newspaper, the agency coordinated the flow of information into and out of the Border Region. When it began operations in Yan'an, the NCNA had only three radio receiving sets and a 100-watt transmitter.[8] During the Anti-Japanese war, it increased that capacity in order to monitor its own eight branches and eleven substations throughout the anti-Japanese bases along with broadcasts from the United States, Great Britain, the Soviet Union, and Japan. The agency provided information not only to the print media but to the the Border Region's radio station as well. Station XNCR transmitted from Yan'an, often sending information in code to underground Party members elsewhere.[9]

Bo Gu, a leading figure in the Internationalist faction, headed both the NCNA and the *Liberation Daily*.[10] He was one of several staff members to work for both. Nevertheless, even though the two news organizations shared many of the same leaders and had a history of strong cooperation, they were not equal. During the Anti-Japanese war, the newspaper played the more important role, but when the civil war began and Communist Party influence extended over ever larger areas of China, the NCNA took precedence.[11]

Moreover, even though it was the official newspaper of the Central Committee, the *Liberation Daily* was not the only newspaper published in the base areas. In the spring of 1940, there were at least fifty-one newspapers and journals in Communist-held territories.[12] The dailies included the *War of Resistance Daily (Kangzhan ribao)*, *Weihe Daily (Weihe ribao)*, *Taiyue Daily (Taiyue ribao)*, and *The Chinese Daily (Zhongguo ren bao)*.

The most important newspaper, apart from the *Liberation Daily*, was the Jin-Cha-Ji base area's *Resistance News (Kang di bao)*, edited by Deng Tuo. If the *Liberation Daily* was used to fight inner-Party battles, the *Resistance News* was used to fight the revolution. Published behind Japanese lines, the newspaper's goal was to give more power to the peasantry and to disenfranchise the local elite. Declared the official publication of the Jin-Cha-Ji Political Department, *Resistance News* first appeared on December 11, 1937; Deng Tuo assumed control in April 1938. By May 1940, the newspaper was printing an amazing twenty-one thousand copies per edition. Originally published every three days, it became a daily on November 7, 1940, appearing under the new name *Jin-Cha-Ji Daily (Jin-Cha-Ji ribao)*.[13]

Another daily, the *People's Daily (Renmin ribao)*, a two-page newspaper and the precursor of the current Beijing publication, served as the official organ of the Jin-Ji-Lu-Yu Border Region government until 1948. At that time, Party leaders combined the border regions of Jin-

Ji-Lu-Yu, Jin-Cha-Ji, and Jin-Sui into one North China base. In the process, the original *People's Daily* merged with Kalgan's *Jin-Cha-Ji Daily* to form the present *People's Daily*, which appeared first in Shijiazhuang in 1948 and moved to Beijing in 1949.[14]

## The Early Period (May 16, 1941–March 31, 1942)

Housed in a cave on Qingliang Mountain, the *Liberation Daily* first appeared on May 16, 1941. Until September, the newspaper printed only two-page editions. When it expanded to four pages, each edition contained approximately forty-eight thousand characters.[15] Maoist critics later charged that the *Liberation Daily* lacked direction and definition during the early period. It is true that, like other areas of Communist policy then, the one for the newspaper failed to give the firm guidelines needed for it to become a powerful propaganda organ. Furthermore, many of the urban intellectuals who staffed it were ignorant of life in the barren Northwest and remained insensitive to local conditions. While these factors contributed to the vagueness seen throughout the *Liberation Daily*, it is also important to remember that the newspaper during its early period reflected the Internationalist ideology of its editor-in-chief, Bo Gu. Moscow-trained and oriented toward an urban-based revolution, he may well have found wire service international and national news more interesting than news of the Border Region.

Bo Gu, Yang Song (general editor and an Internationalist), and Yu Guangsheng (assistant general editor) ran the *Liberation Daily* in the beginning. Yu Wen, Zhang Yingwu, Wang Yi, Yang Pingzhen, Zhu Zhideng, Miao Haileng, Ding Jicang, and Chen Quanbi transferred from the *New China Daily* to work on the paper. Intellectuals from the Marx-Lenin Institute, *Liberation Weekly*, the Lu Xun Art Academy, and other literature-oriented units joined the staff as well. Ding Ling, Wu Lengxi, Li Rui, Huang Caoliang, Chao Yinmin, and Yang Fangzhi all transferred to the newspaper.[16] The first editors' meeting took place on May 14 with Ding Ling, Zhang Yingwu, Bo Gu, and Yang Song in attendance. At that time, General Editor Yang reminded his staff that as the principal propaganda organ of the Party the *Liberation Daily* needed clear-cut positions and lively writing.[17] He provided no further instructions, and there is no evidence from the writing style of early articles that the staff followed those instructions.

New China Bookstore sold the newspaper at a subscription rate of thirty yuan per year, sixteen yuan for six months, three yuan a month, and one jiao per week.[18] A severe shortage of paper (the staff either used paper made from grass or smuggled it through the Japanese lines) and primitive printing facilities ruled out individual subscriptions. At most only 7,600 copies appeared at any one time, and most of these circulated no farther than a twenty-mile radius of Yan'an city and even then went primarily to organizations. Paper alone cost four times the subscription rate, forcing the government to subsidize the newspaper heavily.[19] The expense and difficulty of printing and distribution accounted for its high cost. Technical problems in publishing the newspaper alone were enormous. Printing facilities were nearly as ancient as the Cave of Ten Thousand Buddhas, which housed them.[20]

To help with finances, the *Liberation Daily* published advertisements, although because of prohibitive costs, fewer appeared over the years. The May 23, 1941, edition established the policy. All advertisements had to be paid for a week in advance. Advertisers could submit a personal draft, but all copy was subject to the limits of typesetting and printing facilities. Running an advertisement was not cheap and, as a result, few ran. If an ad appeared alongside the masthead, it cost thirty yuan a day, with each five lines costing between six and eight yuan; if it ran on page 2, it cost four yuan for ten lines. The first advertisement, one for the Shaan-Gan-Ning Border Region Bank, appeared on May 24, 1941, and read: "Expanding the Border Region's economy; improving people's livelihood."

Like headlines in the later *People's Daily*, those in the *Liberation Daily* often told as much about the subject matter as the ensuing article. Designed to convey a simple message or appeal to emotions, many were quite long. Other headlines appeared in larger type, around and under which a series of special articles were grouped. Frequently, they contained numerical titles or campaign slogans to communicate an idea as directly as possible. Because many readers were semiliterate, appeals had to be efficiently phrased and in a simpler vocabulary than the text that followed.

Throughout its life, the *Liberation Daily* maintained a straightforward format, with the most important story on all pages appearing in the upper right-hand corner or across the top of the page. Page 1 contained the major news story of the day. During its first year, headlines for the war in Europe, Asia, or China along with major policy statements dominated the top right-hand headline. After the 1942 reform, news of important Border Region events also appeared there. During the mid-1940s, however, it was not unusual to see articles on European or American elections or some international convocation occupying the top right-hand corner. Photographs did not appear until the fall of 1944. Of poor quality, they were rarely run.

Subject matter also formed a pattern. Major policy decisions always appeared in full on the front page to arouse attention for what would be discussed in detail later. Editorials rationalized and explained Party policy. Stories about martyrs and model workers strove to appeal to people's motives and expectations; their purpose was to promote conformity. When a major campaign occurred, the entire newspaper focused on it, with the language of the campaign pervading the language of the articles.

For much of its life, the *Liberation Daily* refrained from attacks on the Guomindang government in Chongqing or from obvious references to revolution. Even after the reform, few overtly revolutionary terms appeared. This reticence stemmed from the fact that until the mid-1940s, the Communist Party adhered in theory to a united front with the Guomindang against the Japanese. The attempt to maintain a truce meant excluding attacks on such oppressor classes as landlords, promotion of radical land reform, and criticism of the national government. Revolutionary terminology crept into articles on domestic and national issues during the summer of 1943 and increased in 1944. This was partly due to the assumption of control by the Maoists, who were not as willing to subordinate their policies to the United Front as were the Internationalists, and who were more interested in carrying out the rural revolution. Furthermore, as tension between the Guomindang and the Communist Party increased, so did the rhetoric. By the end of 1944 and clearly in 1945, anti-Guomindang language pervaded all national and Border Region news as the government turned from the war with Japan to the impending civil war.

Between May 16 and September 16, 1941, the *Liberation Daily* had only two pages. Page 1 featured international news and some important national news. An editorial appeared each day, generally focusing on international problems. International and national news received equal treatment on page 2. National issues included the base areas, Guomindang-controlled areas, and Japanese-occupied areas, with an occasional article on art or theory.

On September 16, 1941, the paper expanded to four pages. The new layout reflected the strong influence of the Internationalist faction during the *Liberation Daily*'s first year of publication. An edition now looked like this: page 1—news of the European war, some national news, editorials; page 2—European war news; page 3—national news; page 4—Border Region news in the top half, columns in the bottom half.[21] The September 16 edition contained the first "Literature and Art" (*wenyi*) column on the bottom of page 4 and "Short Opinions" (*xiao yanlun*) in the Border Region section. Page 3 carried an essay by Deng Qiaomu entitled "Why We Must Persist in the Ruthless Struggle Against Subjective Statements." Yang Song edited pages 1 and 2 while Yang Fangzhi edited pages 3 and 4.[22]

Page 4 provides a good example of the variety of information found in the *Liberation Daily*. In today's terminology, page 4 would be called the "features" page because it contained "soft news" articles. Readers read regular columns; topics of special interest such as the pages devoted to unequal treaties on February 4–8, 1943; campaigns like that for reduction of rent running from February 1942 until November 1943; and important Party documents, particularly those found in "Study" columns beginning on May 13, 1942. What made page 4 unique compared with other pages was that today's article on crops or tying tourniquets might follow yesterday's short story and song and be replaced by tomorrow's essay on Marx or Lenin. This diversity made it a special target of the Maoists in 1942.

With Bo Gu in control, international news, editorials, and essays dominated the *Liberation Daily* during the early period. Articles concerning World War II took precedence over other news as the newspaper used foreign news service wire stories to report on the war against Germany and Italy, the Soviet Union's battle against the Germans, and the war in Asia. National news followed international in importance, with articles concentrating on the Eighth Route Army, the New Fourth Army, guerrilla struggles, Japanese imperialism, and conditions in occupied areas. Topics given the least consideration included Border Region news, the first stages of rectification, the Guomindang, public opinion, and literature. In other words, events not related directly to life in the Border Region formed the backbone of the newspaper.

That is not to say that Border Region events or policy statements were ignored. Elections, political meetings, and campaigns received coverage as did important policy statements from the Central Committee. Nor did readers lack input; they could express their opinions in "Letters" and "Short Opinions."[23] In addition, the editors invited readers to submit material. To the right of the masthead in the first edition was a public notice that the newspaper sought political comments, translations, literary pieces, poetry, songs, and short stories. How many readers contributed manuscripts is difficult to tell. The numbers must not have been great, however, because in September 1942, Mao Zedong established an advising group to solicit and review manuscripts from the people.[24] Short stories, songs, and poems also appeared. What it does say is that the content of the majority of articles during the early period reflected the distance of the staff from the people they served. It also indicated the control the Internationalist faction exerted over the newspaper's affairs.

The best example of this aloofness is the "Eight Specialized Columns" (ba da zhuanlan), a feature that appeared four or five times a week on page 4 between September 16, 1941, and March 31, 1942.[25] When the newspaper expanded to four pages, the first "Literature and Art" column appeared. Prior to that time, according to the literary column's first editor Ding Ling, "Bo Gu believed that literature should not have a separate column. Good literature could be found on any page."[26] At the outset, "Literature and Art" had four charges: (1) publish known writers; (2) promote young writers; (3) reflect life in the Border Region, the anti-Japanese base areas, and the army; and (4) improve the quality of literature and art. To a certain extent, the column carried out these responsibilities. From manuscripts totaling more than five million characters, editors selected the best for publication. Among these were contributions by more than thirty new writers from the Border Region.[27] That is an impressive record for a column that appeared only a hundred times over a six-month period. Nevertheless, "Literature and Art" possessed serious shortcomings. Most important, manuscripts were long, dull, and cautious and failed to portray life among the people.

The other columns added almost nothing. Those seven columns and the date of their first appearance were: Youth (September 21), Workers (September 24), Enemy (September 27), Women (September 28), Science (October 4), Army (October 29), and Health (November 24). All were basically editorials aimed at the professional reader and drew support from a comparable specialized organization. This resulted in technical columns based on intimate relationships. Examples of such relationships include "Literature and Art" with the Lu Xun Art Academy, "Youth" with the Youth League, "Workers" with the Worker's Society, "Women" with the Central Committee's women's committee, and "Health" with the Central Committee's health office.[28]

Herein lay the principal criticism of the *Liberation Daily* during its first ten months. Lu Dingyi, a supporter of Mao Zedong who later became the newspaper's general editor, summarized in an article entitled "Our Fundamental Viewpoint Regarding Journalism" the Maoist criticisms of the newspaper at the time. He argued that those writing for the *Liberation Daily* came from the old society and still adhered to old theories of journalism. Such theories were often dishonest and unscientific, and always confused. Reform was needed so that journalists could understand their mistakes. Truly revolutionary journalists had a materialistic viewpoint and realized that every piece of news had a political character. That political character, however, was secondary to and determined by the political character of reality. [29]

Clearly, a cultural gap did exist between staff members and the mass of people living in the Border Region. Employees of the newspaper were men and women of artistic and literary talent and not trained news reporters. They also had no representation on the Central Committee or the Party's Northwest Bureau. To make matters worse, below the Yan'an staff, no local support staff existed who could serve as sources.[30] Simply put, writers and editors had little idea about what was going on in the Border Region.

To be fair to the newspaper's staff, life was far from easy in Yan'an. The *Liberation Daily*'s principal editors lived in stone caves, but the majority of the staff made do in damp, cold, earthen ones. All contained simple furnishings—a table, bench, lantern, and pen. In winter, they received charcoal burners. The newspaper possessed one old automobile, which Bo Gu used only when he attended important meetings. Everyone else walked. The entire staff ate the same monotonous meals of millet and sliced sweet potatoes, and they generally wore similar uniforms. They received one set of unlined clothes every second year and one set of quilted clothes every third year. During the winter the unlined garments served as long underwear. (Cloth was scarce in the Border Region.) Each person collected a salary of one to three yuan a month.

During the Great Production Drive, staff members were required to participate in production, which contributed in a small way to alleviating shortages. Some grew pumpkins, tomatoes, tobacco, and potatoes and raised chickens; others established spinning and weaving groups. Eventually, wool socks and sweaters were added to winter clothing allowances. Contributions to the cause went beyond producing food and clothes, however. *Liberation Daily* staff members organized laundry groups and established a barber shop and shoe-making service. In addition, they collected manure for fertilizer and spent artillery shells for iron, made paper bags, and even did the unheard of (for this less than egalitarian world)—they carried their own water. Their efforts paid off. When food became more plentiful, each person was entitled to the unprecedented luxury of three jin of meat per month (about 3.3 pounds).[31]

Life was not all work, however. The *Liberation Daily* sponsored sports teams and held dances and songfests. Staff attended performances at the Lu Xun Art Academy and put on their own plays.[32] Nevertheless, despite the attempts at entertainment, most of the staff, especially those from urban areas, must have found life in Yan'an very dull.

Although complaints against the staff had some basis in fact, there were larger targets awaiting critics of the newspaper. During the summer of 1941, the first rumblings of rectification were heard as Mao Zedong worked to consolidate his dominant position within the Party. Although Wang Ming acknowledged Mao as undisputed leader at a May 1940 speech opening the Zedong School for Young Cadres, he had attacked Mao in March with the republication of his controversial 1932 polemic, "Struggle for the Further Bolshevization of the Communist Party of China."[33] But Wang's attacks carried little weight. His final fall from power came in September 1941 at a Mao-dominated session of the Politburo.

Events at the top levels of Party leadership could not help but affect the *Liberation Daily*. While his close associate was being permanently removed from the Party's power structure, Bo Gu was trying to retain his own position as editor-in-chief. He succeeded by not only acquiescing to but leading a major reform of the newspaper.[34] He heralded the impending changes at a September 9, 1941, meeting. The newspaper failed as an instrument of struggle, he argued. Furthermore, it lacked direction and analysis because it did not reflect policy and provide concrete help to readers.[35] Recognizing the failure to meet the needs of the Party and people, Bo Gu cited problems with layout and editorials. These reforms changed the *Liberation Daily* markedly, but Bo Gu lost control of the newspaper's contents to Mao and the Central Committee, although he did remain at the head until 1944.

Bo Gu's assessment had merit; the *Liberation Daily* did need to be reevaluated. His inflexible layout rules meant that international news—information derived entirely from foreign wire services—overshadowed regional and national news. Originally, staff reporters simply copied down international news reports as received without editing, so major news items escaped Party control. Articles concerning the Communist Party, the Eighth Route Army, and practical reports on the Border Region or China often went unnoticed because they were almost hidden. For example, Mao Zedong's first report to the Central Committee on rectification appeared on February 2, 1942, in the lower right-hand side of page 3 in a small three-column piece.[36] Few articles dealt with matters of real concern to the general population, such as the decrease in the grain levy.

According to Bo Gu's analysis, editorials were the second problem area. They made the same mistakes as did news reports because they considered international issues primary and Party, army, and Border Region matters secondary. As a result, the newspaper never assumed the leadership or agitation propaganda role intended for it. Bo Gu's citation of editorials as problematic is surprising because most people considered him to be the source of the problem. When the *Liberation Daily* began publication, the editor-in-chief insisted that an editorial appear daily in the fashion of Shanghai's *L'Impartial* and *News Daily* and the Soviet Union's *Pravda*. He argued that each edition should contain news, communication coverage, and an editorial. To lack one was to have no newspaper, so the daily editorial became an unalterable feature. If the burden of producing editorials was not heavy enough for the editorial board, Yang Song declared in January 1942 that each member must also write a weekly column.[37] And if that was not enough, each month they must contribute an "essay" (*zhuanlun*), proofread three articles, and translate two articles of three thousand to five thousand characters each.[38] The board could not maintain that pace even if events called for daily editorials, which they did not. Like page 4, editorials became a particular target of reform.

**The Middle Period (April 1, 1942–November 19, 1946)**

By 1942, the conflict between Mao and the Internationalists was over virtually everywhere but the *Liberation Daily*. The reforms announced by Bo Gu in his September speech were all part of rectification. Because the movement radically affected the course of Communist Party history, and because the *Liberation Daily* played a decisive role in it, the following chapter is devoted to it. Here I discuss only reform within the *Liberation Daily* itself and how it affected the structure and reporting in the newspaper.

Throughout late 1941 and early 1942, unrest pervaded certain elements of the Party. Discontent surfaced in March and April 1942 when the *Liberation Daily* published a series of essays (*zawen*) by critical writers (see section 4 of chapter 2 for a list of the essays and articles responding to them). In "Wild Lilies" (March 13 and 23, 1942), considered to be the most inflammatory of these, writer Wang Shiwei accused the Party leadership of elitism and aloofness.

Because they could be seen as a negative example without damaging the fabric of Party organization, critical writers became a convenient target of rectification. This was a lucky break for Bo Gu and others among the Internationalists who still had power. They could easily have been the movement's primary targets, but not one of the group, not even Wang Ming, was targeted for struggle. Only Wang Shiwei achieved that distinction.[39]

Reverberations from Wang Shiwei's essay spread quickly as Party leaders moved to tighten the reins on what they saw as maverick elements within the newspaper. The day after "Wild Lilies" appeared, Mao Zedong sent a telegram to Zhou Enlai stating: "Regarding improving the *Liberation Daily*, [we] have already had discussions to strengthen its Party nature and to reflect the [ideas] of masses."[40] Two days later, the Central Committee charted the course for change in its "Notification of Reform in the Party's Newspaper." It said: "The newspaper is the Party's strongest tool for 'arousing' work because each day it influences 100,000 people. Therefore, managing the newspaper well is a central factor in Party work."[41] And so reform began.

On March 31, 1942, more than seventy writers and leading cadres met with Mao Zedong to discuss the reform. At that time Mao said: "The *Liberation Daily* is one of the organs of daily business [for the Party]. . . . Today we are reforming and must put the newspaper to better use."[42] Before they faced the future, however, they had to clear the air of the past. Once again, Bo Gu acquiesced to the Maoists when in a self-criticism he admitted that the *Liberation Daily* had not tried sufficiently hard to do its best.[43] It failed to implement the Party line and published too few articles about life in the Border Region.[44] The next day's editorial, entitled "To the Readers," proclaimed: "Beginning today, we will implement reform in the newspaper's layout in order to make the *Liberation Daily* into the official newspaper of the Party's true struggle." The editors all took the Maoist pledge to "implement the Party line, reflect mass conditions, strengthen the struggle in thought, and help reform all Party work."[45]

Timothy Cheek argues that Deng Tuo's experiences with the *Resistance News* in the Jin-Cha-Ji base area served as a model for Mao Zedong's statements concerning the press. Specifically, he cites Deng's June 1938 review of the newspaper's work. In that editorial Deng said:

> Of course, the production of *Resistance News* has its mission. It must become the propagandizer and organizer of the border region's mass resistance [and] salvation movement, it must represent the needs of the broad masses, reflect and pass on the real conditions and experience of the broad masses' struggle, promote various aspects of work, [and] educate the masses themselves. At the same time, from the promotion and assistance of the broad masses, [the paper] itself progresses. It is the paper of the masses; it gives impetus to others, and at the same time is taught by others.[46]

While Deng believed news must reflect the needs of the masses, he labored under no illusions that the press was free from Party control. In a late 1938 editorial entitled "Propaganda and Agitation in a Time of War," he wrote that people learned what to do from Party newspapers. Therefore, what appeared in them had to be written carefully and in consultation with Party leaders. Lu Dingyi, who controlled the post-reform *Liberation Daily*, later praised Deng's work in the Jin-Cha-Ji base area, citing this editorial as an excellent principle of statement. Cheek concludes: "Thus, what would become Maoist dicta on the Party-controlled press . . . was for Deng Tuo both his standard operating procedure and a matter of painstaking work." Deng also beat Mao in carrying out a reform in his newspaper. Beginning in May 1941, Deng Tuo implemented a small rectification movement designed to "regularize" thought and strengthen the Party character of work.[47]

Reform changed the *Liberation Daily* from a newspaper adhering to a "bourgeoisie news theory" to one following a "proletarian news theory." The remoteness that characterized the prereform *Liberation*

*Daily* ended, as reporters and editors sought to bridge the gap between the newspaper and the masses. In other words, they sought to carry out the mass line. To effect that transformation meant major changes in the newspaper's administrative policy and personnel. The Central Committee and leading editors retained what they considered to be good about the prereform *Liberation Daily*, reinforcing it with strict guidelines from above. The principal propaganda organ of the Central Committee could not be allowed to deviate from the Party line nor openly question policy in its pages. Above all that meant tightening the Central Committee's control over the *Liberation Daily*. Freedom had no place in the Party's official propaganda organ, and to promote that idea, Party leaders issued the slogan: "The Party and newspaper are one. The newspaper cannot be independent from the Party."[48] The Central Committee established its own propaganda committee (*xuanchuan weiyuanhui*), composed of Mao Zedong (chair), Wang Jiaxiang, Kai Feng, and Bo Gu, to direct the course of the newspaper and oversee its reform. Except for Mao, all the members of the committee were members of, or had once been associated with, the Internationalist faction. He had not won the battle yet.

The committee proposed four steps to strengthen the Party's leadership of the *Liberation Daily*.[49] First, the Central Committee and Politburo would take a more active role in the *Liberation Daily*'s affairs, which included writing editorials and essays. Mao Zedong, Zhou Enlai, Liu Shaoqi, and Zhu De all contributed essays, editorials, and opinions.[50] Several went so far as to visit the newspaper's office to talk with the staff. During a September 4, 1943, visit, Zhou Enlai met with reporters and editors to discuss how the *Liberation Daily* should report news concerning the Guomindang. "We certainly want to pin down Chiang Kai-shek and the Guomindang," he said, "and not let them surrender [to the Japanese]. We continuously want to bring their positive spirit into play."[51] In addition, the Central Committee was supposed to examine all articles and editorials prior to their publication. It is impossible to determine how many they actually saw. Nevertheless, the Party leadership had exercised its right of control, and that threat alone could be all that was needed to keep the staff in line.

Second, the Central Committee, the Northwest Bureau, and the army's political bureau published guidelines for using the *Liberation Daily*. On September 9, 1942, for example, the Northwest Bureau passed "The Decision Concerning the *Liberation Daily* Work Problem.'' The resolution stipulated how to use the *Liberation Daily*, how to contribute to it correctly, how to support those working in communications, and how to criticize the *Liberation Daily*. The following March the bureau issued a second proclamation, ''Information Concerning Several Problems in the *Liberation Daily*.'' Among the matters discussed there were the procedures by which Party people outside the newspaper could make contributions to it.[52]

Third, leaders of the Party and newspaper would meet together on a regular basis to assess the *Liberation Daily* and discuss communication problems. One important change the Maoists imposed in the hierarchy of the newspaper was to name Lu Dingyi, former head of the propaganda bureau of the Eighth Route Army's political department, to be general editor following the death of Yang Song in August 1942. Lu had spent his career doing propaganda work and had some editorial experience, but that may not have been the reason why Mao chose him. According to Wang Ming, Lu was an avowed opponent of the Comintern and the Internationalists.[53] Although not a member of the Politburo, he attended its meetings along with Bo Gu. On their return, they met with the editors to impart directives and determine policy.[54] Strengthening the relationship between the Party's official newspaper and the government did have its positive side. For one thing, it made *Liberation Daily* editors privy to discussions at high levels; for another, it made the newspaper the recipient of all policy pronouncements.

After Lu arrived in August 1942, the relationship among the Party, government, and *Liberation Daily* looked like this: Lu Dingyi and Bo Gu attended meetings of the Politburo and Northwest Bureau. Likewise, members of those organizations attended staff meetings at the *Liberation Daily*. Each reported back to their respective home body. Lin Boqu, representing the Central Committee, checked and approved manuscripts concerning the government while He Long of the army checked manuscripts concerning the military. Any unforeseen problems had to wait for discussion by the Northwest Bureau. Heads of departments within the *Liberation Daily* took responsibility for general news.[55] The system propagandized policy well but gave insufficient space to reporting on organizational work. During the Great Production Drive of 1943 editors attempted to correct that imbalance.

Fourth, in theory the Central Committee directed the newspaper's work, but in reality Mao controlled its course. As he was doing simultaneously within the Communist Party, he was working to consolidate his power within the communications system. At the *Liberation Daily*, Lu Dingyi represented his interests. But Mao did not content himself with behind-the-scenes manipulation; he reviewed policy, selected and revised manuscripts, and wrote articles and editorials. His first editorials appeared on October 12, 14, and 16, 1942. He then had the newspaper staff read and discuss each one in order to "raise their own Marxist thinking."[56] Between October 1942 and November 1946, Mao wrote or revised forty-nine known editorials, essays, and articles (see chapter 4 for dates).

By the late fall of 1942, the *Liberation Daily* was carrying out its propaganda role very efficiently. It employed the Party viewpoint and position to analyze problems. It announced all Party policy and the accompanying slogans. It simplified its language to be more intelligible to the general population, sent its reporters "down to the villages," and in general tried to be more mass oriented. Finally, it worked to mobilize the masses. The *Liberation Daily* was more than the Border Region's official propaganda organ, however. Although members of the Internationalist faction still retained some power over the newspaper, the *Liberation Daily* in late 1942 exhibited the basic characteristics of an official Maoist propaganda organ.

The *Liberation Daily* became the vehicle through which the Central Committee carried out rectification in other areas. Implementation took two forms. First, the newspaper gave wide coverage to study meetings, mass movements, and other activities related to the reform movement. This went beyond thought reform; it included articles on economic reforms as well. Second, the paper served as a textbook for the process of thought reform taking place at all levels of the Party. The *Liberation Daily* published the official study documents for the movement along with numerous other rectification essays (see section 1 of chapter 2 for a list of those documents). The newspaper also published two columns concerned with the Party in the rectification movement. "Party Life" (*dang de shenghuo*), which appeared between September 15, 1942, and March 23, 1943, sought to reform Party members accused of incorrect thinking by publishing positive things about the Party and promoting proletarian thought.[57] "Study" (*xuexi*) appeared on page 4 between May 13, 1942, and January 6, 1943 (see chapter 4 for dates for both columns). The Central Committee took more interest in the second column than the first, assigning Peng Zhen (a close associate of Mao's and a member of the Central Commission, which directed rectification) and Lu Dingyi to edit it. The goal of "Study" was "to help the study movement of the Border Region and Yan'an by creating a pronounced study atmosphere, expounding problems and difficulties, exchanging opinions, developing the good, and criticizing the bad."[58] Lu Dingyi wrote the lead article of the first column, "Why Rectifying the Three Styles Is the Party's Thought Revolution." In all, twenty-four columns appeared (see chapter 4).

As with every other work unit, the *Liberation Daily* staff conducted its own rectification. Following Mao's February 1942 speeches on "Rectifying the Party's Work" and "Oppose Party Formalism," the staff mobilized for rectification. A committee directed the intensive three-month study program, which began April 20 and lasted until July 20.[59] Discussion of long-term changes in the format and structure appear below, but the study movement also produced some immediate effects. Of the 245 articles reviewed during the study sessions, the committee deemed 138 good, the rest bad. Specifically, beyond articles on the labor hero Wu Manyou, they concluded that the *Liberation Daily* had failed to write enough articles about the struggle between man and nature. (For articles on Wu Manyou and labor heroes/heroines, see chapter 4.) It had also failed to provide sufficient articles on political life in the Border Region outside of those on study.[60] To correct that flaw, editors dispatched reporters to do more local reporting. In criticizing the content of articles, the staff was responding to Mao's desire to link theory and practice in all aspects of Party life. In other words, Mao was more concerned with concrete issues than he was with theoretical ones. In a 1948 address to the editorial staff of the *Shanxi-Suiyuan Daily*, Mao made clear exactly how he thought reporters should be educated. Although made several years after the *Liberation Daily*'s reform, his remarks reflect his thinking on the subject in 1942. He said:

> To teach the masses, newspaper workers should first of all learn from the masses. You comrades are all intellectuals. Intellectuals are often ignorant and often have little or no experience in practical matters. You can't quite understand the pamphlet "How to Analyze the Classes in the Rural Areas" issued in 1933; on this point, the peasants are more than a match for you, for they understand it fully as soon as they are told about it. . . . To change from lack of understanding to

understanding, one must do things and see things; that is learning. Comrades working on the newspaper should go out by turns to take part in mass work, in land reform work for a time; that is very necessary. When not going out to participate in mass work, you should hear a great deal and read a great deal about the mass movements and devote time and effort to the study of such material.[61]

After completing the three-month study program, the staff undertook an examination of individual histories. Those who worked for the *Liberation Daily* came from all over China and from various backgrounds. They had little in common except that they were intellectuals. The examination of personal histories did not take long, but for some of the staff it was a nightmare. Several people (names unknown) were taken into custody, although there were no reports of killings or torture.[62] After the first rush of accusations, senior cadres took responsibility for staff investigations, reinstating some they believed unjustly targeted. The Internationalists did not escape; in a self-criticism Bo Gu confessed to taking an "incorrect" line.[63]

It is appropriate here to discuss Party life at the newspaper. Originally, the *Liberation Daily* shared a Party branch with the NCNA. Zhang Yingwu served as secretary. Later, however, the newspaper established its own branch, with Chen Dan as secretary. As was common in the Border Region's capital, the newspaper organized the lives of its staff in a strict military fashion. Party branch representatives regimented everyone's life down to distributing toilet paper (a highly sought-after item in a world where paper was so scarce) and scheduling the room married couples used for Saturday conjugal visits. Political meetings took place every week or two. In theory, meetings were democratic, with everyone from leading cadres to general staff allowed to speak without limitations. The leadership encouraged people to launch criticisms and self-criticisms and, supposedly, kept no files of personal enmities.[64]

Rectification created a new *Liberation Daily*. Lu Dingyi assumed control on August 15, 1942, but other personnel changes took place prior to and after his arrival. After writing her own critical essay and printing others, Ding Ling lost her job as editor of the literary page to Shu Qun, who himself was replaced by a committee in September 1942. Ai Siqi took charge of "Supplements" in 1943. On March 16, 1942, the editing committee made further personnel changes, dividing responsibilities and making the *Liberation Daily* more of a committee effort. Transfers included: from page 1—Zhang Yingwu and Ye Lan; from page 2—Deng Youxing and Yang Pingzhen; from page 3—Wang Yi, Wu Lengxi, and Huang Caoliang. An example of the resulting change was page 3. Cao Ruoming was responsible for the lead news articles, with the remainder of the page divided among Zhang Yingwu, Deng Youxing, and Wu Lengxi. You Wen, Chao Dingyi, and Li Qianfeng took responsibility for the column "Party Life," while Lu Dingyi oversaw editorials; Yu Guangsheng, "Essay"; and Shu Qun, "Art and Literature." Lu Dingyi had veto power over important manuscripts; department heads declined general ones.[65]

Change occurred not only in the resident staff but at all levels of the *Liberation Daily*, and, indeed, in newspapers throughout Communist-held territory.[66] At the *Liberation Daily*, editors implemented a mass line in an effort to eradicate the gap between the staff and readers. In the spring of 1942, the editors divided the Border Region into five districts and sent a reporter and an editor or editors to each to open branch offices. Districts and staff were: Yan'an—Lin Lang (reporter); Longdong—Miao Haileng (reporter), Zhang Tiefu (editor); Suide—Tian Haiyan (reporter), Tian Fang (editor); Guanzhong—Pu Qianjian (reporter), Han Shengben (editor), Ge Ling (editor); Sanbian—Jiang Kefu (reporter), Liu Mobing (editor).[67] The newspaper also set up communications centers in other Party-held areas. In addition, beginning on January 26, 1943, the *Liberation Daily* published on page 4 a column entitled "News and Communications" (*xinwen tongxun*) (see chapter 4 for dates). Among other things, it sought to encourage communications workers to submit manuscripts that reflected readers' opinions. When the *Liberation Daily* published its thousandth issue on February 16, 1944, it had a communications network of six hundred people reporting to it every day.[68] This was a much different newspaper than the one begun by the original staff of twenty-three, three years before.[69]

In a September 1, 1943, article entitled "Our Fundamental Viewpoint Regarding Journalism," Lu Dingyi set forth the revised guidelines for reporting. Adhering to the five "W's" of who, what, when, where, and why, articles must accurately reflect mass viewpoints even though they were written by professionals. The focus of articles must be real problems, with production, military affairs, and mass-based literature given particular emphasis. Reform could not be implemented from above entirely; it had to also be internal and ongoing. Therefore, the *Liberation Daily* began to investigate itself through articles that discussed the propaganda experience and system of implementation; analyzed and calculated misprints for the newspaper during 1942; analyzed various expressions of formalism in its writing; and raised the style and form of coverage.[70]

All four pages and editorials were devoted to mass-viewpoint reporting. According to the new scheme, Border Region matters received more emphasis than international news. Articles concerning working people became, for a time, the lead stories on page 1 (see chapter 4 for dates of articles on labor heroes). Page 2 focused on news of the liberated areas; page 3, the whole country; and page 4, international news.[71] Columns also underwent revision. Strengthening synthesis and commentaries so more readers could understand them became the goal of columns on page 1. Those on page 2 sought to place actual problems in a broader context. Page 3 worked on broadening readers' horizons by better international reporting, and page 4 columns attempted to increase the quality of people's lives.[72]

Once again, page 4 provides a representative example of change. At a September 11, 1942, meeting, three leading Party people made suggestions for the page. According to one report, Lu Dingyi believed page 4 should contain many articles adapted to the demands of dissimilar people. Mao Zedong wanted to have more mass input and, in fact, set up a sixteen-person watchdog group on September 20, 1942, to help choose and edit manuscripts submitted by the public. Finally, Bo Gu envisioned a page 4 filled with shorter, snappier, more mass-oriented articles aimed at a general audience.[73] (This was a far cry from Bo Gu's original idea for page 4. His vision may not be true or may reflect his acquiescence to Mao.) With those aspirations in mind, the page underwent reform. In October, editors advertised for manuscripts in three categories: (1) literary sketches, reports, songs, short stories, cartoons; (2) scientific thought, translations; and (3) worker/peasant/soldier writings and popular works of fiction.[74] The specialized columns that dominated the early period ended, victims of their own aloofness. "Comprehensive Reports" (*zonghexing fukan jieduan*) appeared between April 1, 1942, and November 19, 1946. They differed from the specialized columns that preceded them. Rather than occupying a half page, they now took up a whole page. Their content went beyond art and literature, women, youth, workers, and so forth to include politics, economics, philosophy, history, and literary criticism, among other things. Finally, they actively sought worker/peasant/soldier participation and stopped relying so heavily on professional reporters. As for staff reporters, many now found themselves living in villages to gain the knowledge they needed to write from a mass viewpoint.[75]

That experience deeply affected many of the people who contributed to the *Liberation Daily*. A case in point is Ding Ling. After her dismissal as literary editor of the newspaper, she spent the following two years studying at the Party school and working in the countryside. Assigned to the Border Region's Cultural Association in early 1944, Ding Ling returned to writing. What she wrote after the reform differed from her earlier Yan'an work. Many of her previous characters were individualistic, fraught with anxiety, and, while sympathetic, lacked the idealization of her post-1944 characters. After her return from the countryside, her characters were based on model workers and uplifting real-life incidents. All were involved in some kind of collective work.[76] (For Ding Ling's postreform *Liberation Daily* articles, see chapter 4.)

The writings of Ding Ling are but one example of the different role the *Liberation Daily* played in the Border Region by 1943. No longer emphasizing international news, the newspaper's staff concentrated on articles that reflected the complexities of life in the Border Region. Coverage of the Great Production Drive and military affairs are good illustrations. The Great Production Drive was a campaign begun in 1943 to achieve self-sufficiency for the base area. To promote the campaign and induce everyone to join in production, the newspaper performed its agitation role well as it related heroic life stories, reported production figures, and sponsored contests between model workers. Shortly after Mao Zedong's 1942 speech on "Economic Problems and Financial Problems," the *Liberation Daily* initiated its propaganda campaign.[77] First, it published numerous articles on outstanding workers. In agriculture, it spotlighted Wu Manyou, Yang Chaochen, and the father-daughter team Ma Pi'en and Ma Ke'er; in industry, it focused on Zhao Zhangui and Zhang Ke. The advanced cooperatives of Nanniwan, Jinpenwan, and Nanqu all became the subjects of indepth articles that examined everything from farming methods to organizational structure (see chapter 4 for examples). It organized and reported on competitions between Wu Manyou and Yang Chaochen, Zhao Zhangui and Zhang Ke. Reporters were encouraged to develop personal relationships with those whom they covered. Mo Ai, for example, became friends with Wu Manyou; Mo Ai and Li Yunhui befriended the people of Nanqu cooperative.[78]

By selecting specific models and writing about them, the newspaper wanted to accomplish two goals. First, it sought to show through specific examples how following Party policy improved people's lives. Those examples then became materials for the study movement that accompanied the production campaign. Second, by summarizing production experiences and records, the *Liberation Daily* was able to introduce new economic realities like mutual-aid and cooperatives, or help disseminate scientific information concerning agriculture. The whole campaign fulfilled the agitation and organization role of the newspaper as originally conceived better than ever before.

The *Liberation Daily* employed the same techniques to report on the war against Japan. Again, it highlighted specific heroes, battles, and acts of heroism to rally the Border Region's people behind the Communist armies. If the Chinese committed act after act of heroism, then the enemy committed act after act of treachery. The best reporters traveled to battlefields and guerrilla areas with instructions to report promptly in vivid and lively detail. As with reporting on the Great Production Drive, politics determined success or failure in the army and on the battlefield. Workers, according to the *Liberation Daily* articles, achieved production excellence because they followed the correct line of the Party. Likewise, soldiers won battles because they, too, adhered to the correct line and maintained strict discipline.

What was intended to be was not always so. In my own research on labor heroines based on articles from the *Liberation Daily*, I found that with rare exception the most successful heroines did not follow the accepted Party line. In fact, most pursued independent capitalistic courses working for their own material benefit rather than for any belief in the correctness of current policy. Most were apolitical and expressed little interest in either the Communist Party or revolution. Nevertheless, the *Liberation Daily* printed article after article detailing the lives and production techniques of these famous workers. Why? Because even though they did not achieve excellence because they followed Party policy, they were successful. Therefore, they presented an important lesson for *Liberation Daily* readers to learn: through hard work and persistence, a man or woman would raise their family's standard of living and, in the process, contribute to the goal of economic self-sufficiency for the Border Region. By a roundabout route the policy goal was achieved.[79]

The writing style adopted for the postreform articles merits some attention. Critics of the prereform *Liberation Daily* charged that its articles lacked a clear and vivid style. After the reform, reporters received instructions to write in a clearer, more lively style. Speaking several years later to the editors of the *Shanxi-Suiyuan Daily*, Mao summarized his ideas on the matter: "Newspapers run by our Party . . . should be vivid, clear cut and sharp and should never mutter and mumble. . . . A blunt knife draws no blood."[80] Despite Mao's pleas for lively reportage, articles in the *Liberation Daily* remained, for the most part, turgid and stereotyped. On the one hand it was a way for journalists, nervous about the swing of the political pendulum, to protect themselves. They had no way to guarantee their safety even if they faithfully followed the official line, which had been known to change rapidly. On the other hand, some journalists may well have retained that style as a protest against a manipulative leadership.

Maverick articles did occur. On April 10, 1942, an article described the suicide of a student from the Party school.[81] Repeatedly during the reform movement, Party leaders referred to that article as an example of deviant reporting. It was deviant because it showed that not all people were happy with the course chosen by the Party. Another "offensive" article appeared on page 1 of the August 9, 1945, edition. Entitled "Wartime Technological Revolution, Atom Bomb Surprise Attack on the Enemy's Hiroshima," it used foreign service dispatches to relate the events of the first atomic bomb. The next day an irate Mao Zedong called members of the *Liberation Daily* staff to his cave and criticized them for having a "bourgeois world view." Specifically, he accused them of crediting Japan's surrender to the atomic bomb rather than to the Soviet Union's entrance into the war. They had made a grave political error.[82]

Sometimes articles did not deviate from the Party line as much as they presented controversial issues. An April 1944 page 1 article and editorial on shamans created a great stir because the editors could not agree if it was the place of the newspaper to publish news of superstitions, even though the article discussed a death that resulted from treatment by a shaman. The articles ignited a whole antishaman campaign.[83] Although articles such as these were infrequent, they reinforce the idea that while the Central Committee oversaw the *Liberation Daily*, the paper was also an entity unto itself.

Throughout the Anti-Japanese war period, the *Liberation Daily* maintained its editorial policy of supporting the united front. However, beginning in the summer of 1943, its tone grew more revolutionary. As it became increasingly clear that the war would end in Japan's defeat, Party leaders turned their attention to the impending civil war. Alongside articles urging all Chinese to unite to defeat the Japanese were articles revealing the evils of Guomindang rule. At the same time, the leadership recognized its ever-growing power in China by expanding the newspaper's coverage to include other liberated areas, Guomindang-controlled regions, and world events in addition to the Border Region. It also allowed foreign and Guomindang journalists to take a grand tour of Yan'an and the surrounding areas to gather information to tell the world about life among the "Reds."[84]

The defeat of Japan portended radical changes in the *Liberation Daily*. Civil war loomed on the horizon; articles now called for democratic elections in liberated areas to form strong governments. Direct attacks on the Guomindang pervaded the newspaper.[85] The leading members of the staff differed, too. Lu Dingyi had taken the position of chief of the Central Committee's propaganda bureau; Yu Guangsheng replaced him as general editor. Ai Siqi assisted him while Gao Yangwen edited news for the liberated areas and Liao Gaixiang handled that for the Guomindang areas. Yang Yingwu edited page 1; Yang Pingzhen, international news, Wen Jize, the supplements; and Li Feitian directed proofreading.[86]

While these changes altered the style and form of the newspaper, more fundamental changes were in store. Peace meant that the Party leaders had to reform their communications system to adapt to the current situation and to meet new demands. On August 25, 1945, the editing committees of the *Liberation Daily* and the NCNA met to discuss the future. Bo Gu, Yu Guangsheng, Ai Siqi, Yu Jiansheng, Cao Ruoming, and Chen Kehan attended.[87] As a result of that meeting a three-member delegation from the *Liberation Daily* and the news service set out in October to establish a branch office in the Jin-Cha-Ji base area. Because of unstable conditions there, however, they moved onto the Northeast where they set up operations. The Party's communications system in the Shaan-Gan-Ning Border Region had relinquished its monopoly on the news. As Party-held territory expanded, so did the news. One central newspaper was not enough, so at the beginning of 1946 the Beiping Communist Party sponsored the *Beiping Liberation Daily* (*Beiping jiefang ribao*). The NCNA and the *Liberation Daily* transferred Qian Junruan and Yu Guangyuan there to work. The first edition appeared on February 22, 1946, and thereafter at three-day intervals.[88]

In Yan'an, although the newspaper remained important, its preeminence had been usurped by Yan'an's radio station. On September 11, 1945, station XNCR began daily broadcasts, concentrating on current affairs, news of the liberated areas, and editorials. Because its broadcasts reached the entire nation, it became the official voice of the Central Committee.[89]

When Bo Gu left the NCNA in February 1946 to represent the Party at the Political Consultative Conference, Yu Guangsheng took over for him, once again merging the leadership of the *Liberation Daily* and the NCNA.[90] The Central Committee Secretariat confirmed that merger on May 28, 1946, when it ratified "The NCNA–*Liberation Daily* Management Principles." According to that document, new historical developments determined that the center of the Party's communication system should be the NCNA. To conform to that directive, both news organizations restructured themselves. The idea was to strengthen the dissemination of Party propaganda and to adapt foreign wire-service articles to Party policy. Therefore, all news came via the NCNA; it controlled station XNCR and the *Liberation Daily*'s international, Guomindang area, and liberated area news reporting. The newspaper maintained an editing office responsible for page 1 and supplements on page 4. In July 1946, Liao Chengzhi assumed the concurrent posts of head of the news service and of the *Liberation Daily*.[91] The *Liberation Daily* retained its position as the leading Communist Party newspaper but lost it as the official voice of the Central Committee.

## The Last Period (November 20, 1946–March 27, 1947)

The civil war, unrest in Guomindang-controlled areas, and surging anti-Americanism dominated the *Liberation Daily* during its last four months. War news dominated page 1. Between November 20, 1946, and December 20, 1946, for example, coverage of the war led the headlines for eighteen straight days. Editors used news reports, news bulletins, essays, special reports, songs, and short stories among other formats to reinforce positive war news. Often reporters detailed special case studies to describe general military situations. The goal was two-fold: proclaim the victories of the Communist army, and expand support for the Party and its policies.

But not all news was good. On November 17, 1946, Guomindang calvary attacked the Border Region's Sanbian district. On November 20, 1946, the *Liberation Daily* went from four pages to two as the Central Committee dispersed communications workers to other areas. "A wily hare has three burrows" became the work plan, with Yan'an, Wayaobu, and Shexian (in Hebei) as the three burrows. To protect the newspaper even further, the printing presses were moved from Yan'an to Fengjiacha in Hebei.[92]

The two-page editions presented problems. The reduced space did not allow for a literature and art or a features section. At first, editors attempted to merge these sections to page 2 and even adopted smaller print for literature and art. That did not prove successful, however, so they began to publish a "Sunday supplement" (*Xingqiri zengkan jieduan*), expanding the newspaper to four pages. That lasted until March 15, 1947.

On March 11, 1947, and again on March 13, the Guomindang bombed Yan'an. Although most staff members had already fled to Shijiapan near the presses in Fengjiacha, those who remained behind doggedly published the *Liberation Daily*. Their last edition, number 2,118, appeared on March 14. That same day the Guomindang's 16th Brigade began an all-out invasion of Yan'an, pitting its 204,000 soldiers against the Communists' 25,000. Along with remaining Central Committee members, the *Liberation Daily*'s skeleton staff fled the city. Fang Changjiang directed publication work in Shijiapan and published edition number 2,119 on March 16. While staff from the NCNA the *Liberation Daily* traveled various routes to Shexian, Fang and his staff continued to publish regular-sized two-page editions. The loss of manpower affected reporting, however; international news, for example, was reduced to the one-column "International Week" (*guoji yizhou*). An edition appeared daily between March 16 and March 27. On March 27, 1947, with the enemy perilously near, the last edition of the *Liberation Daily*, number 2,130, appeared at 10:00 A.M. That afternoon, the remaining staff fled.[93] A few months later, the Communist army switched from a strategic defense to a strategic offense on a nationwide scale. The drive for victory was on.

The *Liberation Daily* had an enormous impact on the history of the Party during the Yan'an years. Not only was it the repository for all major policy pronouncements, it also played a crucial role in the struggle taking place within the Party itself. The Communist Party that claimed victory in 1949 in large part wrote its own history on the pages of the *Liberation Daily*.

# Two

# The Medium and Rectification

In the early 1940s the Communist Party carried out a massive reform movement that consisted of several campaigns and lasted until 1945. The rectification of styles campaign (*zhengfeng*), the focus of this chapter, took place between February 1942 and July 1943. Primarily a study movement, it had three goals: (1) to reeducate cadres in Marxism-Leninism and its specific application to the problems of China; (2) to make the Border Region an economically and politically independent area with change initiated by the masses; and (3) to establish Mao Zedong as the Party's undisputed ideological and political leader. One of Mao's chief objectives in the campaign was to rid himself of the Internationalists once and for all.

The term *zhengfeng* is a contraction of *zhengdun* (to correct) and *zuofeng* (work style) and connotes reform rather than purge. What took place in the Communist Party during the early 1940s was a reform in the sense that it concentrated on "nonantagonistic" contradictions (i.e., among the people), whereas a purge eliminated "antagonistic" contradictions (i.e., between us and the enemy).[1] For many undergoing it, however, it may have seemed more like a purge than a reform.

## Sources of Rectification

Rectification resulted from the tension pervading the Border Region Party organization during the late 1930s. Both the Guomindang and the Japanese watched apprehensively as Communist Party activity, military and otherwise, proliferated in North and East China. Each responded in characteristic fashion. The Japanese crippled the Communist army with an all-out attack on North China launched in reaction to the Hundred Regiments Campaign of August–December 1940. Likewise, in January 1941, Guomindang troops attacked and virtually annihilated the New Fourth Army headquarters in Anhui Province. To make matters worse, the Communist army itself was suffering from morale problems. Reports emerged of soldiers shooting deserters without authorization, beating up villagers, and torturing prisoners of war.[2] Combined with the tightening of the blockade imposed by the Nationalist government on the Border Region in 1939, these crises put a terrible strain on the resources and leadership of the Shaan-Gan-Ning Border Region.

If Party leaders had been united and the membership well-disciplined, the external crises might not have created the chaos they did. Such was not the case. One problem was that between July 1937 and July 1940, membership in the Communist Party increased from 40,000 to 800,000.[3] On the one hand, the young intellectuals and uneducated peasants who formed the core of the new recruits failed to fully understand Marxism-Leninism, the philosophical basis of the revolution they championed. On the other hand, many of those with a thorough background in Marxism-Leninism, like the Internationalists, had little experience with a mass-based rural revolution. This ignorance of policy and reality prevented both groups from adequately implementing a program that would advance the Border Region toward socialism. It also caused dissension within the ranks of the Party.

**Format for Rectification**

An equally divisive problem was factionalism within the top levels of the Party. Rectification was more than a movement to reform and reeducate errant cadres. It was also the instrument Mao Zedong used to consolidate his position in the Party, and to defeat those who opposed him or were even thought to oppose him. To take charge, Mao appointed the Central Commission to Lead Rectification composed of Liu Shaoqi, Kang Sheng, Chen Yun, Peng Zhen, Gao Gang, and Li Fuchun, all supporters of Mao. Kang Sheng served as chairman until January 1943 when Liu Shaoqi returned from Central China and took over.[4] Kang was responsible for implementing the rectification study program in the Party while Li Fuchun was responsible for it at the Central Party School.[5]

According to the theory of rectification proposed by Frederick Teiwes, a revolutionary organization generally suffers from leadership cleavages when ascending to power. Such cleavages force it to adopt coercive techniques for internal control. When the organization is unified, however, it can use persuasive control techniques. In like manner, where such an organization has a secure environment, it may develop systematic educational methods. Where its external environment is threatening, coercive methods work better. Although an external crisis existed in late 1941, the Border Region's security was never threatened.[6] In the early 1940s, the environment was conducive to persuasive change.

The idea of using persuasion rather than coercion to maintain discipline within the Party ranks was not new with Mao. Although pre-1935 leaders, including the Internationalists, often treated deviationists harshly, they recognized a need to limit inner-Party struggle. Therefore, while people like Chen Duxiu were expelled from the Party, others, like Qu Qiubai, retained positions without power. Mao himself held prestigious posts in the early 1930s when his power was at its lowest.[7]

Although dissension still existed, by early 1942 the Communist Party was ideologically, politically, and organizationally sound. Mao, therefore, began to consolidate his power through persuasion. He chose as his base of operation the system of Party schools, which the Central Committee established at its 1938 Plenum. Top-level cadres no longer went to Moscow to study. Educating them within the Border Region became the norm, as more than four thousand cadres took part in a study movement during 1939 and 1940. They attended the Central Party School, the Anti-Japanese Military and Political University, the Lu Xun Academy of Arts and Literature, or the Academy of Natural Sciences in Yan'an. Power over this system gave Mao ideological control over the Party.[8] The *Liberation Daily* was an integral part of that system.

Not everyone supported Mao's plan to consolidate his power and elevate himself. Even among those in the Party's higher echelons who supported Mao, many opposed using his works as the focal point of a study campaign. Zhu De, for example, was a Maoist but feared that his own accomplishments would be overshadowed in the rush to elevate Mao. Liu Shaoqi also supported Mao but questioned his soundness as a theoretician.

The Internationalists and other opponents of Mao charged that he did not advocate a process that "creatively" developed Marxism-Leninism but one that would "revise and/or distort" it. Their opponents made the countercharge that targets of rectification—subjectivism, secretarianism, and formalism—were remnants of the "three left lines" promoted when the Internationalists controlled the Party.[9] Not one of the documents used in the study movement was written by a member of the Internationalists, and several (including Mao's "Oppose Party Formalism" and Liu Shaoqi's "Liquidate Menshevik Thought") attacked the foreign formalism and dogmatism attributed to that group.[10]

Realizing the need to reorganize the political and economic structure of the Border Region to survive the external crises, and determined to clear the obstacles to unchallenged power, Mao Zedong formally initiated the rectification of styles campaign. More than a thousand Party members gathered at the Central Party School on February 1, 1942, to hear him inaugurate the movement with his address, "Reform Learning, the Party, and Literature." A week later he gave his second major address, "Oppose Party Formalism."[11] In both speeches, Mao promoted the "sinification of Marxism." He criticized those, such as the Internationalists, who studied Marx, Lenin, and Stalin without relating them to the Chinese revolution, and he urged Party members to relate experience to theory.

If cadres were to transform the Border Region into a self-sufficient revolutionary society, there could be no dissension in the ranks. Cadres had to be dedicated to defeating the Japanese and committed to a complete social change well-grounded in Marxism. Party leaders attempted to integrate the various components of the rank and file into a coherent whole by motivating and inspiring them. At the same time, they tightened ideological standards and decreed a uniform Maoist methodology. Ironically, that meant moving from the earlier formalistic and bureaucratic procedures in Party and government administration toward a more decentralized and informal structure. It also meant increasing production to make the Border Region self-sufficient and to improve the people's standard of living.

### The Critical Writers

Many of the urban writers who had come to the Shaan-Gan-Ning Border Region to join the revolution did not share Mao's concept of rectification. They mistook the confusion during the early stages of the campaign as an open invitation to indulge in a free exchange of ideas. Accordingly, they unleashed a barrage of critical essays on the literary page (page 4) of the *Liberation Daily*. Edited by one of their own,

Ding Ling, page 4 provided an excellent forum for their vigorous, if short-lived, outburst between mid-March and mid-April 1942. (Section 4 below lists articles written by the critics and those attacking them.)

Critical essays, however, grew out of more than confusion. Timothy Cheek argues that in 1941–42, two agendas existed for rectification: Mao's and the revolutionary writers'. Mao wanted to insure his own preeminence by attacking the Internationalists and the entrenched Yan'an bureaucracy. The writers, on the other hand, had broader social aims. Wang Shiwei and Ding Ling are good examples of the critics' thinking. In "We Need Critical Essays," which appeared in the October 23, 1941, *Liberation Daily*, Ding Ling called for writers to follow the example of the dean of Chinese literature, Lu Xun, in using the short critical essay called *zawen* to seek out and tell the truth. Several months later, Wang Shiwei wrote "Statesmen-Artists," which appeared in the popular literary journal *Grain Rain*. There he suggested that writers act as loyal but vigilant critics of the rectification process. Neither of these concepts was what Mao had in mind. He believed that intellectuals must be subordinated to the Leninist Party structure. In other words, they should tow the Party line.[12]

But it was too late; Wang Shiwei and Ding Ling had set the guidelines and other writers quickly took up the banner. Using the critical essay, the protesters went to work as the Party's loyal but independent censors.[13] Never one to avoid controversy, Ding Ling took the lead by publishing the first critical essay. On March 9, 1942, "Reflections on March 8" appeared attacking the Party's policy concerning women. Within the month, seven more critical essays appeared on page 4.

Party leaders could not tolerate such vehement protest and launched a counterattack during the first week of April. The critical essay ceased to appear in the newspaper. Their vehicle denied to them, the critics tried a new route: passive resistance to studying rectification documents and to attending the increasingly widespread self-criticism sessions. That route did not escape censure as editorials appeared on April 2, 4–8, and 11, 1942, criticizing that type of protest as well.

As is often the case in a Chinese Communist Party campaign, the leadership singled out certain errant elements to illustrate ideas unacceptable to the Party. In this case, it was writers and intellectuals. The campaign to reeducate them was in full swing in May when a conference convened in Yan'an to discuss the role of art and literature in society. On May 2 and 23, 1942, Mao Zedong announced the orthodox line for the arts: all literature was to be mass-oriented and reflect the class stand of the proletariat.[14] In his second speech, Mao, without making direct accusations, called upon critical intellectuals to recant their views.[15] None of the critics escaped censure, but Wang Shiwei was targeted for special criticism.

Why Wang Shiwei? Wang joined the Party in 1926 and soon became known as a translator of Marxist-Leninist writings from Russian. He was involved with the Chinese Trotskyites during the late 1920s and corresponded with Chen Duxiu until 1936. His reputation as an ideology and literature specialist ensured him a research position at the Marx-Lenin Institute when he arrived in Yan'an in the late 1930s. "Statesmen-Artists" was not Wang's only inflammatory essay. On March 13 and 23, 1942, he published an essay entitled "Wild Lilies." Consisting of a preface and four short critical essays, "Wild Lilies" was modeled on Lu Xun's "A Rose Without Blooms," two satirical essays written in 1926 criticizing literary leaders' hypocrisy.[16] In his essay, Wang accused Party leaders of creating an elite aloof from the masses and called for constant vigilance against evil.

Rectification began at the Central Research Institute on March 19, 1942, in the midst of the publication of "Wild Lilies." It could not have come at a worse time for Wang Shiwei. Although he had attacked the Internationalists in his critical essay, calling them " 'great masters' who can't open their mouths without talking about 'Ancient Greece,' " he was associated with them through his mentor at the institute, Luo Mai. Luo, along with the other Internationalists, saw the campaign against Wang as an opportunity to divert attention from themselves. They joined enthusiastically in denouncing Wang Shiwei.[17]

The small Party group to which Wang belonged at the Central Research Institute also contained Chen Boda, Mao's cultural adviser and Wang Shiwei's enemy. When Wang sought to ignore the Party's rectification of styles program of self-criticism and document study, Chen attacked. The animosity between the two men stemmed from an article Wang wrote during the fall of 1940 entitled a "A Short Essay on National Forms in Art and Literature." Angry at the article's contents, Chen wrote a response demanding a revision. Their quarrel was a continuation of the 1935–37 debate during which Lu Xun and Hu Feng resisted Zhou Yang's demands that writers use "national" forms instead of the Western forms they preferred.

Under pressure, Wang refused to retract and agreed to revise only after the two men reached a compromise. Chen waited to publish his 1941 criticism after the attack on Wang began in the late spring of 1942. Given the bitterness of the debate, Chen might well have convinced Mao to make Wang and other critical writers the campaign's targets.

Moreover, Wang's article appeared during the winter of 1940–41 at a time when the Maoists were beginning to worry about the leftist tendencies they perceived in the leading research and propaganda organs. It may have also influenced Mao's decision to crush ideological deviation by reviving the cadre education movement. Moreover, Wang was a perfect scapegoat for Mao's campaign. He was not widely known and, along with the other critical intellectuals, was isolated enough that attacks against him would not cause a major upheaval in the Party organization.

Finally, the anti-Wang campaign coincided with a Japanese blockade of the base area and a time when the Border Region's economy was in a disastrous state. A vituperative campaign would be just the thing to divert attention from critical internal problems.[18]

The above reasons all played a part in determining the decision to target Wang, but Mao Zedong had basic ideological differences with Wang Shiwei. Wang's proposals ran counter to Mao's concept of rectification struggle, which called not for intellectuals using the critical essay but for small Party-led groups engaged in face-to-face criticism/self-criticism. Wang also disagreed with Mao's argument that dissenting opinions fueled the fires of Japanese and Guomindang propaganda. Moreover, Wang represented the remnants of what Cheek calls the "cosmopolitan strain of May Fourth intellectual experimentation inside the [Party]." This group did not fit into Mao's nativist concept of the Party. Therefore, Wang's voice had to be silenced if Mao was to achieve preeminence. The whole literary rectification was the final battle between the cosmopolitan and nativist trends in the Communist movement.[19]

Attacks on Wang began in May and raged throughout June and July 1942. On June 8, a thousand people from schools and Party organs in Yan'an met to charge Wang with being a Trotskyite subversive and a petty-bourgeois idealist. A second meeting held from June 15 to 18 accused Wang of plotting secretly with the international Trotskyite movement. Chaired by Ding Ling, Zhou Yang, and Sai Kesan, it was the first major public exercise in ideological education found in the rectification movement.

The June 18 session ended the struggle meetings against Wang, but the *Liberation Daily* continued to carry articles denouncing him for another month. These anti-Wang articles used their own alternative to the critical essay. By employing a distorted kind of textual analysis, they sought to demonstrate Wang's "guilt."[20]

## The Role of the *Liberation Daily*

The *Liberation Daily* not only published the critics' essays, it also published the attacks against them. That lapse into intellectual debate was brief, however. The *Liberation Daily* was the principal propaganda organ and, as such, supported the Party's position during rectification despite being headed by an Internationalist, and a target of the campaign, for most of the period. As Mao Zedong assumed control of the newspaper during the spring of 1942, he used it increasingly as a vehicle for his own ideas. He declared it the official organ of daily business at an April 1942 meeting held to discuss its part in the campaign. Then he directed the newspaper to publish reform documents along with news of the campaign's progress at all levels of the Party.[21] Between 1942 and 1944, the newspaper functioned as it always had—announcing policy goals, promoting slogans that insured their acceptance, and creating the enthusiasm needed for their successful implementation. Nevertheless, the role of the newspaper changed and extended beyond its routine activities. Certainly, the *Liberation Daily* served as the authoritative source through which the Maoists asserted their ideology. But its articles did not address implementation so much as implementors and the problem of making sure they were educated in the politically correct line. If propaganda is meant to modify expectations about the future, then what is seen in the *Liberation Daily* during rectification is the process of educating cadres to accept, understand, and promote those modified expectations in the right way. The expectations themselves were not crucial; the attitude of the Party members toward them was.

The reform movement itself was more than the rectification of styles campaign, which lasted from February 1942 until July 1943. After a preparatory period (September 1941–February 1942) and the rectification of styles campaign, there was the counterespionage campaign (summer of 1943–summer of 1944) and the campaign to rewrite Party history. Attention turned from investigating cadres' history to counterespionage activities in the spring of 1943. Party organizations had screened cadres looking for spies since the late 1930s, but there had never been a widespread purge. Mao called for increased vigilance against spies in 1942 and for an all out movement against them in 1943. By August 1943 some four thousand "Guomindang agents" and other hostile elements had been uncovered in the Border Region.[22] Wang Ming later claimed that the campaign was directed against the Internationalists, including himself, Bo Gu, Luo Fu, Wang Jiaxiang, Kai Feng, Yang Shangkun, and Zhu Rui.[23]

In 1944, the Maoists moved again to eliminate opposition when they began a campaign to rewrite Party history. Discussions among senior cadres on the subject had been going on since September 1941, but there was no move to begin the process until 1944. During this campaign, many of the remaining Internationalists who held positions in the propaganda system were removed.[24] Although he remained head of the NCNA, Bo Gu left the *Liberation Daily* at this time.

Overall, the reform movement sought to "indoctrinate and train an elite that was clearly distinct from the masses in the eyes of top [Communist Party] leaders, despite their repeated urging that members of that elite get close to the masses and unite with them."[26] While some parts of it, like the counterespionage campaign, were mass campaigns in the true sense, other parts, such as the "to the village" campaign, were conducted like mass campaigns even though they were directed at the elite.

Mao believed that propaganda consisted of popularization, simplification, and correlation to political tasks. His chief method of propaganda was always the mass campaign (or in this case a variation of it). Because the rectification campaign of the early 1940s was carried out like a mass campaign, the media—specifically the *Liberation Daily*—played a critical role. Through it, Party leaders publicly announced the campaign, reported on mass meetings, and published all the materials necessary to make it flourish. The newspaper provided a convincing interpretation of Party goals set forth in a logical and easy-to-understand way.

## Rectification: A Case Study

The rectification of styles campaign provides an excellent case study for the *Liberation Daily*. Analysis of the reform movement as reported in the newspaper includes the "official" documents of the movement; related articles such as reports of meetings, examples of conflict among the leadership and the evolving cult of Mao, and essays written by major rectification figures; "Study" columns; editorials; and articles from the campaign on art and literature. I have restricted the case study to the rectification of styles campaign because it is a good excellent example of inner-Party struggle and Mao's consolidation of power. Many other events in the Border Region are connected in some way to the overall reform movement. For example, the Production Drive or the counterespionage campaign, both of which gained momentum in 1943, are not included here. Citations for these are found in chapter 3.

There were twenty-two official study documents for the reform campaign listed in an April 3, 1942, Central Committee report. Those that appeared in the newspaper are cited below. Other editorials and articles were selected according to several criteria. Included are articles that reflect major policy issues and ideological struggle cited in Compton's *Mao's China* and other major secondary works or in the *Liberation Daily* itself, and editorials and articles cited in *The Great Victory of the Chinese Communist Party's First Rectification Campaign* (*Zhongguo gongchandang diyici zhengfeng de weida shengli*), "Important Events in Yan'an's *Liberation Daily*" (Yan'an 'Jiefang ribao' dashiji), and *The Yan'an Rectification Movement* (*Yan'an zhengfeng yundong*).[26] *The Great Victory* is a treatise on the rectification campaign compiled in 1957. Although primarily a history, it discusses the *Liberation Daily*'s role in the campaign and includes articles and editorials that the Party considered important. "Important Events in Yan'an's *Liberation Daily*" is an analytical chronology of important events in the newspaper compiled in 1984 for the journal *Journalism Research Materials* (*Xinwen yanjiu ziliao*). *The Yan'an Rectification Movement* is a compilation of important rectification writings found in Party publications of the period.

This chapter ends in September 1943. By that time all the major reform documents had appeared, the "Study" column in the *Liberation Daily* had ended, the campaign in art and literature had concluded, and the Maoists were in power. There is no attempt here to included all articles on the campaign, but only those from four categories: major articles and documents, editorials, "Study" columns, and art and literature.

## The Survey

### I.  Articles and Documents

During the fall of 1941 articles on political study and other issues preceding the actual campaign appeared:

1. "Fandui xuexizhong de jiaotiaozhuyi" (Oppose dogmatism in study), September 2, 1941 (editorial).
   *Synopsis:* At the Sixth Plenum in 1938, Mao had called for the sinification of Marxism as an antidote to the dogmatism within the Party. But in the intervening three years, nothing had been done. That was wrong because sinification was in accordance with Lenin and Stalin. Mao Zedong was developing Marxism-Leninism according to the situation in China at that time.
2. "Jiaqiang dangsheng de duanlian" (Strengthening party discipline), September 6, 1941 (editorial).
3. "Fandui zhuguanzhuyi" (Oppose subjectivism), by Ai Siqi, September 19, 1941, p. 3 (continued September 20).
   *Note:* A leading Marxist philosopher, Ai Siqi arrived in Yan'an in mid-1937 from Shanghai where he had been active in the intellectual world. He remained in the Border Region for a decade, serving as the Party's leading philosopher through his writing, teaching, and translating. Mao Zedong openly admired his work and was greatly influenced by him. Ai's writings apparently were the source of Mao's information on contradictions and dialectics. Along with Zhou Yang, Zhang Ruxin, and Chen Boda, Ai Siqi was a member of Mao's personal think tank.[27]
4. "Zhuguanzhuyi de laiyuan" (The source of subjectivism), by Ai Siqi, October 14, 1941, p. 3.
5. "Ruhe yu zhuguanzhuyi zuo douzheng" (What does subjectivism struggle with?), by Wang Ziye, November 8, 1941, p. 3.
6. "Zhonggong zhongying guanyu Yan'an ganbu xuexiao de jueding" (The CCP Central Committee's decision regarding the Yan'an cadre school), December 20, 1941, p. 1.
   *Official document:* Translated in Compton, pp. 74–79.

In February 1942 Mao Zedong officially launched the reform movement. The newspaper printed the complete text of most major speeches and study documents. These included discussions of the campaign itself and examples of personal and group experiences and reform. Items 7 through 30 below are the official documents of reform plus materials related to or explaining them. Several of the documents listed in the April 3, 1942, Central Committee report on the rectification of styles campaign as "official" did not appear in the *Liberation Daily*. Also cited in this section are the principal articles on the important Senior Cadre Conference.

7. "Zhengfeng 'xuefeng,' 'dangfeng,' 'wenfeng' " (Reform in "writing," "the party," and "literature"), February 2, 1942, editorial.

*Synopsis:* Discusses Mao's speech at the opening ceremonies of the Party school (see no. 22 below). Focused on the call for reforming the "three styles," stressed that cadres need not fear criticism or self-criticism, or exposing their weaknesses because their responsibility was to the people and the revolution, not to themselves. The Party line was the correct one; cadres must implement it in the real world and utilize it to analyze concrete matters. The real theorist was one who could take the spirit and methods of Marxism-Leninism and solve practical problems. Cadres were to "continuously study and keep on fighting despite setbacks."

8. "Jiaqiang difang zai zhiganbu jiaoyu" (The education of cadres in service), February 5, 1942 (editorial).

9. "Guanyu zai zhiganbu jiaoyu de jueding" (Decision regarding professional cadre), March 2, 1942, p. 1.

*Official document:* The actual statement was issued on February 28, 1942, but appeared in the *Liberation Daily* on March 3, 1942. Translated in Compton, pp. 80–87.

10. "Gaizao women de xuexi" (Reform our study), by Mao Zedong, March 27, 1942, p. 1.

*Official document:* Translated in Compton, pp. 59–68.

11. "Guanyu zai Yan'an taolun Zhongying jueding ji Mao Zedong tongzhi zhengfeng sanfeng baogao de jueding" (The decision of the Central Committee on Mao Zedong's reform the "three styles" report), April 7, 1942, p. 1.

*Official documents:* The actual statement was issued on April 3, 1942, but did not appear in the *Liberation Daily* until April 7, 1942. Translated in Compton, pp. 1–8.

Between April 10 and 20, 1942, the *Liberation Daily* published the "Rectification 'Three Styles' Discussion Materials Special Edition" (Zhengfeng sanfeng taolun ziliao teji). These issues of the newspaper were intended as a study guide for cadres undergoing reform.[28] They contained most of the twenty-two articles targeted for study in the reform movement.[29]

12. "Fandui dangnei jizhong bu zhengque de qingxiang" (Oppose several incorrect tendencies in the Party), by Mao Zedong, April 10, 1942, p. 4.

*Official document:* Translated in Compton, pp. 239–45.

13. "Fandui ziyouzhuyi" (Oppose liberalism), by Mao Zedong, April 10, 1942, p. 4.

*Official document:* Translated in Compton, pp. 184–87.

14. " 'Nongcun diaocha' xu" (Preface to "Village Investigations"), by Mao Zedong, April 10, 1942, p. 4.

*Official document:* Translated in Compton, pp. 54–58.

15. "Lun dang de Buershiweikehua," by Joseph Stalin, April 10, 1942, p. 4.

*Official document:* Translated in Compton, pp. 269–71.

16. "Zenyang zuo yige gongchandangyuan" (How to be a member of the Communist Party), by Chen Yun, April 12, 1942, p. 4.

*Official document:* Translated in Compton, pp. 88–107.

17. "Lun gongchandangyuan de xiuyang" (How to be a good Communist), by Liu Shaoqi, April 13–14, 1942, p. 4.

*Official document:* Translated in Compton, pp. 108–55. See also Liu Shaoqi, *Three Essays on Party-Building*, pp. 1–97. For a discussion of Liu's role in rectification, see no. 26 below.

18. "Sudalin lun lingdao yu diaocha" (Stalin on leadership and investigation), April 18, 1942, p. 4.

19. "Liening Sudalin deng lun dang de jilu yu minzhu" (Lenin, Stalin, and others on Party discipline and democracy), April 18, 1942, p. 4.

*Official document:* Listed in Compton, p. 7, but not translated.

20. "Sudalin lun pingjunzhuyi" (Stalin on egalitarianism), April 20, 1942, p. 4.

21. "Zenyang yanjiu zhongxuanbu siyue sanhao jueding" (How to study the April 3d decision of the Central Committee propaganda department), by Kang Sheng, April 22, 1942, p. 1.

*Synopsis:* Advised cadres to study the reform documents conscientiously and to work to grasp the "weapons of criticism and self-criticism." Free rein must be given to party members so that they reflect the opinion of the grass roots. Nevertheless, democracy within the Party cannot extend beyond reasonable limits because it will destroy Party unity. If there is democracy then there must also be strong leadership, but that group cannot become tyrants. "The top level must allow lower-level democracy." Where there are mistakes, all levels must work to recognize, understand, and correct them. Nevertheless, various levels cannot become too independent; there must be discipline within the Party. All Party members must uphold the idea of "one heart, one mind" and "concern for the country and the people."

*Note:* This is part of the report on the April 18, 1942, Yan'an cadre study meeting. Compton mentions two reports by Kang Sheng as important reform documents on p. 6. This may be one of them.

Kang Sheng served as the chief security and intelligence officer in the Border Region and, as such, probably headed the Social Affairs Department, the principal security organ. Li Kenong replaced him in that position in 1946. In addition, he was also believed to have held a high position in one of Yan'an's Party Schools. He also chaired the Central Commission to Lead Rectification until 1943. Furthermore, he was reported to have been elected to the Central Committee at the Seventh National Party Congress (April–June 1945), the Congress where Mao established his preeminent position in the Party.[30]

22. "Zhengfeng xuefeng, dangfeng, wenfeng" (Reform in learning, the Party, and literature), by Mao Zedong, April 27, 1942, p. 1.

*Official document:* This is the official text of Mao's February 1, 1942, address at the opening ceremonies of the Party school. See no. 7 above. Translated in Compton, pp. 9–32.

23. "Zhonggong zhongying xuanchuanbu guanyu zai quandang jinxing zhengfeng sanfeng xuexi yundong de zhishi" (The CCP's Central Committee propaganda department directs the whole Party to advance the study movement to rectify the "three styles"), June 12, 1942, p. 1.

24. "Fandui dangbagu" (Oppose party formalism), by Mao Zedong, June 18, 1942, pp. 1 and 2.

*Official document:* This is the official text of Mao's February 8, 1942, address at the Party school. Translated in Compton, pp. 33–53.

25. "Du 'Zhongying guanyu diaocha yanjiu jueding' ji 'nongcun diaocha xuyan er' yihou" (After reading the "Central Committee's decisions concerning investigation and research" and "Second preface to village investigations"), June 27, 1942, p. 4.

*Note:* The two articles analyzed here did not appear in the *Liberation Daily.*

26. "Lun dangnei douzheng" (On inner-Party struggle), by Liu Shaoqi, October 9, 1942, pp. 1 and 2.

*Note:* This is translated in Compton, pp. 188–238, but not listed as an official study document in the April 3, 1942, Central Committee report on the rectification of styles campaign. See also Liu Shaoqi, *Three Essays on Party-Building,* pp. 101–61.

This last article, "On Inner-Party Struggle," is one of the most important documents of the reform movement and established Liu Shaoqi as a major theorist and the principal ally of Mao Zedong. As director of the Cadre Training Department and simultaneously as secretary of the CCP's Central Plains Bureau, Liu achieved a high position within the Party between 1938 and 1939. During rectification he served as secretary general of the Party's Central Secretariat, vice-chairman of the Party's Military Affairs Commission, and from 1943, chair of the Central Commission to Lead Rectification. In those capacities he was instrumental in orchestrating the reform movement.

His theoretical contributions to the movement were threefold. In 1939 Liu delivered a series of lectures at the Party school entitled "How to Be a Good Communist." Liu drew upon ideas of Marx and Confucius to argue that Party members must steel themselves through practical struggle, subordinating their own interests to those of the Party. His 1941 lecture, "On Inner-Party Struggle," replaced Wang Ming's 1931–32 pamphlet of the same title. In his essay, Liu stressed the ideas of criticism/self-criticism and supported issue-oriented struggle. He also argued that the earliest stages of rectification (pre-February 1942) lacked leadership, relying instead on a plethora of slogans. Part of the process of establishing a strong leadership, according to Liu, was purging Mao's leftist opponents from the hierarchy of the Party. His attacks on that group culminated in his 1943 essay, "Liquidate Menshevist Thought," in which he accused the Internationalists of being doctrinaire.[31]

27. "Bianqu dang gaoganhui shengli bimu" (The curtain falls on the victorious meeting of the Border Region's senior cadre meeting), January 31, 1943, p. 1.

*Note:* Held between October 19, 1942, and January 14, 1943, under the auspices of the Party's Northwest Bureau, the Senior Cadre Conference met to solve three major problems facing local Party organizations: (1) the quest for unified leadership, (2) the definition of the Party's tasks in the area, and (3) the revision of Party history of the Border Region. Mao Zedong, representing the Politburo, and Gao Gang, representing the Northwest Bureau, dominated the conference. One of its important tasks was to consider rewriting Party history, particularly that of the Border Region. This was of particular importance to Gao Gang, who had been called a "rightist" when the Internationalists led the Communist Party and who had been rehabilitated only after Mao Zedong and Zhu De arrived in Shaanxi. He believed that those responsible for the leftist line in the Border Region had not been thoroughly exposed, and that local history ought to be rewritten to exonerate him.

During this same conference it was also decided to begin restructuring the social, economic, political, and military dimensions. The early "crack troops and simple administration" and "to the village" movements had heralded a full-scale move in this direction. Such a restructuring meant placing an emphasis on a new approach to agricultural production. The programs in administrative reform and rent reduction paved the way for larger mutual-aid units. These were designed to revolutionize and stimulate the rural economy and create the nucleus for new forms of social and political life. If peasants cooperated fully, they could expect personal gain.[32]

28. "Gao Gang tongzhi zongjie guoqu lishi jiaoxun" (Gao Gang's lecture summarizing past history), January 31, 1943, p. 1.

*Note:* During the early 1930s, Gao was one of the leaders of the Communist guerrillas who tried to establish a viable peasant-based movement in Shaanxi. After the arrival of Mao Zedong in 1935, Gao served in several posts. From 1938 until 1940 he was secretary of the Party Committee for the Shaan-Gan-Ning Border Region; from 1940 until the end of the war he was secretary of the Party's Northwest Bureau; and throughout the Yan'an period he chaired the Border Region assembly. He consolidated his own position in the bureau at the Senior Cadre Conference, which he convened. In the address cited above, Gao gave his version of the history of the Party's Northwest branch. Part of the attack on the "leftism" of the Internationalists and of Mao's own move to consolidate his power, the address signaled Gao's victory over his former rivals and established his preeminence in the Border Region. Mao relied heavily on Gao's local power in his attempt to topple Wang Ming. About Gao he said: "I came to northern [Shaanxi] five or six years ago, yet I cannot compare with comrades like [Gao Gang] in my knowledge of conditions here or in my relations with people of this region."[33]

29. "Zhonggong zhongying guanyu lingdao fangfa de jueding" (The CCP Central Committee's decision on methods of leadership), June 4, 1943, p. 1.

*Official document:* Translated in Compton, pp. 176–83.

30. "Qingsuan dangnei de Menshiweizhuyi sixiang" (Liquidate Menshevik thought), by Liu Shaoqi, July 6, 1943, p. 1.

*Official document:* Translated in Compton, pp. 255–68.

Items 31 through 119 are important policy statements, documents explaining policy, and articles written by prominent Party members showing the evolving cult of Mao and discussing reform within the *Liberation Daily.* These are not found among the official study materials.

31. "Jinian Zhongguo gongchandang nian zhounian" (Commemorate the CCP's twentieth anniversary), July 1, 1941, p. 2.

*Synopsis:* Announced the beginning of a study campaign. The Party's successes were due to the combination of Marxism-Leninism and Chinese reality. Because he correctly grasped theory, Mao Zedong had successfully led the Party.

32. "Zhongguo gongchandang yu geming zhanzheng" (The CCP and revolutionary war), by Zhu De, July 1, 1941, p. 2.

*Note:* In this article, Zhu De deliberately ignored Mao's contribution to military theory, the area where Mao made his most significant contribution to theoretical knowledge.

33. "Mao Zedong tongzhi de shaonian shidai" (The era of Mao Zedong's youth), by Xiao San, December 14, 1941, p. 4.

*Note:* This article signaled the beginning of the cult of Mao Zedong. The stature of both Mao and his writings rose significantly during rectification despite an initial reluctance on the part of leading Party officials to push things too far. They wanted to promote Mao as the most important leader while maintaining the prestige of the Central Committee. However, a combination of internal and external events—rectification, the publication of Chiang Kai-shek's *China's Destiny*, the dissolution of the Comintern in May 1943, and Chiang's own elevation in stature—enabled Mao to rise meteorically between 1943 and 1945. White and Jacoby reported that by 1944, the Border Region suffered from "Mao Zedong mania" as senior members of the Party vied with each other to flatter Mao.[34]

34. "Bianfu yiji jiguan chengli xuexi zhidao weiyuanhui" (Top level offices in the region government establish a committee to guide study), February 4, 1942, p. 4.

*Synopsis:* Lin Boqu headed the committee, with Zhou Wen as secretary. The committee's purpose was to advance and guide study in various offices.

35. "Zhongguo gongye yu Zhongguo zichanjieji" (Chinese industry and Chinese bourgeoisie), by Chen Boda, February 4–5, 7–9, 1942, p. 3 (dated May 15, 1941).

*Synopsis:* Analyzes the major types of industrial organizations in China relating the differing attitudes toward the war with Japan to particular socio-economic interests and concerns.[35]

*Note:* During rectification, Chen Boda was the leading "interpreter" of Mao's thought. Before he emerged as a leading idealogue and polemicist in the early 1940s, Chen was a relatively obscure professor and member of the Communist underground. After his arrival in Yan'an in 1937 he worked as an instructor in the Central Party School and directed the Propaganda Department's Research Section. He also served as Mao's personal secretary for a time. Chen rose to prominence in 1941 when he disagreed with Wang Shiwei over literature. When Wang became the chief target of rectification, Chen became his principal accuser.[36]

36. "Yanda jianli zhenggui xuezhi" (Yan'an University establishes a standard educational system), February 10, 1942, p. 4.

*Synopsis:* Discusses changes in the educational system based on the Central Committee's decision concerning cadre education.

37. "Women zenyang xuexi" (How do we study?), by He Deli, February 12, 1942, p. 3.

*Synopsis:* Summary of an article written in the *Study Newspaper* (*Xuexi bao*) published by the North China Bookstore. It discussed attitudes of study, saying that there should be mutual study, mutual criticism. There should be no viewpoints from Party cliques, only truth in learning.

38. "Xuexi he zhangwo Mao Zedong de lilun he celüe" (Studying and

grasping Mao Zedong's theory and tactics), by Zhang Ruxin, February 18 and 19, 1942, p. 3.

*Note:* Studying and grasping Mao's thought is the main task of the Party, according to the article. This was the first attempt to systematize the study of Mao's writings and provide an annotated bibliography of them. It was also the first public mention of Mao's lectures, which are known today as "On Practice," "On Contradiction," and "Lecture Notes on Dialectic Materialism."

39. "Ganbu huiyishang, Kang Sheng tongzhi baogao, fandui zhuguanzhuyi, zongpaizhuyi, zhong xuanbu haohao quandang zhankai relie taolun" (At the cadre meeting, Comrade Kang Sheng reports, oppose subjectivism and factionalism, central propaganda bureau summons whole Party to launch an enthusiastic discussion), February 22, 1942, p. 3.

40. "Zhonggong zhongying guanyu zai zhiganbu jiaoyu de jueding" (CCP's Central Committee's decision concerning local cadre education), March 2, 1942, p. 1.

41. "Zai zhiganbu jiaoyu de jueding, guiying yewu jiaoyu, zhengzhi jiaoyu, wenhua jiaoyu, lilun jiaoyu wei fanwei" (The education decision for local cadre stipulates that professional education, political education, and theoretical education be the model), March 2, 1942, p. 1.

42. "Zai Yan'an ganbu dahuishang, Kang Sheng tongzhi dang bagu" (At the Yan'an cadre meeting, Comrade Kang Sheng denounces Party formalism), March 8, 1942, p. 1.

*Note:* Kang Sheng was the leading Maoist in the campaign to study Mao and provided the guidelines for rectification. He did not exempt current leadership and policies from criticism but made it clear that the Maoist line was not a target of criticism. The critical essays followed this article.

43. "Wei dadao zhuguanzhuyi zongpaizhuyi yu dangbagu er douzheng" (Struggle to overthrow sectarianism, subjectivism, and party formalism), by Zhang Ruxin, March 8, 1942, p. 3.

*Synopsis:* Discusses the remnants of sectarianism, formalism, and subjectivism found among Party bureaus, cadres, and Party members. Analyzes the relationship among the three "isms."

44. "Shenru minjian liaojie qingkuang Gao yizhang SuiMi guilai" (Penetrating the people, understanding the conditions—President Gao returns from Suide and Mizhi), March 23, 1942, p. 4.

45. "Dao shemma difang xuexi" (Where do we go in study?), by Chen Yun, March 24, 1942, p. 1.

46. "Zhongying yanjiuyuan taolun zhengdun sanfeng" (The Central Committee Research Institute discusses rectifying the three styles), March 28, 1942, p. 1.

47. "Zhongying dangxiao zaidu gaizu gaojun" (The Central Committee completes another reorganization of the Party school), April 1, 1942, p. 1.

48. "Mao Zedong tongzhi haozhao zhengfeng sanfeng yao liyong baozhi" (Comrade Mao Zedong calls for using the newspaper in rectifying the three styles), April 2, 1942, p. 1.

*Synopsis:* On the eve of reform, Mao Zedong and Editor-in-Chief Bo Gu convened a meeting of more than seventy writers and responsible people in Yan'an Party branches. Asked for direction and guidance in reform.

49. "Zhonggong zhongying xuanchuanbu wai gaizao dangbao de tongzhi" (The CCP's Central Committee uses "Information" to reform the newspaper), April 1, 1942, p. 2.

*Synopsis:* Expounds on the opinions, uses, and responsibilities of the Party newspaper, and ways to handle the problems of the Party newspaper. Along with "Information" were three articles concerning the roles of Party newspapers in the international Communist movement.

50. "Mao Zedong tongzhi kouhao zhengfeng sanfeng yao liyong baozhi" (Comrade Mao Zedong's slogan: We must use the newspaper to rectify the three styles), April 2, 1942, p. 1.

*Synopsis:* Recent demands from critics for "absolute equality" were illusions and their methods of criticisms were harmful to the Party.

51. "Ertong jiaoyuzhong de zhuguanzhuyi" (Sectarianism in children's education), by Dong Chuncai. April 4, 1942, p. 4.

*Synopsis:* There are incorrect leanings in children's education. People must pay attention to the sickness of "too much politicalization" in teaching materials and among teachers. As it was, there was no relationship between educational materials and what was happening in children's lives.

52. "Junshi xueyuan de dangxing jiancha shimo" (The whole story of the military affair's academy investigation into Party nature), by Wu Qiang, April 6, 1942, p. 2.

53. "Zhengfeng sanfeng yundong zhandai" (Launch the rectifying the three styles movement), April 8, 1942, p. 2.

*Synopsis:* The administrative institute, the Lu Xun Art Academy, and the youth theater convened a rectification propaganda committee or report committee. They also established a rectification investigation committee to advance study and investigation work.

54. "Guanyu piping fangfa wenti de yanjiu" (Regarding research into the problems of the methods of self-criticism), by Shi Lu, April 11, 1942, p. 2.

*Synopsis:* Raised the attitudes and methods that criticism and self-criticism should have.

55. "Baoanchu jibu shi zenyang taolun zengqiang dangxing de jueding" (The security office's decision on how to discuss strengthening party nature), by Lu Dingyi. April 14, 1942, p. 2.

56. "Zhengdun sanfeng" (Rectifying the three styles), April 14, 1942, p. 2.

*Synopsis:* Concerns the rectification process at the youth theater.

57. "Chengli bianqu xuexi zongwuhui" (The general meeting to set up study in the Border Region), April 16, 1942, p. 2.

58. "Chengli bianqu zong xuexi weiyuanhui guanyu zhixing Zhongying xuanchuanbu xiyue sanhao jueding de jihua" (A Border Region general study committee is established to implement the plan of the Central Committee's Propaganda Bureau's April 3 decision), April 16, 1942, p. 2.

*Synopsis:* The plan contained two parts: (1) Establishing three study committees consisting of Party and mass groups, government systems, and military systems; (2) Regulating the limits of study organizations and those participating, and the time allotment for studying and researching the study articles.

59. "Yanjiu Mao Zedong tongzhi zhengfeng sanfeng baogao de fanying xinde" (Reflect and study what one has gained from researching Comrade Mao Zedong reform the "three styles" report), April 17 and 19, 1942, p. 2.

60. "Zhongying xuexi zongwuhui chengli lingdao yanjiu nianer wenjian" (The Central Committee's study group establishes and leads research on the twenty-two articles), April 19, 1942, p. 2.

61. "Ganbu xuexi dongyuan dahui" (A meeting to mobilize cadre study), April 20, 1942, p. 1.

*Note:* There are related articles and an editorial on the same page.

62. Buyao wujie 'shishi qiushi' " (One does not want to misunderstand "seeking truth from facts"), by Ai Siqi, April 22, 1942, p. 4.

*Synopsis:* How a person with incorrect leanings learns to seek truth from facts. The author suggests four ways to do that.

63. "Zhonggong zhongying guanyu wuyijie de zhishi" (The CCP's Central Committee's instructions concerning the May 1 celebration), April 22, 1942 (Doylun).

*Synopsis:* The instructions discuss the problems of sectarianism, formalism, and subjectivism in the labor movement. Points out that rectification is a long-term struggle to reform thought and work styles.

64. "Bianqu ganbu xuexi dongyuanhui" (Border Region cadre study mobilization meetings), April 23, 1942, p. 2.

65. "Zhongying shujichu gebu zhengfeng xuexi rechao gaozhang" (The enthusiastic upsurge of rectification study among the varous branches of the Central Committee's secretariat), April 30, 1942, p. 2.

66. "Zhengfeng sanfeng shi dang zai sixiangshang de geming" (Rectifying the "three styles" is a revolution in party thinking), by Kai Feng, May 13, 1942 (Dailun).

67. "Linghui ershierge wenjian de jing yu shizhi" (Grasp the spirit and essence of the twenty-two articles), by Peng Zhen, May 14, 1942 (Dailun).

*Synopsis:* The spirit and essence of the twenty-two articles is the standpoint and method by which to analyze and solve problems. A proletarian standpoint must be used in articles.

68. "Wenxue zhi lu" (The road of cultural study), by He Qifang, May 19, 1942, p. 4.

69. "Shaan-Gan-Ning bianqu, wugeyue gongzuo gaogao: shieryue yijiusiyinian–liuyue yijiusiernian" (The Shaan-Gan-Ning Border Region's five-month work report: December 1941–September 1942), June 1, 1942, p. 1.

70. "Yan'an xian daishi du wenjian" (Yan'an *xian* begins reading the articles), June 1, 1942, p. 2.

*Synopsis:* Beginning June 1, *xian*-level cadres would study the rectification study articles for four hours a day. *Qu*-level cadres studied for two hours a day. Every other month cadres took five complete days out for advanced study.

71. "You taolun dao fansheng" (From discussion to self-examination), by Xie Juezai, June 13, 1942 (Dailun).

*Synopsis:* Examines the relationship of practical work and self-examination, giving the following example: "Articles are like swords and practice is like a pig. If you don't have a sword then you can't kill the pig. If you have a good sword then you can slaughter the pig."

72. "Xibeiju guanyu zai ge fenqu ji gexian xuexi Mao Zedong tongzhi zhengfeng sanfeng baogao deng nianerge wenjian de zhishi" (The Northwest Bureau's directive to various districts and subregions regarding the study of Comrade Mao Zedong's reforming the "three styles" report and the other twenty-two articles), June 16, 1942, p. 2.

73. "Zhongying dangxiao juxing kaoshi" (The Central Committee party school holds an examination), June 24, 1942, p. 2.

*Synopsis:* When the Central Committee Party School completed the first stage of its study on opposing sectarianism, it held an examination on the materials.

74. "Jiu jieji benxing de gaizao" (Transformation of old class nature), June 27, 1942, p. 4.

75. "Jinian dang de ershiyi zhounian" (Commemorating the Party's twenty-first anniversary), by Zhu De, July 1, 1942, p. 1.

*Synopsis:* The most important work of the Party at that time was to advance the slogans of rectification, eradicate evil elements, build a strong new Party, reform cadre's thinking and work styles, and cause the whole Party to go along the road to Bolshevism.

76. "Chedi shixing jingbing zhengce" (Thoroughly implement the crack troops' policy), July 3, 1942, p. 1 (continued on following pages).

77. "Gengjia tigao budui de pinshi" (Raise the quality of troops even higher), by Wang Zhen, July 10, 1942 (Dailun).

*Note:* This was originally published in the 359th Brigade's publication, *Battle Voice*.

78. "Lun women de baozhi" (Our newspaper), July 20, 1942, p. 4.

*Synopsis:* "In order for our newspaper to be even better, to be able to oppose Party formalism to begin building a new style of writing, we will publish articles concerning the newspaper and writing."

79. "Jiu jiao yu Chen Boda tongzhi" (Some elucidation from comrade Chen Boda), by Yu Bingran, July 23, 1942, p. 4.

80. "Huida Yu Bingran tongzhi" (In reply to Comrade Yu Bingran), by Chen Boda, July 23, 1942, p. 4.

*Note:* Chen Boda's emphasis on the need for petty-bourgeois intellectuals to remold their ideology led to a debate with Yu, who believed individuals should be judged on their own merits, not their class background.

81. "Yanjiuyuan dangfeng xuexi jieshu" (The research institute concludes its party nature study), July 26, 1943, p. 2.

82. "Zhengfengzhong nuli gaizao ziji" (In rectification make an effort to reform yourself), July 31, 1942, p. 2.

83. "Bianqu xitong ge jiguan kaishi zongjie diyiqi xuexi" (Various offices in the Border Region system begin to summarize the first period of study), August 7, 1942, p. 2.

84. "Women yinggai you de zuofeng" (The style of work we should have), by Xie Juezai, August 8, 1942 (Dailun).

*Synopsis:* This is a summary of a speech the author made to the Border Region Assembly's permanent committee regarding the establishment of a work style.

85. "Duoshu tongzhi renzhen fanshen" (A great many comrades earnestly examine themselves), August 8, 1942, p. 2.

*Synopsis:* Summarizes the first period of study at the Military Affairs Institute.

86. "Xinsijun quanti zhizhanyuan nuli xuexi zhengfeng wenjian" (All the officers and men of the New Fourth Army are making an effort to study the rectification articles), August 10, 1942, p. 1.

87. "Jianquan women de tongxunwang" (Perfecting our communications network), by Yang Pingzhen, September 1, 1942, p. 2.

*Synopsis:* Analyzed existing problems in communication workers' organizational work.

88. "Zhongying xibeiju zhishi ge difang gaijin xuexi" (The Central Committee's Northwest Bureau directs various places to improve study), August 21, 1942, p. 2.

89. "Zhongying zhishu dangwei guanyu zhengfeng xuexiqizhong zhibu gongzuo wenti de tongzhi" (The Central Committee notifies subordinate Party committees regarding problems of branch work in the rectification study period), September 13, 1942, p. 2.

90. "Guanyu weiwulun de jiduan zaji" (Some notes regarding materialism), by Ai Siqi, September 17, 1942, p. 4.

*Synopsis*: Discussed three problems: (1) reality, experience, theory; (2) analysis; (3) synthesis.

91. "Luyi dangfeng xuexi relie" (The Lu Xun Art Academy fervently studies party nature), September 30, 1942, p. 2.

92. "Huazhong ge budui ge jiguan zhengfeng xuexi pubian zhankai" (Troops and officers in Central China universally launch rectification study), October 3, 1942, p. 1.

93. "Women dedao xuexi de xiaoguo" (The results we achieve from study), October 17, 1942, p. 2.

*Synopsis*: Reflects on rectification in Ganquan *xian*.

94. "Zhengfeng xuexui zong du Lu Xun" (Reading Lu Xun in rectification study), by Xiao San, October 18, 1942, p. 4.

95. "Yanda jixu jingxing fan ziyouzhuyi dahui" (Yan'an University's ongoing meeting to oppose liberalism), October 28, 1942, p. 2.

96. "Zhongying yanjiuyuan zhengfeng yilai sixiang gaizao zongjie" (Summary of the research administration's reform in thinking since rectification), by Zhang Ruxin, October 31 and November 1, 1942, p. 4.

97. "Zhongying zhishu jiguan tongzhi dangfeng xuexi rechao gaozhang" (The enthusiastic upsurge for Party nature study among comrades from the subordinate offices of the CCP's Central Committee), November 3, 1942, p. 1.

98. "Zhongying Shandong fenju zongjie xuefeng xuexi" (The Central Committee's Shangdong branch summarizes the study of study nature), November 15, 1942, p. 2.

99. "Luyi dangfeng xuexi diyi jieduan gaozao jieshu" (The conclusion of the Lu Xun Art Academy's first stage of reform of Party nature study), November 18, 1942, p. 2.

100. "Zhongying mishuchu zhengfeng xuexi zongjie peihe diaocha gongzuo" (The Central Committee's secretariat rectification study summarizes investigative work), December 6, 1942, p. 2.

101. "Zenyang gaizaole womende xuexi" (How we reformed our study), by Ai Siqi, December 26 and 27, 1942, p. 4.

102. "Zhexue zhanxianshang de Liening shidai" (The Leninist period's philosophical battlefront), by Ai Siqi, January 21, 1943, p. 4.

103. "Mantan xinwen bagu" (Informally discussing formalism in journalism), January 26, 1943, p. 4.

*Synopsis*: Discusses the manifestations of journalistic formalism found in the Border Region's newspapers.

104. "Shixing dang de wenyi zhengce Yan'an zuojia fenfen xiaxiang" (Implementing the party's literature and art policy, one after another, Yan'an writers go down to the villages), March 15, 1943, p. 2.

*Synopsis*: Concerns the experience of writers, among them Ding Ling, who had been sent to the villages.

105. "Renxing, dangxing, gexing" (Human nature, Party nature, revolutionary nature), by Chen Boda. March 27, 1943, p. 4.

*Synopsis:* In a true proletarian political party, the interests of the party and those of the individual should be the same. If personal interests clash with party interests, then personal interests must be subordinated.

106. "Xibeiju guanyu jiefang ribao jige wenti de tongzhi" (The Northwest Bureau's statement regarding several problems in the *Liberation Daily*), March 30, 1943, p. 1.

107. "Huazhong de zhengfeng yundong" (The rectification movement in Central China), April 3, 1943, p. 3.

108. "Yinianlai Jin-Cha-Ji junqu zhengfeng xuexi" (Last year's rectification study in the Jin-Cha-Ji military district), April 11, 1943, p. 3.

109. "Yan'an xian ju ganbu xuexi de jidian jingyan" (The experiences of Yan'an *xian*-level cadre in rectification study), by Liu Yiyun, April 24 and 25, 1943, p. 2.

*Synopsis:* Sums up experiences in four areas: (1) preparation work of thought leadership, (2) mutual problems of study and work, (3) the relation of theory to practice, (4) leadership and study methods.

110. "Zhengfeng lingdao zerenshang de sange wenti" (Three problems in the responsibilities of rectification leadership), by Li Zhuoran, May 6, 1943 (Dailun).

111. "Huigu Yanshu gexian zhengfeng xuexi" (Reviewing rectification study in the various *xian* of Yanshu), by Cao Wen, May 22, 1943, p. 2.

*Synopsis:* Summarizes the results and existing problems of rectification study in the ten *xian* of Yanshu during the last half year.

112. "Zhongying Huazhongju guanyu yijiusisannian zhengfeng xuexi de zhishi" (The Central Committee's Central China Bureau's directive regarding rectification study in 1943), June 5, 1943, p. 1.

113. "Zhongguo gongchandang yu Zhongguo minzu jiefang de daolu" (The CCP and the road to China's national liberation), by Wang Jiaxiang, July 8, 1943, pp. 1–2.

114. "Zai Mao Zedong de qizhi xia, wei baowei Zhongguo gongchandang er zhan" (Fight to defend the CCP under the banner of Mao Zedong), by Bo Gu, July 13, 1943, p. 1.

*Note:* This is a good example of Bo Gu's acquiescence to the Maoists.

115. "Mao Zedong tongzhi shi Zhongguo renmin de jiuxing" (Comrade Mao Zedong is the liberator of the Chinese People), July 17, 1943, p. 2.

116. "Shandong de zhengfeng xuexi" (Rectification study in Shandong), October 24, 1943, p. 3.

*Synopsis:* Discusses the experience and discipline of the rectification process among Shandong Party branches and military districts.

117. "Guanche dang de wenyi zhengce zuzhi jutuan xiaxiang gongzuo"

(Implementing the party's literature and art policy, organizing theater groups to go down to the villages to work), November 24, 1943, p. 2.

118. "Luyi gongzuotuan jingyan" (The experiences of the Lu Xun Art Academy work group), March 15, 1944, p. 4.

119. "Xibeiju xuanchuanbu jiangli wenhua xuexi mofan" (The Northwest Branch propaganda bureau rewards model workers in cultural study), July 31, 1944, p. 2.

## II. Editorials

1. "Jiangli ziyou yanjiu" (Reward unrestrained research), June 7, 1941.

*Synopsis*: Scholars can do earnest research within a Marxist framework.

2. "Fandui xuexi zhong de jiaotiaozhuyi" (Oppose dogmatism in study), September 9, 1941.

*Synopsis*: Mao's call for the signification of Marxism did not contradict Marxism-Leninism. The time was ripe for "creative" Marxism; Mao was adding to Marx based on the practical experiences of China.

3. "Jiaoyushang de geming" (The revolution in education), January 13, 1942.

4. "Tigao bianqu guomin jiaoyu" (Promote nationalistic education in the Border Region), January 14, 1942.

*Synopsis*: There was great development in the quantity of nationalistic education in the Border Region, but quality was still lacking.

5. "Zhangwo Ma-Liezhuyi de suoyao (Grasp the key to Marxism-Leninism), January 21, 1942.

*Note*: This was the first time the media made it clear that the writings of Mao should take precedence over the writings of Marx, Lenin, Stalin, and Engels. It marked an end to the ideological diversity that had plagued the Party since 1921. There was no ideological unity at this time, but the Maoist position expressed in the *Liberation Daily* prevailed.

6. "Xuanbu dang bagu sixing" (Propagandizing the death of party formalism), February 11, 1942.

*Synopsis*: The best method for smashing Party formalism was to establish the correct style of propaganda work. Correct propaganda must raise the problems and solve them.

7. "Zhankai xuanchuan gongzuoshang de xin zhenrong" (Launch the new lineup of propaganda work), February 13, 1942.

8. "Tigao ganbu de wenhua shuiping" (Raising cadres' cultural level), February 15, 1942.

9. "Peizhi difang ganbu" (Training local cadres), March 7, 1942.

10. "Yewu jiaoyu he zhengzhi jiaoyu" (Professional education and political education), March 10, 1942.

11. "Fayang minzhu zuofeng" (Develop a democratic style), March 19, 1942.

12. "Dang de jueding—xingdong de zhizhen" (The party's decision—an indicator of action), March 21, 1942.

13. "Ba wenhua gongzuo tuijin yibu" (Advance cultural work a step), March 25, 1942.

14. "Zhi duzhe" (To the readers), April 1, 1942.

*Note:* Signaled beginning of the reform movement in the *Liberation Daily.* See related article on page 2 "Zenyang bian dangbao" (How to distinguish the party's newspaper).

*Synopsis:* The *Liberation Daily* was the most important propaganda instrument of the Party. It must make Party policy clear and reflect the life of the masses. Articles must be written simply enough so illiterate people can understand concepts when they are read to them and so barely literate people can read and understand articles. Dissimilar viewpoints could be debated, but no guidelines were given as to how to do that.

15. "Zai youji zhanzheng huanjing zhong zai zhiganbu jiaoyu shi kenong he biyaode" (Under guerrilla battle conditions, that which is possible and necessary in professional cadre education), April 4, 1942.

16. "Zhengfeng sanfeng bixu zhengque jinxing" (Correctly advance rectifying the "three styles"), April 5, 1942.

*Synopsis:* There were two ways to carry out reform work—one correct, the other incorrect. The incorrect methods are subjective and factional, while the correct methods are practical and realistic. Cadres need to conform to the idea of "curing the sickness to save the person." That means examining oneself deeply and forgiving others.

17. "Ziwoping cong he zhuo shou" (How do you start a self-criticism?), April 6, 1942.

18. "Chungeng, zhengce yu xuexi" (Spring plowing, policy and study). April 8, 1942.

19. "Guanche jingbing jianzheng" (Carry out crack troops and simple administration), April 9, 1942.

20. "Dangnei minzhu wenti" (Problems of democracy within the Party), April 11, 1942.

21. "Poxiao qian de heian" (Darkness before the dawn), April 15, 1942.

22. "Fandui jiaoyu gongzuo zhong de jixingbing" (Oppose the acute illness in educational work), April 17, 1942.

23. "Taolun zhengfeng sanfeng de jutihua" (Discuss the details of rectifying the three styles), April 18, 1942.

24. "Yingjie kunnan jiaqiang tuanjie" (Welcome difficulties, strengthen unity), April 20, 1942.

*Synopsis:* The Party was more united at that time than ever before in its twenty-year history. Nevertheless, the present conditions are not satisfactory. By studying the reform documents, the Party's important work can be consolidated.

25. "Zaocheng xuexi rechao" (Create a study fervor), April 23, 1942.

*Synopsis:* A guide to the twenty-two study documents. Although studying the twenty-two articles had been the focus of cadre attention for several months, there were groups who still went about it incorrectly. For example, some men and women did not try to understand the articles thoroughly or see any point in careful study of them. But the articles were important because they represented the crystallization of long experience in the revolutionary movement. To achieve significant gains in the future, it was important to create an enthusiasm for study.

26. "Bianqu ganbu de renshi wenti" (Recognizing the problems of Border Region cadre), April 28, 1942.

27. "Yiding yao xuexi nianerge wenjian" (One certainly wants to study the twenty-two articles), May 5, 1942.

*Synopsis:* Discussed the mistaken attitudes in studying the articles. People refused to research and to consider the articles, and to follow the decisions of the Central Committee. But that was wrong because editorials reflected current correct Party thinking. This was the only means of correcting deviations and completing reforms.

28. "Zhengfeng sanfeng zhong de liangtiao zhanxian douzheng" (The two-line struggle in rectifying the "three styles"), May 9, 1942.

*Synopsis:* Implementation of the Party's correct line must be guaranteed. To do this one must oppose leftist tendencies and expand the two-line struggle to the greatest possible limits.

29. "Fandui qunzhong gongzuozhong de zhuguanzhuyi" (Oppose sectarianism in mass work), May 11, 1942.

30. "Linghui ershierge wenjian de jingshen yu shizhi" (Grasping the spirit and essence of the twenty-two articles), by Peng Zhen, May 14, 1942.

*Synopsis:* Grasping the spirit and essence meant understanding the articles' standpoints, viewpoints, and essence. The standpoint was the class stand of the proletariat; the viewpoint was that of dialectical materialism; and the essence was understanding the contents of each article. Although on the surface that may have appeared simple, in reality it was not. The contents of the articles were more important than the style.

31. "Yiding yao fanxing ziji" (You certainly want to examine yourself), May 23, 1942.

*Synopsis:* Explained the April 3 decision of the Central Committee.

32. "Yan'an yigeyue xuexi yundong de zongjie" (A one-month summary of the study movement in Yan'an), June 5, 1942.

*Synopsis:* Divided the summary into two parts: (1) present conditions of the movement and ten existing tendencies; (2) methods to be used from that point on, and thirteen concrete examples. People concentrate on consolidating study and deepening the movement. The nature of rectification was the struggle of proletarian and petty-bourgeois thinking.

33. "Xuanchuan weiwulun" (Propagandize materialism), June 10, 1942.

34. "Guanyu junduizhong de zhengfeng sanfeng" (Rectification in the army), July 2, 1942.

35. "Xianji zhengfeng xuexi kaishi" (Begin *xian*-level rectification study), July 3, 1942.

36. "Ba women de baozhi ban de geng haoxie" (Running our newspaper office even better), July 18, 1942.

*Synopsis:* Discussed the reform process in the *Liberation Daily* in effect since April. "We must first politically educate ourselves and with regard to the newspaper get everyone to replace old attitudes with new ones. We must also have technical education so everyone will learn how to supply the newspaper with appropriate manuscripts."

37. "Baozhi he xin de wenfeng" (The newspaper and the new style of writing), August 4, 1942.

38. "Fanxing" (Self-examination), August 16, 1942.

*Synopsis:* Discussed problems people faced in undertaking a self-examination. These included relating theory to practice, reading the study articles thoroughly, and discussing them once read. The articles were "theory," self-examination was "practice." If people examined themselves deeply then they discovered more mistakes and found it more difficult to correct them, but they also realized that they were advancing slowly.

39. "Zhankai tongxunyuan de gongzuo" (Expanding the work of communication workers), August 25, 1942.

40. "Dihou xingshi yu wo jun zhengzhi gongzuo" (The situation behind enemy lines and our army's political work), September 9, 1942.

41. "Jianli xiangcun dangzheng gongzuo de zhengque guanxi" (Establishing the correct relationship in village Party political work), September 17, 1942.

42. "Dang yu dangbao" (The Party and the Party's newspaper), September 22, 1942.

43. "Zhengque xuefeng zhengque dangfeng" (The correct study style, the correct Party style), September 24, 1942.

44. "Dangyuan jiaoyu yingyou chedi zhuanbian" (There should be a thorough reform of party member's education), October 30, 1942.

45. "Tigao lingdao gaizao zuofeng" (Raising reform work among the leadership), November 10, 1942.

*Synopsis:* Stressed the responsibility of the Party's leadership organ in understanding conditions and grasping policy. It cannot replace government work or sink into a locked daily routine.

46. "Gei dangbao de jizhe he tongxunyuan" (For the benefit of the Party newspaper's reporters and communication workers), November 17, 1942.

47. "Fandui guanliaozhuyi" (Oppose bureaucratism), December 18, 1942.

48. "Ba laodongli zuzhiqilai" (Organizing the labor force), January 25, 1943.

*Synopsis:* Delivered at the Senior Cadre Conference. Detailed the pitfalls of previous experiences with cooperatives organized as arms of the state. Cooperatives could only work if the entire population participated. The goal was national salvation by strengthening the economy; if cooperatives were successful, then people's lives would improve.

49. "Gaoganhui yu zhengfeng yundong" (The senior cadre conference and the rectification movement), March 4, 1943.

## III. Study Columns

"Study" first appeared on May 13, 1942, and was published twenty-four times thereafter until January 16, 1943. (Columns appeared on May 13, 16, 21, 24, 28; June 1, 8, 11, 15, 17, 20, 27, 30; July 13, 23; August 5, 11, 23, 28; September 8, 25; October 6; November 9; January 16.) Rotating regularly with other page 4 columns, its purpose was to "to further the study movement of the Party in Yan'an and throughout the Border Region." The contents included essays, random thoughts, tales of work experiences, discussions of problems, and other "articles of quality." The following are articles from the "Study" column.

1. "Weishemma zhengfeng sanfeng shi dang de sixiang geming" (Why rectifying the "three styles" is a revolution in Party thought), by Lu Dingyi, May 13, 1942.

2. "Wo dui Zhongxuanbu sisan jueding de renzhi" (My understanding of the Central Committee's propaganda bureau's April 3 decision), by Tao Zhu, May 13, 1942.

3. "Zenyang xuexi ershierge wenjian" (How to study the twenty-two articles), by Peng Zhen, May 16, 1942.

4. "Yanjiu wenjian de shihou zenyang zuo biji" (When you study the articles how do you take notes?), by He Qifang, May 21, 1942.

*Note:* He Qifang was one of the critical writers discussed under "Campaign in Art and Literature." See no. 16 under "Art and Literature."

5. "Xuexi guannian de gexin" (Study ideological innovations), by Ai Siqi, May 21, 1942.

6. "Liang zhong xuexi fangfa" (Two kinds of study methods), by Wu Liangping, May 24, 1942.

7. "Wo de fanxing" (Self-examination), by Tian Xiuzhi, May 24, 1942.

*Note:* This is one of a series of articles on self-examination. See nos. 18, 26, 31, 35, and 46 below, and nos. 17, 31, and 38 under "Editorials."

8. "Shemma jiaozuo 'cong shiji chufa' " (What can be called "being realistic"), by Lu Dingyi, May 28, 1942.

9. "Liangzhong yanjiu wenjian de fangfa" (Two methods for researching articles), by Zhang Ruxin, May 28, 1942.

*Note:* One of three related articles published on that date.

10. "Du 'nongcun diaocha xuyaner' " (Reading "Second preface to village investigations"), by Tong Dalin, May 28, 1942.

11. "Minzhu jizhongzhi" (Democratic centralism), by Fan Wenlan, June 1, 1942.

12. "Lun 'Dengji zhidu' " (On "Hierarchy"), by Jian Nanxiang, June 1, 1942.

13. "Sudalin lun dang de Buershiweikehua" (Stalin on the Bolshevization of the Party), June 8, 1942.

14. "Zhuguanzhuyi de genyuan he kefu de banfa" (The sources of subjectivism and methods of overcoming it), by Tao Zhu, June 8, 1942.

15. "Ruhe dapo jiaotiaozhuyi de xuexi" (How to smash dogmatic study), by Kai Feng, June 11, 1942.

16. "Xuexi yu lingdao" (Study and leadership), by Xu Yixin, June 11, 1942.

17. "Guanyu lilun yu shiji" (Regarding theory and practice), by the editorial committee, June 15, 1942.

18. "Ruhe fanxing ziji" (How to examine yourself), by Feng Wenbin, June 15, 1942.

19. "Zongpaizhuyi qingxiang zai wo shenshang shi shenyang juti biaoxian de" (How factional tendencies in me are concretely expressed), by Cui Zhe, June 15, 1942.

20. "Guanyu Wang Shiwei" (Concerning Wang Shiwei), by Chen Boda, June 15, 1942.

21. "Chedi fensui Wang Shiwei de Tuopai lilun ji qi fandang huodong" (Thoroughly smash Wang Shiwei's Trotskyite theories and anti-party activities), by Zhang Ruxin, June 17, 1942.

22. "Wo lai zhaozhaojing" (Looking in the mirror), by Deng Liqun, June 20, 1942.

23. "Wo shi zenyang fanxing zijide?" (How do I examine myself?), by Han Zuo, June 20, 1942.

24. "Jiu jieji benxing de gaizao" (The transformation of old class nature), by Chen Boda, June 27, 1942.

25. "Du 'Zhongying guanyu diaocha yanjiu de jueding' ji 'Nongcun diaocha xuyan er' yihou" (After reading "The Central Committee's decision

regarding investigation and research'' and "Second preface to 'Village Investigations' "), by Liu Xing, June 27, 1942.

26. "Guanyu fanshen" (Regarding self-examination), by Wang Chaocheng, June 27, 1942.

27. "Mantan" (Informal discussion), June 30, 1942.

28. "Jiaotiaozhuyi de weixian" (The dangers of dogmatism), June 30, 1942.

29. "Zai qingnian juyuan xuexi zongjiehuishang de jiangyan" (Lectures at the youth theater's meeting to summarize study), June 30, 1942.

30. " 'Guan gongdangshi jieshuyu' yu 'Lun dang de Buer-shiweikehua' changsheng de lishi tiaojian" (Historical factors in producing "Concluding remarks on Party history" and "On the Bolshevization of the Party"), by Shi Zhe, July 13, 1942.

31. "Shiwunian sixiang bianhua de fanshen" (A self-examination of fifteen years of thought reform), by Wu Wenlin, July 13, 1942.

32. "Yao bu yao tigao wenhua shiping?" (Do we want to raise the cultural level?), July 13, 1942.

33. "Gaizao ziji de zuofeng" (The method of reforming myself), by Cao Lihuai, July 13, 1942.

34. "Du 'Guanyu Yan'an ganbu xuexiao de jueding' " (Reading "The decision regarding the Yan'an cadre school"), July 23, 1942.

*Note:* For the document see no. 6 under "Articles and Documents."

35. "Sixiang de fanxing" (Examining one's thinking), by Chen Boda, July 23, 1942.

36. "Niu yu zongwu gongzuoshe" (The cow and the general affairs worker), by Wang Zhong, August 5, 1942.

37. "Fandui genjudi gongzuozhong zhi zhuguanzhuyi" (Oppose subjectivism in base area work), by Hu Xikui, August 5, 1942.

38. "Muqian Yan'an zhengfeng xuexi zhongde wenjian yanjiu yu gongzuo jiancha" (Article research and work inspection at present in Yan'an rectification study), by Kang Sheng, August 11, 1942.

39. "Dule 'Gaizao women de xuexi' zhihou" (After reading "Reforming our study"), by Cheng Zhigan, August 11, 1942.

40. "Zenyang zongjiu xuefeng xuexi yu kaishi dangfeng xuexi" (How to summarize learning styles study and begin Party styles study), by Li Fuchun, August 11, 1942.

41. "Guanyu zongjie sanyue lai xuexi jingyan de jidian yijian" (Regarding several opinions which summarize the study experiences of the past three months), by Kuang Yaming, August 11, 1942.

42. "Zenyang zongjie 'xuefang xuexi' yu kaishi 'dangfeng xuexi?' " (How do you summarize "reform in learning" study and begin "reform in party" study?), August 11, 1942.

43. "Quanmian zhankai zhengdun sanfeng de xuexi yu jiancha" (Comprehensively expanding the study and investigation of rectifying the three styles), August 23, 1942.

44. "Ershinian lai wodi jiaotiaozhuyi" (My dogmatism of the last twenty years), by Wang Enhua, August 23, 1942.

45. "Sudalin lun ziwo piping" (Stalin on self-criticism), August 28, 1942.

46. "Sixiang de fanxing" (Examining one's thinking), by Chen Boda, August 28, 1942.

47. "Junwei fenquzong Xue Ji guanyu kaishi dangfeng xuexi de jueding" (The CCP's Central Committee's Military Commission's district general Xue Ji's decision regarding the beginning of the "reform the Party" study), September 8, 1942.

48. "Dui Yueh Tianyu tongzhi 'Du guanyu Yan'an ganbu xuexiao de jueding' zhi shangque" (Regarding Comrade Yueh Tianyu's discussion of "Reading the decision regarding the Yan'an cadre school"), September 25, 1942.

49. "Kaizhan zhengfeng sanfeng yundong" (Expanding rectifying the "three styles" movement), by Rao Soushi, October 6, 1942.

*Note:* This "Study" contained letters from the readers.

50. "Du 'Niu yu zongwu gongzuozhe' hou" (After reading "The cow and the general affairs worker"), by Liu Zhendong. October 6, 1942.

51. "Linghui yu yunyong" (Understand and apply), October 6, 1942.

52. "Zuo zongwu gongzuo de tongzhi zenyang jinxing zhengfeng xuexi?" (How do comrades who do general affairs work advance rectification study?), by Wang Zhong, October 6, 1942.

53. "Guanyu dangxiao taolun dahui de fangzhen wenti" (Regarding the policy questions raised at the discussion meeting at the Party school), by Peng Zhen, November 9, 1942.

54. "Gongnong ganbu yao xue wenhua" (Worker-peasant cadres want to study literature), by Peng Zhen, January 16, 1943.

## IV. Art and Literature

Items 1 through 9 below are the critical writers' essays.

1. "Women xuyao zawen" (We need critical essays), by Ding Ling, October 23, 1941, p. 4.

*Synopsis:* Writers of the day should follow the example of Lu Xun by always seeking and speaking the truth.[37]

2. "Sanbajie you gan" (Reflections on March 8, Women's Day), by Ding Ling, March 9, 1942, p. 4.

*Synopsis:* The leadership of the Party had failed to better the position of women significantly. Although progress had been made, advances were slow because of inadequacies within the Party itself. Translated in Gregor Benton, "The Yenan (Yan'an) Opposition," *New Left Review* 92 (July–August 1975): 102–105.

3. "Liaojie zuojia, zunzhong zuojia" (Understand and respect writers), by Ai Qing, March 11, 1942, p. 4.

*Synopsis:* Writers must take responsibility for the spiritual health of the nation, forcing people to look at themselves carefully.

4. "Haishi zawen de shidai" (Still a period of critical essays), by Luo Feng, March 12, 1942, p. 4.

*Synopsis:* "The dagger (Lu Xun) used to smash through the darkness and to point to the road ahead is already buried underground and rusty, and those who know how to use this weapon are in reality a few." Translated in Benton, pp. 105–106.

5. "Bianzhe de hua" (Words from the editor), by Ding Ling, March 12, 1942, p. 4.

*Note:* Ding Ling left the editorship of the newspaper's literary page shortly after this essay was published.

*Synopsis:* Reiterated her 1941 appeal for the short critical essays.

6. "Ye baihehua" (Wild lilies), by Wang Shiwei, March 13, 1942, p. 4. Continued March 23, 1942.

*Synopsis:* Party leaders had created an elite aloof from the masses. There must be a constant vigil against wrong and a willingness to improve. Translated in Benton, pp. 96–102.

7. "Lun zhongshen dashi" (On marriage), by Xiao Jun, March 25, 1942, p. 4.

*Synopsis:* Voiced many of the same criticisms as expressed by Ding Ling's March 9, 1942, article.

8. "Duoshaoci a wo likaile wo richang de shenghuo" (How many times have I left my everyday life), by He Qifang, April 3, 1942, p. 4.

*Note:* This was a critical poem, not an essay.

9. "Lun tongzhi zhi 'ai' yu nai" (On "love" and forbearance among comrades), by Xiao Jun, April 8, 1942, p. 4.

*Synopsis:* The wine of "comradely" love was being diluted.

Items 10 through 40 reflect the crackdown on the critics and their recantations. Articles attacking Wang Shiwei are included in this section.

10. "Du 'Ye baihehua' yougan" (Some feelings after reading "Wild lilies"), by Qi Su, April 7, 1942, p. 4.

11. "Yehu yishu" (A bunch of wild lilies), by Guang Min, April 7, 1942, p. 4.

12. "Zai Yan'an wenyi zuotanhuishang de jianghua" (Talks at the Yan'an conference on literature and art), by Mao Zedong, October 19, 1943, pp. 1, 2, and 4.

*Note:* These lectures were delivered on May 2 and 23, 1942. Therefore, I have placed them here, which is correct chronologically, even though they did not appear in the *Liberation Daily* until October 1943.

*Synopsis:* Writers and artists were technicians who would get better with training. Art was a political weapon in class struggle so must reflect politically correct proletarian ideas. Translated in Bonnie S. McDougall, *Mao Zedong's "Talks at the Yan'an Conference on Literature and Art": A Translation of the 1943 Text and Commentary,* pp. 55–86.

13. "Duiyu dangqian wenyi zhu wenti de wojian" (Views concerning the present problem in art and literature), by Xiao Jun, May 14, 1942, p. 4.

*Note:* Unlike the other critical writers, Xiao Jun never recanted his views or attacked Wang. He continued his independent position.

14. "Wo duiyu muqian wenyisheng jige wenti de yijian" (My opinion regarding the current problems in art and literature), by Ai Qing, May 15, 1942, p. 4.

*Note:* Although Mao called for writers to recant their view, none did. Rather, there were discussions about the impact and meaning of Mao's talks. This is one such discussion where Ai Qing made a half-hearted attack on Wang Shiwei.

15. "Cong 'zhengzhijia, yishujia' shuodao wenyi" (Speaking about art and literature from "Statesmen-artists"), by Yang Weizhe, May 19, 1942.

16. "Yanjiu wenjian de shihou zenyang zuo biji?" (When you study the articles, how do you take notes?), by He Qifang, May 21, 1942, p. 4.

*Note:* He Qifang was the first critical writer to recant. His disavowal created so much personal enthusiasm that he joined the Party's literary hierarchy.

17. "Du Shiwei tongzhi de 'Zhengzhijia, yishujia' hou" (After reading Comrade Shiwei's "Statesmen-artists"), by Jin Canran, May 26, 1942, p. 4.

*Note:* This is a good example of the distorted textual analysis used to "prove" Wang's guilt.

18. "Lun Wang Shiwei tongzhi de sixiang yiyi" (On the thoughts and opinions of Comrade Wang Shiwei), by Fan Wenlan, June 9, 1942, p. 4.

19. "Yishujia de 'Ye baihehua' " (The artist's "Wild lilies"), by Chen Dao, June 9, 1942, p. 4.

*Synopsis:* Discusses the flaws in Wang Shiwei's thinking. The fourth section concerns Lu Xun.

20. "Ji 'Du "Ye baihehua" yu gan' zhihou" (Additional thoughts on "After reading 'Wild lilies' "), by Li Bozhao, June 9 and 10, 1942, p. 4.

*Note:* Attributed to Chen Boda.

*Synopsis:* Wang Shiwei was like a leech, something that appeared small and harmless but sucked people's blood.

21. "Zhengzhijia yu yishujia-duiyu Wang Shiwei 'Zhengzhijia-yishujia' yiwen zhi yijian" (Statesmen and artists—an opinion regarding Wang Shiwei's "Statesmen-Artists"), by Cai Tianxin, June 10, 1942, p. 4.

22. "Ren zai jianku zhong shengzhang—ping Ding Ling tongzhi de 'Zai yiyuan zhong shi' " (Men grow through difficulties—criticizing Ding Ling's "In the hospital"), by Liao Ying, June 10, 1942, p. 4.

23. "Wentan shang de 'Buerba' jingshen" (The "Bulba" spirit in literary art circles), by Xiao Jun, June 13, 1942, p. 4.

24. "Dao zuoquan tongzhi" (Mourn for the powerful leftist comrade), June 15, 1942, p. 1.

25. "Guanyu Wang Shiwei" (Concerning Wang Shiwei), by Chen Boda, June 15, 1942, p. 4.

*Synopsis:* Wang was an ideological dogmatist and cultural elitist. He was a hypocrite because, while he posed as a morally superior critic of the Party, he was actually an ambitious schemer. Although he advocated a "classless" society, he accepted the rewards of being a cadre.

26. "Cong Lu Xun de zawen tandao Shiwei" (Using Lu Xun's essays to talk about [Wang] Shiwei), by Zhou Wen, June 16, 1942, p. 4.

*Note:* This is another good example of distorted textual analysis.

27. "Wenyijie dui Wang Shiwei yingyou de taidu ji fanxing" (The attitude and self-examination that literary and art circles should have toward Wang Shiwei), by Ding Ling, June 16, 1942, p. 4.

*Note:* This is a transcript of her June 11, 1942, speech to the Central Research Institute struggle meeting.

28. "Chedi fensui Wang Shiwei de Tuopai lilun ji qi fandang huodang" (Thoroughly smash Wang Shiwei's Trotskyite theories and anti-Party activities), by Zhang Ruxin, June 17, 1942, p. 4.

*Synopsis:* This was a summary of the June 10, 1942, Central Research Institute discussion meeting. The article contained four questions: (1) What anti-Party thinking had Wang Shiwei promoted? (2) What were the special characteristics of Wang's anti-Party life? (3) How did Wang Shiwei serve the people? (4) How do we respond to his counterrevolutionary life? It denounced Wang and, in doing so, attempted to pull other writers back into line.

29. "Yan'an wenyi jie chuxing zuotanhui" (The literary circles in Yan'an hold a forum), June 19, 1942, p. 2

30. "Yan'an wenyi ju tanhuahui guanyu Tuopai Wang Shiwei shijian de jueyi" (Resolution of the Yan'an literary circles forum concerning the affair of Wang Shiwei the Trotskyite), June 20, 1942, p. 4.

31. "Xianshi bu rongxu waiqu" (Reality does not permit misrepresentation), by Ai Qing, June 24, 1942, p. 4.

32. "Lun Zhongyang yanjiu yuan de sixiang lunzhan" (On the ideological polemic in the Central Research Institute), by Luo Man, June 28, 1942, p. 4.

*Note:* This is an attack on Wang Shiwei.

33. "Douzheng riji" (Diary of a struggle), by Wen Jize, June 28 and 29, 1942, p. 4.

*Note:* Summarizes events at the forum on Party discipline and democracy held at the Central Research Institute between May 27 and June 13, 1942. At those meetings the Mao faction attacked not only the critics but all opposition. Questions of democracy and discipline were dispensed with quickly as the meetings turned to a denunciation of Wang Shiwei.

34. "Zai Zhongying yanjiuyuan liuyue shiyiri zuotanhui shang de fayan" (The statement of the Central Committee's research administration on the June 11 discussion meeting), by Fan Wenlan, June 29, 1942, p. 4.

*Note:* This article contains excerpts of Wang's agreement to end his disagreement with the Party.

35. "Xie zai Shiwei tongzhi 'Wenyi de wenyiguan minzhu xingshi duanlun' zhihou" (After writing in Comrade Wang Shiwei's "Short essay on national forms in art and literature"), by Chen Boda, July 3 and 4, 1942, p. 4.

*Note:* Dated January 7, 1941.

36. "Wang Shiwei de wenyiguan yu women de" (Wang Shiwei's viewpoints on art and literature and mine), by Zhou Yang, July 28 and 29, 1942, p. 4.

*Synopsis:* The article contained five sections: (1) the questions Wang raised, (2) art and politics, (3) art's theory of human nature, (4) writing brightness or writing darkness, (5) summary.

Zhou Yang's article ended the period of attack and began a period of praising new values.

37. "Yiding yao tigao wenhua" (We certainly want to raise culture), by Wu Tailiang, January 16, 1943.

38. "Weishemma yao xuexi wenhua?" (Why study culture?), by Han Dongshan, January 16, 1943.

39. "Guanyu dang de wenyi gongzuozhe de liangge qingxiang wenti" (Regarding two problems to which Party art and literature workers are inclined), by Chen Yun, March 29, 1943.

40. "Gaizao ziji, gaizao yishu" (Reform the self, reform art), by He Qifang, April 3, 1943, p. 4.

# THREE

# The Medium: A Chronological Survey

The *Liberation Daily* is the best source of information available on life in the Shaan-Gan-Ning Border Region and events within the Chinese Communist Party during the Yan'an years. Because it is impossible to isolate one issue or events from another on the pages of a newspaper, it offers a broader perspective on political, social, economic, and war issues than do government documents or observations by foreign or Guomindang journalists. Some of the best information about Border Region life generally comes not from articles on a particular subject but from those on general topics like health care, production, election activities, and crop news.

Nevertheless, the *Liberation Daily* must be approached cautiously. Information in it cannot be used unqualifiedly to illustrate concrete changes or advances in politics, economics, or society. Production and crop figures, for example, should be checked against other documents if possible. Moreover, fact is occasionally mixed with fiction. That does not mean falsified data but propaganda stories printed in a manner like that used for factual reports. These exist to explain policy or to teach cadres how to do things, and they are so stereotyped that they are easy for the researcher to identify. Although not literally true, they reveal the major concerns of the period. Yet, even with these qualifications, the *Liberation Daily* provides the most detailed and accurate information on the Shaan-Gan-Ning Border Region found anywhere.

This chapter surveys the newspaper's contents and its potential as a source for the study of Communist Party history during the Yan'an period. Although it is a selected survey of the newspaper in four-month periods and not a comprehensive index, it is designed to acquaint the reader with the kinds of information in the *Liberation Daily* and how it might be used. After some general observations on the *Liberation Daily* for each period, seven areas are surveyed: (1) general page and editorial survey, listing subject matter according to frequency of appearance; (2) important editorials, citing those concerned with major

Party or Border Region issues; (3) columns replacing editorials; (4) page 1 articles concerned with the outstanding issues of the day; (5) page 4 articles concerned with the outstanding issues; (6) regular page 4 columns; and (7) significant articles on the remaining pages. Variations are noted as they occur.

Because the newspaper's format changed little during its life, it is relatively easy to assess the primary issues under discussion in it. As a general rule, they appeared in the same location with the same type of headline in the same format for each page. When surveying the newspaper, the lead article on each page of every edition was recorded along with the dominant themes from the remainder of the page. I cite page 1 and page 4 articles and editorials that illustrate primary issues. They were chosen because they addressed the principal social, economic, and political concerns between 1941 and 1947 as well as the international, national, and domestic situation. The contents of the survey also reflect the diminished importance of the Internationalists and the assumption of control by the Maoists. Table 1 compares the newspaper's prevalent themes with important national affairs and the domestic economic, political, educational, and legal situation. Articles from pages 2 and 3 are listed under "other significant articles." As a general rule, the most important articles on page 2 explained those from page 1, and page 3 almost always carried news of the war and international affairs.

---

Table 1

**Articles in the JFRB as a Reflection of Events Occurring in China and in the Border Region**

---

| 1941 | JFRB |
|------|------|

1. War In Europe
2. Impending U.S. war with Japan
3. Organizing for Production
4. Reforming Educaton
5. United Front

---

| 1941 | National Affairs |
|------|------------------|

1. United Front Against Japan
2. U.S. Entry into War
3. Limited Trade with Rest of China

Table 1 *(continued)*

| 1941 | National Affairs *(continued)* |
|---|---|
| | 4. Military Mobilization<br>5. Guomindang Blockade<br>6. Japanese Offensive |
| 1941 | Domestic: Economic |
| | 1. Moderate Reform<br>2. Organizing to Expand Production<br>3. Land Reclamation<br>4. Begin Mutual-Aid |
| 1941 | Domestic: Political |
| | 1. No Revolution–United Front Phase<br>2. New Democracy<br>3. To the Village Movement<br>4. Increased Strength of Bureaucracy<br>5. Organizing Masses to Implement Program |
| 1941 | Domestic: Legal |
| | 1. Three-Three Policy<br>2. 1939 Marriage Law |
| 1941 | Domestic: Education |
| | 1. Educating Village Cadres<br>2. Finding Teachers<br>3. Forming Study Groups<br>4. Separate Education for Men and Women<br>5. New Character Movement |
| 1942 | JFRP |
| | 1. War<br>2. Rectification<br>3. Production<br>4. Labor Heroes<br>5. Elections |
| 1942 | National Affairs |
| | 1. Guomindang |
| 1942 | Domestic: Economic |
| | 1. Rectification—Transforming Economic Life at the Village Level |

Table 1 *(continued)*

| 1942 | Domestic: Economic *(continued)* |
|------|----------------------------------|
|      | 2. Inflation Rises Drastically<br>3. Graduate Income Tax Imposed<br>4. Government Gives Loans for Production |
| 1942 | Domestic: Political |
|      | 1. Rectification—Education on Marxism and Mass Mobilization<br>2. Shift from Vertical to Dual Rule<br>3. Talks at Yan'an Forum |
| 1942 | Domestic: Legal |
|      | 1. Law Passed Forbidding Footbinding |
| 1942 | Domestic: Education |
|      | 1. Cadre Education in Marx<br>2. Emphasis on Unity of Theory and Practice<br>3. Alternative Schools Established<br>4. Emphasis on Practical Education |
| 1943 | JFRB |
|      | 1. Great Production Drive<br>2. War<br>3. Formation of Cooperatives and Mutual-Aid Teams<br>4. Labor Heroes<br>5. Growing Tension with Guomindang<br>6. Reemergence of Revolutionary Terms |
| 1943 | National Affairs |
|      | 1. United Front Breaks Down<br>2. Guomindang Agrees to Discuss Outstanding Issues |
| 1943 | Domestic: Economic |
|      | 1. Great Production Drive/Self-Sufficiency<br>2. Inflation Continues to Rise<br>3. Mass Participation in Production<br>4. Labor Hero Campaign<br>5. Begin Reducing Rent and Interest Campaign |
| 1943 | Domestic: Political |
|      | 1. Rectification—Mass Mobilization<br>2. Tightening Party Discipline |

Table 1 *(continued)*

| | |
|---|---|
| 1943 | Domestic: Political *(continued)* |

3. Simplification of Government Bureaucracy
4. Emphasize Mass Line
5. Anti-Subversive Campaign

| | |
|---|---|
| 1943 | Domestic: Education |

1. Intellectuals Working Among the Peasants
2. Transforming Society Through Community Responsibility

| | |
|---|---|
| 1944 | JFRB |

1. Production/Labor Heroes
2. War
3. Political Situation in China
4. Literacy Campaign
5. Articles More Diverse
6. More Editorials

| | |
|---|---|
| 1944 | National Affairs |

1. U.S. Observer Teams Visit Yan'an
2. Guomindang—CCP Tension
3. Growing Communist Support in China

| | |
|---|---|
| 1944 | Domestic: Economic |

1. Labor Hero Campaign
2. Mutual Aid/Cooperative Work
3. Encourage Cotton Production Making It Exempt from Taxes
4. Rent Reduction Campaign

| | |
|---|---|
| 1944 | Domestic: Political |

1. Renewed Emphasis on Class
2. Decentralization of Government—Simple More Efficient Government
3. Mass Involvement at Local Level

| | |
|---|---|
| 1944 | Domestic: Legal |

1. Emphasis Mediation Not Courts
2. Mass Involvement in Making and Implementing Laws
3. Revised Marriage Law
4. Strengthening *Xiang* Level Government

| | |
|---|---|
| 1944 | Domestic: Education |

1. Emphasis on Part-time Education

Table 1 *(continued)*

| 1944 | Domestic: Education *(continued)* |
|---|---|
| | 2. General Education Major Part of Curriculum<br>3. Retraining Cadres in Education<br>4. Emphasis on Practical Educational Skills |
| 1945 | JFRB |
| | 1. End of War<br>2. Political Situation in China<br>3. Production/Cooperative Work<br>4. Impending Civil War<br>5. Expanding CP-Held Territory |
| 1945 | National Affairs |
| | 1. End of War<br>2. "On Coalition Government" Calls for Reorganizing National Government<br>3. August, Begin Negotiations with Guomindang |
| 1945 | Domestic: Economic |
| | 1. Encourage Private Capital to Increase Economic Development<br>2. Self-Sufficiency<br>3. Reducing Rent-Land Confiscation Abandoned |
| 1945 | Domestic: Political |
| | 1. New Constitution, Elevation of Mao<br>2. Elections<br>3. Specific Program of War, Coalition Government, People's Freedom |
| 1945 | Domestic: Education |
| | 1. Established Vocational Schools |
| 1946 | JFRB |
| | 1. Postwar China<br>2. Civil War<br>3. Land Reform<br>4. Rectification<br>5. Liberated Areas |
| 1946 | National Affairs |
| | 1. Civil War Begins<br>2. January 1946 Political Consultative Conference Begins |

Table 1 *(continued)*

| 1946 | Domestic: Economic |
|---|---|
| | 1. Bourgeoisie Industry and Commerce Protected Under New Democracy |
| | 2. December 21, 1946 Draft Law for Governmental Purchase of Land |
| | 3. Return to More Radical Land Policy |
| 1946 | Domestic: Political |
| | 1. Streamlining Hierarchical Organization of Party |
| | 2. Criticism by Party Especially Land Reform |
| 1946 | Domestic: Legal |
| | 1. Draft Law for the Government Purchase of Land |
| 1946 | Domestic: Education |
| | 1. Professional Schools |
| 1947 | JFRB |
| | 1. Civil War |
| 1947 | National Affairs |
| | 1. July, CCP Declared in Open Rebellion |
| | 2. Yan'an Taken by Guomindang in March |
| | 3. CCP Goes on the Offensive |
| 1947 | Domestic: Economic |
| | 1. Linking Land Reform to War and Production |
| | 2. September, National Land Conference |
| | 3. Mass-Line Importance of Land Reform |
| 1947 | Domestic: Political |
| | 1. Party Reform Winter, 1947–1948 |
| | 2. Rectification |
| 1947 | Domestic: Legal |
| | 1. Agrarian Law |

## THE SURVEY

### May 16, 1941–August 1941

*General Comments:* During its first three and a half months, the newspaper established a regular format in two-page editions. War dominated the news, with attention paid to U.S.-China relations and America's possible entry into the war. At the end of June and July, there was great interest in the Germans fighting on the Russian front. Almost no space was given to national news. On the domestic scene, election news and the organization of men and women for production predominated. Fiction dealt with the war and intellectuals who came to the Border Region.

### *1. General Page and Editorial Survey*

*Note:* In the general page and editorial survey, I use a system of numbers to indicate the relative frequency with which articles on that topic appeared. Number "1" is the subject that appears most frequently, "2" is the second most frequent topic, and so forth. When the same number appears for several topics it means that approximately the same number of articles appeared.

| Subject of article/editorial | Location of article/editorial | | | | |
|---|---|---|---|---|---|
| | Editorial | Pg 1 | Pg 2 | Pg 3 | Pg 4 |
| Economics | 6 | — | — | — | — |
| Education | — | — | 4 | — | — |
| Elections | — | — | 6 | — | — |
| Guomindang | 5 | — | — | — | — |
| Health | — | — | 8 | — | — |
| International | 4 | — | — | — | — |
| Marx | 2 | — | — | — | — |
| Politics (domestic)* | 3 | — | — | — | — |
| Politics (national)* | — | — | 7 | — | — |
| Production | — | — | 3 | — | — |
| Short stories | — | — | 2 | — | — |
| War in China | 1 | 2 | — | — | — |
| War in Europe and Asia | 1 | 1 | 1 | — | — |
| Women | — | — | 5 | — | — |
| Youth | 7 | — | — | — | — |

*National refers to events affecting all China; domestic refers to events affecting the Border Region.

## 2. *Important Editorials*

"Qingkan jinri zhi yuzhong jing shi shejia zhi tianxia" (Please consider whose family will eventually rule the contemporary world), by Mao Zedong, May 18, 1941.

"Shizheng gangling—dao qunzhong zhong qu!" (Administrative program—to the masses!), May 21, 1941.

"Lun jingji yu jishu gongzuo" (On economic and technical work), June 2, 1941.

"Tuixing xin wenzi yu saochu wenmang" (Pursue the new characters and eradicate illiteracy), June 4, 1941.

"Jinnan zhanyi de jiaoxun" (The lessons of the South Shanxi campaign), June 9, 1941.

*Note:* Guomindang's anti-Communist Policy.

"Huanying kexue yishu rencai" (Welcome scientific and artistic talent), June 10, 1941.

"Shijie zhengzhi de xin shiqi" (The new era of world politics), June 26, 1941.

"Su bi sheng, De bi bai" (The USSR must win, Germany must lose), June 29, 1941.

"Jinian Zhongguo gongchandang nianzhounian" (Commemorating twenty years of the Chinese Communist Party), July 1, 1941.

"Renmin shi zhengyi zhanzheng shengli de yuanquan" (People are the just source of battle victory), July 26, 1941.

*Note:* War between Germany and the USSR.

"Fazhan bianqu jingji jianshe de quanjian" (The key to expanding the Border Region economic construction), August 1, 1941.

"Du bianqu zheng gongzuo baogao" (Reading the Border Region work report), August 29, 1941.

## 3. *Columns Replacing Editorials*

"Lun muqian zhanju" (On the present war situation) by Zhou Enlai, June 14, 1941 (Dailun).

"Dao dagong baoshu" (Reaching the disinterested reader), by Zhou Enlai, July 13, 1941 (Dailun).

" 'Qiqi' sinian" ("7–7" four years), by Zhou Enlai, July 30, 31, 1941 (Dailun).

"Wo guo kangzhan sizhounian zhi minzhu zhengzhi" (Democratic politics of our country's anti-Japanese fourth anniversary), by Dong Biwu, August 3, 1941 (Dailun).

## 4. Major Page 1 Articles

"Deguo faxisi jingong Sulian" (Germany attacks the Soviet Union), June 23, 1941.

"Wei kangzhan sizhou nianjihui xuanyan" (Declaration of the commemorative meeting for the fourth anniversary of the anti-Japanese war), July 7, 1941.

"Zhonggong zhongying guanyu zuijin guoji shijian de shengming" (The CCP's Central Committee's announcement regarding the most recent international events), August 20, 1941.

## 5. Major Page 2 Articles (of Two-Page Editions)

"Maliezhuyi he wenyi chuangzuo" (Marx-Leninism and creative work in literature and art), by Ouyang Shan, May 19, 1941, p. 2.

"Mofan de Nanqu hezuoshe" (The model Nanqu cooperative), May 25, 1941.

"Zhongguo gongchandang ershi zhounian jihui teji" (Special issue on the 20th anniversary commemorative meeting of the Chinese Communist Party), July 1, 1941 (all p. 2).

"Qiqi kangzhan sizhou nianji teji" (Special issue commemorating the fourth anniversary of the 7–7 resistance battle), July 7, 1941.

*Note:* Articles by Zhu De and others.

"Wenxue yu shenghuo mantan" (An informal discussion on cultural study and life), by Zhou Yang, July 17–19, 1941, p. 2

"Jingshenjie zhi zhanshi" (The soldier of the spiritual world), by Zhou Yang, August 12–14, 1941.

*Note:* Concerns Lu Xun.

## 6. Regular Page 4 Columns

None.

## 7. Other Significant Articles

None.

## September–December 1941

*General Comments*: The newspaper is now four pages. Until the Japanese surrender, war news usually took precedence over other news. In September there was extensive coverage of the war in the Soviet Union, talks between the United States and Japan, and the possible entry of the United States into the war. The impending war between the United States and Japan was the most frequently found topic for October. September 16, 1941, ushered in the first of the regular page 4 columns. Issues of importance for the Border Region included education, organizing young people and women for the war effort, and production. Between November 2 and 27, 1941, the *Liberation Daily* published biographies of men and women attending the Border Region Assembly.

## *1. General Page and Editorial Survey*

| Subject of article/editorial | Location of article/editorial | | | | |
|---|---|---|---|---|---|
| | Editorial | Pg 1 | Pg 2 | Pg 3 | Pg 4 |
| B.R. Assembly | 11 | 4 | — | 2 | 2 |
| B.R. Government | 10 | — | — | — | 8 |
| Chinese Communist Party | 5 | — | 3 | — | — |
| Communications | — | — | — | — | 8 |
| Cooperatives | — | — | — | 6 | — |
| Economics | 7 | — | — | 4 | 8 |
| Education | 6 | — | 3 | — | 3 |
| Elections | 8 | — | 3 | 8 | — |
| Health | — | — | — | 7 | — |
| International | 2 | — | 3 | 5 | — |
| Law | — | — | — | 8 | 7 |
| Literature and art | — | — | — | — | 1 |
| Military | — | — | — | — | 6 |
| National minorities | — | — | 3 | 5 | — |
| Political study | 4 | — | — | 3 | — |
| Production | 9 | — | — | 3 | — |
| Science | — | — | — | 6 | — |
| Short stories | — | — | 2 | — | — |
| Sino-American relations | — | — | 3 | — | — |
| U.S. entrance into the war | — | 2 | — | — | — |
| USSR | — | — | 3 | — | — |
| War in China | 3 | 3 | — | — | — |
| War in Europe and Asia | 1 | 1 | 1 | 1 | 7 |
| Women | — | — | 5 | — | 4 |
| Workers | — | — | — | — | 5 |
| Youth | — | — | 3 | — | 5 |

## 2. Important Editorials

"Fandui xuexizhong de jiaotiaozhuyi" (Oppose dogmatism in study), September 2, 1941.

"Dapo jiu de yiceng" (One layer in smashing the old), September 11, 1941.

"Tigao bianqu min jiaoyu" (Raising mass education in the Border Region), October 4, 1941.

"Guoqing jihui" (National day commemoration), October 10, 1941.

"Yingjie bianqu canyihui" (Greet the Border Region Assembly), October 12, 1941.

"Jingbing jianzheng" (Crack troops, simple administration), December 6, 1941.

"Taipingyang zhanzheng yu wo guo de renwu" (The Pacific War and our country's responsibility), December 11, 1941.

"Fandui zhengquan jianshezhong de quanmenzhuyi" (Oppose close-doorism in building political rights), December 29, 1941.

## 3. Columns Replacing Editorials

None.

## 4. Major Page 1 Articles

"Mao Zedong tongzhi zai bianqu canyihui de yanshuo" (The address of Comrade Mao Zedong at the Border Region assembly), November 22, 1941.

"Zhongguo gongchandang wei Taipingyang zhanzheng de xuanyan" (The declaration of the CCP on the Pacific War), December 10, 1941.

"Zhonggong zhongying quanyu Taipingyang fanRi tongyi zhanzheng de zhishi" (The CCP's Central Committee's directive on the Pacific anti-Japanese united battlefront), December 13, 1941.

## 5. Major Page 4 Articles

"Bianqu di sifa: Bianqu zaji zhi yi" (Border Region administration: some Border Region notes), October 13–14, 1941.

"Dui bianqu canyihui yijian" (Regarding opinions in the Border

Region assembly), October 25–31; November 2, 4–5, 10–12, 16, 1941.

" 'Zhongguo xinwenzi' chuban" (Publishing "China's new writings"), November 26, 1941.

"Bianqu ziliao" (Border Region materials), December 3, 5, 6, 10, 12, 23, 30, 31, 1941.

### 6. Regular Page 4 Columns

*Literature and Art* (September 16–20, 22, 23, 25, 26, 29, 30; October 1–3, 6, 7, 9, 10, 13, 14, 15–17, 19, 21, 23, 24, 27, 28, 30, 31; November 3–4, 6, 7, 11, 13–16, 18, 20, 22, 25, 27, 28; December 1, 2, 4, 5, 8–11, 15–18, 23–25, 29–31).

*Youth* (September 21; October 5, 20; November 2, 17, 30; December 14, 28).

*Workers* (September 24; October 8, 22; November 5, 19; December 3, 19).

*Women* (September 28; October 12, 26; November 9, 23; December 7, 21).

*Science* (October 4, 18; November 1, 10, 29; December 13, 27).

*Army* (October 29; November 12, 16; December 12, 26).

*Enemy* (September 27; October 11, 25; November 8, 22; December 6, 20).

*Health* (November 24; December 22).

### 7. Other Significant Articles

"Shuangshi guoqing jihui tekan" (Special double ten national day commemorative issue), October 10, 1941, p. 3.

"Tantan gongwen gaige" (Discussing the official reform), by Zhou Yang, October 30–31, 1941, p. 3.

### January–April, 1942

*General Comments*: Rectification began in February, and by April study articles appeared on every page. The survey below does not include rectification articles that were discussed and listed in chapter 2. At the end of April, page 4 columns appeared irregularly, replaced by longer essays or short stories. Although rectification dominated the

Party, news of the war in Europe and China dominated the *Liberation Daily*. The reform movement did lead domestic news, but production and economic news were also important as the spring planting season approached. This four-month period saw the beginning of letters to the editors (February 8), in April the appearance of a daily page 2 "Party life" column, and the first articles on labor heroes and heroines. Wu Manyou and Zhao Zhangui are two famous labor heroes who were the subject of numerous articles.

## 1. General Page and Editorial Survey

| Subject of article/editorial | Location of article\editorial | | | | |
|---|---|---|---|---|---|
| | Editorial | Pg 1 | Pg 2 | Pg 3 | Pg 4 |
| Army | 8 | — | — | 6 | — |
| Arts and literature | — | — | — | — | 1 |
| B.R. Assembly | — | — | — | 7 | — |
| B.R. Government | 4 | — | 3 | 6 | — |
| Communications | — | — | — | — | 9 |
| Cooperatives | — | — | — | 7 | — |
| Economics | 3 | 4 | 2 | 3 | 8 |
| Education | 5 | — | — | 7 | 8 |
| Elections | 9 | 7 | — | 6 | 9 |
| Enemy | — | — | — | — | 6 |
| Essays | — | — | — | — | 4 |
| Guomindang | — | — | — | 7 | — |
| Health | — | — | — | 7 | 7 |
| International affairs | — | — | 3 | — | — |
| Labor heroes/heroines | — | — | 3 | — | — |
| Land policy | 6 | — | — | 4 | 9 |
| Letters to *Liberation Daily* | — | — | — | 7 | — |
| Marxism-Leninism | 11 | — | — | — | — |
| Production | 7 | 5 | 2 | 5 | 2 |
| Rectification | 2 | 3 | — | 2 | 3 |
| Science | — | — | — | — | 6 |
| Three-three system | — | 7 | — | — | — |
| War in China | 10 | 2 | 1 | 1 | — |
| War in Europe and Asia | 1 | 1 | 1 | 1 | — |
| Women | — | — | — | 5 | 5 |
| Women's Day | — | 6 | — | — | — |
| Workers | — | — | — | — | 7 |
| Youth | — | — | 3 | — | 5 |

## 2. Important Editorials

For rectification editorials see chapter 2.

"Jiaoyushang de geming" (Revolution in Education), January 13, 1942.

"Tigao bianqu guomin jiaoyu" (Raise the Border Region's nationalistic education), January 14, 1942.

"Jiaqiang difang zai zhiganbu jiaoyu" (Strengthen local cadre education), February 5, 1942.

"Zai lun jingbing jianzheng" (Again discuss crack troops and simple administration), February 20, 1942.

"Yingjie sanba guoji funüjie" (Welcome March 8, Women's day), March 8, 1942.

"Ba wenhua gongzuo tuijin yibu" (Advancing cultural work a step), March 25, 1942.

"Jianche jingbing jianzheng" (Thoroughly implement crack troops and simple administration), April 9, 1942.

"Bianqu nongmin xiang Wu Manyou kanqi" (Border region peasants emulate Wu Manyou), April 30, 1942.

### 3. Columns Replacing Editorials

See chapter 2.

### 4. Major Page 1 Articles

For page 1 articles on rectification, see chapter 2.

"Zhonggong zhongying guanyu kangRi genjudi zhengce de jueding" (Decision of the Communist Party Central Committee regarding the land policy for the anti-Japanese base areas), February 6, 1942.

"Qingzhu hongjun ershisi zhounian" (Celebrate the red army's 24th anniversary), by Mao Zedong, February 23, 1942.

"Liannian kaihuang shouliang teduo" (For years on end opening a great deal of land and harvesting much grain), April 30, 1942.

*Note:* Concerns labor hero Wu Manyou.

### 5. Major Page 4 Articles

For page 4 articles on rectification, see chapter 2.

"Xianji shixing jingbing jianzheng diyisheng" (The first sounds of implementing crack troops and simple administration campaign at the *xian* level), January 9, 1942.

"Bianqu ziliao" (Border Region materials), January 16, 22, 1942.

"Yijiusiyinian Shaan-Gan-Ning bianqu de jingji jianshe gaikuang"

(A survey of the Shaan-Gan-Ning Border Region's economic construction in 1941), January 20–21, 1942.

"Xin de jiaoyu fangzhenxia" (Under the new educational policy), January 28, 1942.

"Zhixing 'Jingbing jianzheng' " (Carry out "crack troops and simple administration"), February 1, 1942.

"Jinian sanba guoji funüjie tekan" (Special issue to commemorate March 8, Women's Day), March 8, 1942.

"Benbao gexin qianye fangxun gejie yijian" (The newspaper's innovative eve, an inquiry into several opinions), April 2, 1942.

*Note:* Twenty-five readers criticized the newspaper.

"Ertongmen tongjieqilai xuexi zuo xin Zhongguo de xin zhuren" (Children unite to begin studying to become the new masters of new China), by Mao Zedong, April 4, 1942.

## 6. Regular Page 4 Columns

*Literature and Art* (January 1, 7, 8, 10, 13–15, 20–22, 24, 27, 29; February 2–5, 9–12, 15, 17–19, 21, 25–26; March 2–5, 9–12, 17–19, 23–26, 29, 30).

*Enemy* (January 5, 17, 31; February 14, 28; March 28; April 21).

*Army* (January 9, 23; February 6, 20; March 6, 20).

*Women* (January 6, 18; February 1, 16).

*Youth* (January 11, 25; February 8, 22; March 1).

*Science* (January 12, 26; February 7, 24; March 7, 21).

*Workers* (January 16, 30; February 13, 27; March 27).

*Health* (January 19; February 23; March 22, 31; April 19, 29).

## 7. Other Significant Articles

"Makesi de zhixue fangfa" (Marx's political study method), by Wang Ziye, January 16, 1942, p. 3.

"Kang Youwei de datong shehuizhuyi" (The Great Harmony Socialism of Kang Youwei), by Wang Kuang, January 19–21, 1942, p. 3.

"Zhonggong zhongying tongguo genjudi tudi zhengce" (The CCP's Central Committee adopts a land policy for the base areas), February 6, 1942, p. 3.

"Zhonggong zhongying guanyu kangRi genjudi tudi zhengshu jueding de fujian" (Appendix to the CCP's Central Committee's correct decision regarding land in the anti-Japanese base areas), February 6, 1942, p. 3.

"Xinxiang" (Letters), February 8; March 20, 22, 28, 30, 1942, p. 3.

"Balujun xinsijun zhuanbian ganbu jiaoyu gongzuo" (The 8th Route Army and the New 4th Army transform cadre education work), April 1, 1942, p. 2.

"Minxian yingxiong" (People's heroes), April 22, 1942, p. 2.

"Mofan yingxiong Wu Manyou shi zenyang faxiande" (How model worker and labor hero Wu Manyou was discovered), by Mo Ai, April 30, 1942, p. 2.

## May–August 1942

*General Comments*: Apart from the war, production and Party reform were the leading topics during this four-month period. May issues were devoted almost entirely to rectification. Between May 13, 1942, and January 16, 1943, twenty-three "Study" columns appeared on page 4. Articles specifically on rectification are listed in chapter 2 and not repeated in this survey. Finally, there was interesting coverage of the political situation in India at this time.

## 1. General Page and Editorial Survey

| Subject of article/editorial | Location of article/editorial | | | | |
|---|---|---|---|---|---|
| | Editorial | Pg 1 | Pg 2 | Pg 3 | Pg 4 |
| B.R. Assembly | 5 | 6 | 4 | — | — |
| B.R. Government | — | 6 | 7 | — | — |
| Building new China | 4 | 6 | 2* | 2 | — |
| Cadres | — | 6 | — | — | — |
| Commemorations | 3 | 4 | 9 | — | 7 |
| Communist Party | 4 | — | — | — | — |
| Economics | 6 | 6 | — | — | — |
| Elections | 5 | 6 | 7 | — | — |
| Enemy | — | — | — | — | 4 |
| Essays | — | — | — | — | 1 |
| Health | — | — | — | — | 5 |
| Internal conditions | 6 | — | — | 2 | — |
| International affairs | 5 | — | — | 1 | — |
| Labor heroes/heroines | 6 | — | 7 | — | — |
| Letters to the *Liberation Daily* | — | — | 3 | — | — |

| Subject of article/editorial | Location of article/editorial | | | | |
|---|---|---|---|---|---|
| | Editorial | Pg 1 | Pg 2 | Pg 3 | Pg 4 |
| Natural disasters | 5 | — | — | — | — |
| Politics (domestic) | — | 9 | — | — | — |
| Production | — | 3 | 2 | 2 | — |
| Rectification | 1 | 4 | 1* | 2 | — |
| Salt | 6 | — | — | — | — |
| Science | — | — | — | 6 | — |
| Self-defense | 5 | 5 | 6 | — | — |
| Short stories & poems | — | — | — | 2 | — |
| Soviet army | — | — | — | 8 | — |
| Study | — | — | — | 3 | — |
| Taxes | — | — | 9 | — | — |
| War in China | 5 | 2 | 5 | 1 | — |
| War in Europe & Asia | 2 | 1 | 5 | 1 | — |
| Women | — | — | 8 | 3 | — |

*These generally found under heading "Party life."

## 2. Important Editorials

For rectification editorials, see chapter 2.

"Wu Manyou—mofan nongmin" (Wu Manyou—model peasant), May 6, 1942.

"Bianfu kai ganbu dongyuan dahui" (The Border Region government opens the cadre mobilization meeting), May 21, 1942.

"Sansanzhi de yunyong" (Utilizing the three/three system), May 25, 1942.

"Jiaqiang duiyu xuexi de lingdao" (Strengthen study leadership), June 2, 1942.

"Zai lun dihou jingbing jianzheng" (Again discuss crack troops and simple administration behind enemy lines )June 23, 1942

"Chedi shixing jingbing zhengce" (Thoroughly carry out the crack troop policy), August 3, 1942.

"Baozhi he xin de wenfeng" (The newspaper and the new style of writing), August 4, 1942.

"Qingbing jianfu dangqian gongzuo de zhongxin huanjing" (The core environment of crack troops simple administration's present work), August 23, 1942.

"Zhankai tongxunyun gongzuo" (Expand reporters' work), August 25, 1942.

### 3. Columns Replacing Editorials

"Banyue junshi dongtai" (Semimonthly military developments), May 15, 31; June 16, 30; July 15, 31; August 15, 31.

"Zhandou de wuyi jinian" (The May 1 anniversary of battle), by Deng Fa, May 1, 1942 (Dailun).

"Zengyan" (Parting words of advice), by Xie Juezai, June 4, 1942 (Dailun).

"Gengjia tigao budui de pinzhi" (Raise the quality of troops even more), by Wang Zhen, July 10, 1942 (Dailun).

"Jianjue zhixing jingbing zhengce" (Resolutely implement the crack troop policy), by Zuo Quan, July 13, 1942 (Dailun).

"Zuo Quan tongzhi jingshen busi" (The spirit of Comrade Zuo Quan is not dead), by Zhou Enlai, July 30, 1942 (Dailun).

"Women yinggai you de zuofeng" (The style of work we should have), by Xie Juezai, August 8, 1942 (Dailun).

### 4. Major Page 1 Articles

For page 1 articles on rectification, see chapter 2.

"Jinian dang de ershiyi zhounian" (Commemorating the Party's 21st anniversary) by Zhu De, July 1, 1942.

"Zhongguo gongchandang zhongying weiyuanhui wei jinian kangzhan wu zhounian xuanyan" (CCP's Central Committee makes a declaration on the 5th anniversary of the anti-Japanese war), July 7, 1942.

*Note:* See related page 1 and page 4 articles.

### 5. Major Page 4 Articles

For page 4 articles on rectification, see chapter 2.

"Dang de zuzhi he dang de wenxue" (Party organization and Party cultural study), by Lenin, May 14, 1942.

"Makasizhuyi yu wenyi" (Art, literature, and Marxism), May 15, 1942.

"Lun women de baozhi" (Our newspaper), by Lenin, July 20, 1942.

### 6. Regular Page 4 Columns

*Science* (May 3, 30; July 1, 31; August 30).
*Enemy* (May 6, 17, 22; June 7, 21; July 6, 21; August 6, 21).
*Health* (May 18, 29; June 14; July 22, 30; August 14).

*Study* (May 13, 16, 21, 24, 28; June 1, 8, 11, 15, 17, 20, 27, 30; July 13, 23; August 11, 23).

### 7. Other Significant Articles

"Chi Chen Duxiu de touxiang lilun" (Denounce the capitulation theory of Chen Duxiu), by Li Xinqing, May 8, 1942, p. 3.

*Note:* Criticized an article Chen wrote on March 21 for Chongqing's *Dagong bao.*

"Jingbing jianzheng zai Jin-Ji-Lu-Yu bianqu" (Crack troops, simple administration in the Jin-Ji-Lu-Yu border region), by Mao Duo, August 19, 1942, p. 2.

### September–December 1942

*General Comments:* War and rectification again led in number of articles. Those specifically on rectification are listed in chapter 2 and not repeated here. In September there were several articles on Lenin, the elections and an increasing number on labor heroes/heroines. In late November and December, fewer editorials appeared. Their absence reflected reforms in the newspaper.

### 1. General Page and Editorial Survey

| Subject of article/editorial | Location of article/editorial | | | | |
|---|---|---|---|---|---|
| | Editorial | Pg 1 | Pg 2 | Pg 3 | Pg 4 |
| Army | 4 | — | — | — | — |
| B.R. Assembly | 7 | 4 | — | — | — |
| B.R. Government | 2 | 6 | 8 | — | — |
| Cooperatives | — | 7 | 8 | — | — |
| Crack Troop campaign | — | 6 | 6 | — | — |
| Education | 5 | — | 7 | — | — |
| Elections | 7 | — | 5 | — | — |
| Enemy | — | — | — | — | 3 |
| Essays | — | — | — | — | 1 |
| Factories | — | 7 | — | — | — |
| Health | 7 | | — | — | — |
| International affairs | 5 | — | 1 | — | — |
| Labor heroes/heroines | — | 7 | 8 | — | — |

| Subject of article/editorial | Location of article/editorial | | | | |
|---|---|---|---|---|---|
| | Editorial | Pg 1 | Pg 2 | Pg 3 | Pg 4 |
| Land policy | — | 7 | — | — | — |
| Letters to *Liberation Daily* | — | — | 4 | — | — |
| Lu Xun anniversary | 7 | — | — | — | — |
| National affairs | — | 7 | — | — | — |
| Norman Bethune | 7 | — | — | — | — |
| Politics (domestic) | 6 | — | — | — | — |
| Postwar China | — | 7 | 10 | — | — |
| Production | 1 | 3 | 1 | 2 | — |
| Rectification | 2 | 6 | 2* | — | — |
| Reducing rent | 7 | 7 | 3 | — | — |
| Russian revolution | 7 | 5 | 9 | 2 | 6 |
| Science | — | — | — | — | 4 |
| Short stories | — | — | — | — | 2 |
| Study | — | — | — | — | 5 |
| Taxes | — | — | — | — | 5 |
| Textiles | — | — | 9 | — | — |
| War in China | 3 | 2 | — | 1 | — |
| War in Europe & Asia | 1 | 1 | — | 1 | — |
| Women | — | — | 9 | 3 | — |

*These generally found under heading "Party life."

## 2. *Important Editorials*

For rectification editorials, see chapter 2.

"Women shizhong yao tongzhi laobaixing zai yizi" (We must all along unite with comrades among the ordinary people), September 4, 1942.

"Jianli xiangcun dangzheng gongzuo de zhengque guanxi" (Establish the correct relationship with Party political work in rural areas), September 17, 1942.

"Dang yu dangbao" (The Party and the Party's newspaper), September 22, 1942.

"Hongjun de weida shengli" (Great victory of the red army), by Mao Zedong, October 12, 1942.

*Note:* Chinese Communist Party's appreciation of the Battle of Stalingrad.

"Lishi jiaoxun" (Historical lesson), by Mao Zedong, October 14, 1942.

*Note:* War between U.S.S.R. and Germany.

"Ping Bailin shengming" (Criticize the Berlin declaration), by Mao Zedong, October 16, 1942.

"Jinian Lu Xun xiansheng" (Commemorating Mr. Lu Xun), October 19, 1942.

"Zhuanru shengchan zhongqu" (Shift to production), October 21, 1942.

"Zhu shiyue geming nianwu zhounian" (Congratulations on the 25th anniversary of the October Revolution), by Mao Zedong, November 7, 1942.

"Gei dangbao de jizhe he tongxunyuan" (For the benefit of reporters and communication workers), November 17, 1942.

"Jiaqing lingdao xiangcun zhibu jianshe" (Strengthen the leadership in establishing rural Party branches), November 19, 1942.

"Jiji jinxing 'Nanniwan zhengce'!" (Positively advance the "Nanniwan policy"!), December 12, 1942.

### 3. Columns Replacing Editorials

"Banyue junshi dongtai" (Semimonthly military developments), September 15, 20; October 17, 31; November 15; December 1, 17, 31.

"Zhu jiuyue yundong dahui" (Best wishes to the September mobilization assembly), by Zhu De, September 2, 1942 (Dailun).

"Diwei 'sici zhiqiang yundong' zongjie de zongjie" (A summary of the puppet government's summary of the "4th political strengthening movement"), by Nie Rongzhen, September 16, 1942 (Dailun).

"Mian dongbei tongbao" (Encouraging our Northeast compatriots), by Zhu De, September 18, 1942 (Dailun).

"Tichang gongnong tongzhi xue wenjian—Kang Sheng tongzhi gei 'Bitanhui' bianji tongzhi de xin" (Promoting essays written by workers and peasants—Comrade Kang Sheng sends a letter to the editors of "Conversations by writing"), October 4, 1942 (Dailun).

"Ping Dongjing guangbo" (Criticize Tokyo's broadcasts), December 11, 1942 (Pingshi).

"Ping de paiqian jundangju tanhua" (Criticize the enemy's dispatch of army authorities for discussion), December 15, 1942 (Pingshi).

"Lixing wuzhi shenghuo de jieyue" (Rigorously enforce the practice of thrift in material life), by Huo Weide, December 20, 1942 (Lunzhuan).

"Jisu zhankai Zhao Zhankui yundong" (Continuously expand the Zhao Zhankui movement), by Gao Zhangjiu, December 22, 1942 (Lunzhuan).

"Baoxing yu canbai" (Violent conduct and crushing defeat), by Nie Rongzhen, December 24, 1942 (Dailun).

"Zai lun hongjun dongji zhengshi" (Again discuss the Red Army's winter offensive), December 25, 1942 (Pingshi).

"Wanchang zhengliang de zuihou gongzuo" (Complete the last work of collecting the grain levy), December 30, 1942 (Pingshi).

### 4. Major Page 1 Articles

For specific titles on rectification, see chapter 2.

"Guanche jianzheng zhengce, bianfu haokai dongyuan dahui, yiji jiguan jinxing jiancha gongzuo" (Implement a policy of simple administration, the Border Region government convenes a mobilization meeting, top level organizations advance investigation work), September 11, 1942.

"Fazhan shengchan jiaoyu ganbu, guanche jingbing jianzheng zhengce" (Expand production, educate cadres, implement the crack troop simple administration policy), December 14, 1942.

"Tudizu ge tiaoli caoan" (Draft resolution for land rent), December 30, 1942 (continued page 2).

### 5. Major Page 4 Articles

For specific titles on rectification, see chapter 2.

" 'Jiu yi' kuoda yundonghui tekan, #1" ("September 1" expanding mobilization meeting special edition, #1), September 5, 1942.

"Zhao Zhankui tongzhi" (Comrade Zhao Zhankui), by Deng Muqing and Zhang Tiefu, September 13–14, 1942.

"Zhongying yanjiuyuan zhengfeng yilai gaizao sixiang zongjie" (A summary of thought reform since rectification at the Central Committee's Research Institute), by Zhang Ruxin, October 31, November 1, 1942.

"Jinian de nongdai gongzuo" (This year's agricultural loan work), December 22, 1942.

## 6. Regular Page 4 Columns

*Health* (September 2, 15, 29; October 15, 29; November 15, 29; December 14, 29).
*Enemy* (September 6, 21; October 7, 22; November 6, 21; December 8, 21).
*Science* (September 30; October 30; November 30; December 30).
*Study* (September 8, 25; October 6; November 9).
*Taxes* (November 10; December 6, 18).
*News and Communication* (October 28).

## 7. Other Significant Articles

"Jianquan women de tongxunwang" (Perfecting our communication network), by Yang Pingzhen, September 1, 1942, p. 2.
"Dang de shenghuo" (Party life), September 15; October 3, 7, 12, 15, 18, 22, 29; November 2, 4, 11, 28, 30; December 5, 9, 12, 19, 22, 25, 27, 31, 1942, p. 2.
"Yanda chengli zhounian jinian" (Yan'an University sets up an anniversary commemoration), September 24, 1942, p. 2.
"Mofan gongren Zhao Zhankui" (Model worker Zhao Zhankui), by Deng Muqing, September 29, 1942, p. 2.

## January–April 1943

*General Comments*: News of the European war concentrated primarily on the Soviet Union while that of the Border Region focused on production. Beginning in January, the emphasis was on raising agricultural production. In late February and early March there were numerous articles on labor heroes/heroines as the Great Production Drive sought to achieve economic self-sufficiency throughout the Border Region. Throughout March and April, the lead article was production; opening up new land dominated April issues. Page 4 contained reports on new economic plans. Between February 4 and 8, a series discussed the unequal treaties that remained with Western powers.

## 1. General Page and Editorial Survey

| Subject of article/editorial | Location of article/editorial | | | | |
|---|---|---|---|---|---|
| | Editorial | Pg 1 | Pg 2 | Pg 3 | Pg 4 |
| Army | — | — | — | — | 6 |
| B.R. Assembly | 5 | 7 | — | — | — |
| Cadres | — | 7 | 9 | — | — |
| Cooperatives | — | 7 | 8 | — | — |
| Crack Troop campaign | — | — | — | 3 | — |
| Economics | 4 | — | 10 | 3 | — |
| Education | — | — | 7 | 3 | — |
| Enemy | — | — | — | — | 4 |
| Essays | — | — | — | — | 1 |
| Factories | — | 3 | 10 | 3 | — |
| Health | — | — | — | — | 3 |
| Internal conditions | — | — | 11 | — | — |
| Labor heroes/heroines | 3 | 2 | 2 | 3 | 3 |
| Letters to *Liberation Daily* | — | — | — | — | 6 |
| Mutual aid | — | 7 | 10 | — | — |
| Politics | 5 | 7 | 11 | — | — |
| Production | 1 | 1 | 1 | 2 | — |
| Rectification | 4 | 6 | 3 | 3 | — |
| Reducing rent | — | — | 9 | — | — |
| Refugees | — | 7 | 6 | — | — |
| Science | — | — | — | — | 5 |
| Short stories | — | — | — | — | 2 |
| Simplify gov. campaign | 5 | 7 | 7 | — | — |
| Study | — | — | — | — | 7 |
| Textiles | — | 7 | 5 | 3 | — |
| Thought reform | — | 7 | — | — | — |
| Unequal treaties | 3 | 4 | — | — | 7 |
| War in China | 5 | 5 | — | 1 | — |
| War in Europe and Asia | 2 | 1 | — | 1 | — |
| Women | — | — | 4 | 2 | 5 |

## 2. Important Editorials

"Kaizhan Wu Manyou yundong" (Expand the Wu Manyou movement), January 11, 1943.

"Ba laodong zuzhiqilai" (Begin organizing production), January 25, 1943.

"Yongzheng aimin yundong" (Movement to support the government, cherish the people), February 1, 1943.

"Zhongguo gongchandang yu feichu bupingdeng tiaoyue" (The CCP and abolishing the unequal treaties), February 4, 1943.

"Shengchan da jingsai" (The great contest for production), March 3, 1943.

"Ganbuhui yu zhengfeng yundong" (Cadre meeting and rectification), March 4, 1943.

"Kaizhan Wu Manyou yundong" (Expand the Wu Manyou movement), by Zhao Changyuan, March 15, 1943.

### 3. Columns Replacing Editorials

"Banyue junshi dongtai" (Semimonthly military developments), January 15; February 2, 16; March 1, 16; April 1, 15.

"Sanlun hongjun dongji zhengshi" (Three discussions on the red army's winter offensive), January 9, 1943 (Pingshi).

"Wang Ni de chouju" (The ugly play of Wang Ni), January 13, 1943 (Pingshi).

"Zhong-Mei Zhong-Ying xinyue" (New Sino-American Sino-British treaties), January 14, 1943 (Pingshi).

"Silun hongjun dongji gongshi" (The fourth discussion of the red army's winter offensive), January 24, 1943 (Pingshi).

"Kaizhan yongzheng aimin yundong" (Launch the support the government, cherish the people movement), by He Long, February 1, 1943 (Dailun).

"Xiangying shengchan haohao kaizhan Zhao Zhankui yundong" (The response to production, the summons to expand the Zhao Zhankui movement), by Deng Fa, February 7, 1943 (Dailun).

"Wulun hongjun dongji zhengshi" (The fifth discussion of the red army's winter offensive), February 8, 1943 (Pingshi).

"Dajin jun de haojiao" (The bugle call of the great advancing army), February 17, 1943 (Pingshi).

"Gongwubuke hongjun" (The ever-victorious red army), February 19, 1943 (Pingshi).

"Zhunbei 'juezhan' de diguo yihui" (The enemy assembly which prepares for the "decisive battle"), March 7, 1943 (Pingshi).

"Yingjie funü gongzuo de xin fangxiang" (Welcome the new direction of women's work), by Cai Chang, March 8, 1943 (Dailun).

"Ping Qiu Guer yanshuo" (Criticize Qiu Guer's speech), March 25, 1943 (Pingshi).

"Kefu chungeng yundongzhong lingdaoshang de ruodian" (Overcome the weak points of leadership in the spring planting movement), by Gao Gang, April 17, 1943 (Dailun).

"Xiang Liu Zhiran tongzhi xuexi" (Toward studying Comrade Liu Zhiran), by Gao Gang, April 24, 1943 (Dailun).

"Xiang xiji zizu de mubiao majin" (Move the target of self-sufficiency forward), April 28, 1943 (Dailun).

### 4. Major Page 1 Articles

"Yan'an gejie relie qingjia xinnian, dangzhongying ji bianfu haokai ganbu wanhui, Mao zhuxi haohao jin shengchan jiaoyu" (Various circles in Yan'an enthusiastically celebrate the new year, the Party's Central Comittee and the Border Region government convene a cadre meeting, Chairman Mao summons [everyone] to bind together production and education), January 4, 1943.

"Bianqu de tudizu ge xingshi" (The format for Border Region land), January 23, 1943.

"Yongzheng aimin yundong" (Movement to support the government, cherish the people), February 1, 1943.

"Nianerwei shengchan yingxiong" (Twenty-two production heroes), February 3, 1943, all p. 1.

"Zhonggong zhongying guanyu ge kangRi genjudi muqian funü gongzuo fangzhen de jueding" (The decision of the CCP's Central Committee on the present direction of women's work in the anti-Japanese base areas), February 26, 1943.

"Guanyu Wu Manyou de fangxiang" (Concerning Wu Manyou's direction), March 15, 1943, (con't. p. 2.

### 5. Major Page 4 Articles

"Guanyu dangnei shenghuo" (Regarding inner-Party life), by Chen Boda, January 10, 1943.

"Bianqu di tudi zudian xingshi" (The Border Region's practice of renting out land to tenants), by the NW Party Bureau research office, January 23, 1943.

"Laodong yingxiong jianyue dahui" (Labor heroes' review meeting), by Mo Ye, January 25, 1943.

"Qingzhu feichu bupingdeng tiaoyue tekan" (Special issue to congratulate the abolition of the unequal treaties), February 4–8, 1943.

"Shaan-Gan-Ning bianqu jianzheng shishi gangyao" (Outline to implement the simplification of the Shaan-Gan-Ning Border Region government), March 6, 1943, all p. 4.

"Renxing-dangxing-gexing" (Human nature—party nature—individual nature), by Chen Boda, March 27, 1943.

"Guanyu yishu gongzuozhe xiaxiang de wenti" (The problem of artists going down to the villages), by Kai Feng, March 28, 1943.

"Guanyu dang de yishu gongzuozhe de liangge qingxiang wenti" (Regarding two potential problems of party artists), March 29, 1943.

"Mantan baozhi de cuozi" (Discussing the mistakes of the newspaper), by Ji Cang, April 8, 1943.

"Xiongmei kaihuang" (Elder brothers and younger sisters open land), April 25, 1943.

*Note:* First published *yangko* (a rural folk dance).

### 6. Regular Page 4 Columns

*Enemy* (January 6, 22; February 9, 25; March 11, 25; April 27).
*Health* (January 15, 31; February 3, 16, 27; March 15, 21, 22; April 10, 29).
*Study* (January 16).
*News and Communication* (January 26; March 5; April 8).
*Science* (January 30; March 2–4).
*Army* (April 1, 16).

### 7. Other Significant Articles

"Dang de shenghuo" (Party life), January 6, 9, 13, 25, 28; February 2, 8, 11, 18, 26; March 2, 4, 6, 7, 8, 16, 17, 22, 23, 1943, p. 2.

"Dangqian dahoufang de gongye" (The work facing the rear areas), April 15, 1943, pp. 3, 4.

### May–August 1943

*General Comments:* The Great Production Drive was in full swing as articles about production replaced the war as the major news story. The government began to promote cooperatives and mutual-aid teams and to organize factories; all these received extensive coverage in the newspaper. Revolutionary rhetoric absent from Party writing during the United Front reappeared as the *Liberation Daily* emphasized the role of the Communist Party in the Anti-Japanese war as compared with that of the Guomindang. In July, the Border Region government began a campaign against traitors and spies.

## 1. General Page and Editorial Survey

| Subject of article/editorial | Location of article/editorial | | | | |
| --- | --- | --- | --- | --- | --- |
| | Editorial | Pg 1 | Pg 2 | Pg 3 | Pg 4 |
| Army | — | — | — | — | 5 |
| Arts and literature | — | — | — | — | 7 |
| Backward elements | — | — | 9 | — | — |
| Cadres | — | — | 10 | — | — |
| Communist Party | 2 | 4 | — | — | — |
| Cooperatives | — | — | 7 | — | — |
| Democracy | 4 | — | — | — | — |
| Education | — | — | 11 | — | 5 |
| Essays | — | — | — | — | 1 |
| Factories | — | 7 | 4 | 3 | — |
| Fascism | 3 | — | — | — | — |
| Government reform | — | — | 10 | — | — |
| Guomindang | 3 | 11 | — | 3 | — |
| GMD/CCP fighting | 4 | 10 | 9 | 3 | — |
| GMD/CCP relations | 1 | 9 | — | — | — |
| Health | — | — | — | — | 6 |
| International affairs | — | 11 | — | 2 | — |
| July 7 commemoration | — | 6 | — | — | 4 |
| Labor heroes/heroines | — | 11 | 2 | 3 | 7 |
| May 1 | — | 10 | — | — | — |
| Media | — | — | — | — | 8 |
| Mutual aid | — | 11 | 5 | — | — |
| National affairs | — | — | — | 3 | — |
| Production | — | 2 | 1 | 3 | — |
| Questions and answers | — | — | — | — | 3 |
| Rectification | — | 8 | 7 | — | — |
| Reducing rents | — | — | 11 | — | — |
| Refugees | — | — | 9 | — | — |
| Self-defense | — | 5 | 8 | — | — |
| Short stories and poems | — | — | — | — | 2 |
| Textiles | — | — | 3 | — | — |
| Village reform | — | 9 | — | — | — |
| War in China | — | 1 | 11 | 3 | — |
| War in Europe and Asia | — | 3 | 11 | 1 | — |
| Women | — | — | 6 | 3 | 7 |

## 2. Important Editorials

"Lun gongchan guoji di jiesan" (On disbanding the Communist International), May 28, 1943.

"Zai lun gongchan guoji de jiesan" (Again on disbanding the Communist international), June 27, 1943.

"Zhongguo gongchandang yu Zhonghua minzu" (Chinese Communist Party and the Chinese people), July 1, 1943 (continued page 2).

"Qilai! Zhizhi neizhan! Wanjiu weiwang!" (Rise up! Prevent civil war! Remedy the peril!), July 9, 1943.

"Zhiwen Guomindang" (Interrogate the Guomindang), by Mao Zedong, July 12, 1943.

"Zai jie zai li xiaomiao neizhan weiji" (Again connect, again experience the civil war crisis), July 18, 1943.

"Qing Chongqqing kan Luoma" (Inviting Chongqing to watch Rome), August 21, 1943.

"Meiyou gongchandang, jiu meiyou xin Zhongguo" (If there is no Communist Party, then there is no new China), August 25, 1943.

## 3. Columns Replacing Editorials

"Banyue junshi dongtai" (Semimonthly military reports), May 2, 15; June 1, 17; July 19; August 5, 17.

"Zai gongying gongchangzhong ruhe kaizhan Zhao Zhankui yundong?" (In publicly owned factories how do we launch the Zhao Zhankui movement?), by Deng Fa, May 7, 1943 (Dailun).

"Guanyu nonghu jihua de wenti" (Regarding the problems in the peasant household plan), by Zhang Bangying, May 9, 1943 (Dailun).

"Beifei mengjun dasheng" (The great North Africa victory of the allied forces), May 10, 1943 (Pingshi).

"Zhankai chucao yundong" (Develop the hoe-the-weeds movement), by Zhang Bangying, May 29, 1943 (Dailun).

"Xiaji fangyi gongzuo" (The summer's epidemic prevention work), May 31, 1943 (Pingshi).

"Mengguo dajin jun de qianxi" (The eve of the allied forces great advancing army), June 13, 1943 (Pingshi).

"Cong diyihui kan dikou guonei weiji" (From the enemy assembly see the national crisis of internal enemies), June 24, 1943 (Pingshi).

## 4. Major Page 1 Articles

Note: At this time long articles, some with the author's name, frequently replaced editorials and opinion columns. They are cited here and not with editorials or columns.

"Guanyu gongchan guoji zhiwei zhuxituan tiyi jiesan gongchan guoji de jueding" (Regarding the decision of the Communist International's presidium to disband the Communist International), May 27, 1943.

"Lun gongchan guoji di jiesan" (Discuss disbanding the Communist International), May 28, 1943.

"Zhonggong zhongying guanyu lingdao fangfa de jueding" (The CCP Central Committee's decision regarding methods of leadership), June 4, 1943.

"Zhonggong Huazhong ju guanyu yijiusisannian, zhengfeng xuexi de zhishi" (Directives for the 1943 rectification study by the Central China branch of the central committee), June 5, 1943.

"Zhengzhi yu jishu: dangbao gongzuozhong de yige zhongyao wenti" (Red and expert: An important problem in the world of the Party's newspaper), June 10, 1943.

"Guanyu hezuoshe de jige wenti" (Several problems regarding cooperative societies), June 12, 1943.

"Guanyu jianquan junren hezuoshe gongzuo de zhishixin" (A directive letter regarding the strong cooperative work between the army and the people), June 22, 1943.

"Zhongguo gongchandang zhongying weiyuanhui wei kangzhan liuzhounian jinian xuanyan" (The CCP's Central Committee's declaration for commemorating the 6th anniversary of the war), July 2, 1943.

*Note:* See related articles page 2.

"Zhongguo gongchandang yu Zhongguo minzu jiefang de daolu" (The Chinese Communist Party and the road of Chinese national liberation), by Wang Jiaxiang, July 8, 1943, pp. 1–4.

"Zai Mao Zedong de qizhixia, wei baowei Zhongguo gongchandang er zhan!" (Under the banner of Mao Zedong, defend the Chinese Communist Party and fight!), by Bo Gu, July 13, 1943.

"Zhongguo zhengzhi heian kangzhan buli, Ying-Mei mengbang dabu manyi" (Chinese political reactionary's weak resistance, the U.S.–Great Britain alliance is really insufficient), by Mao Zedong, July 13, 1943.

"Ping 'Zhongguo zhi mingyun' " (Criticizing "China's Destiny"), by Chen Boda, July 21, 1943, pp. 1–4.

"Zonggong zhongying beifangju guanyu zhengfeng jingyan de jieshao" (An introduction to the CCP's Central Committee's northern bureau's rectification experiences), August 2, 1943.

"Guogong liangdang he Zhongguo zhi mingyun" (The Guomindang, the CCP, and China's fate), by Lu Zhenyu, August 7, 1943, (continued p. 4).

" 'Zhongguo zhi mingyun' jiduan weixinlun de yumin zhexue" (The foolish philosophy of the extreme idealism of "China's Destiny"), August 11, 1943.

"Guogong liangdang kangzhan chengji de jiao" (A comparison of the Guomindang and the CCP's resistance achievements), August 24, 1943.

### 5. Major Page 4 Articles

"Guanyu gongying gongchang de jige wenti" (Concerning several problems of publically owned factories), by Luo Fu, May 1, 1943.

"Lun gongying gongchangdang yu zhigonghui gongzuo" (Discussing Party and labor-management work in publically owned factories), by Deng Fa, May 1, 1943.

"Sanwujiu lu de kaihuang gongzuo" (The clearing land work of the 359th brigade), by Wang Simao, May 6, 1943.

"Women shi zenyang jinxing shengchan he jiaoyu de?" (What should we do to advance production and education?), by Liu Huang, June 13, 1943.

"Shengchan jihua" (Production plan), by Yi Wei, June 16, 1943.

"Qiyi Zhongying nianer zhounian, qiqi kangzhan diliu zhounian jinian tekan" (July 1, the 22d anniversary of the Central Committtee, July 7, the 6th anniversary of the Anti-Japanese war), July 2–8, 1943.

"Bo Jiang Jieshi de wenhua guan" (Refute Chiang Kai-shek's cultural outlook), August 9, 1943.

"Bo Jiang Jieshi de falu guan" (Refute Chiang Kai-shek's legal outlook), August 10, 1943.

### 6. Regular Page 4 Columns

*Army* (May 3, 17; June 2, 19; July 1, 31; August 18).
*Health* (May 15, 31; June 17, 28, 29; August 14).
*Enemy* (May 25; June 25; August 28).
*News and Communication* (August 8).

### 7. Other Significant Articles

"Nanniwan kenqu zhengfu chengli de yiyi ji qi gongzuo fangzhen" (The significance of establishing a Nanniwan reclaimed land government and its work direction), May 19, 1943, p. 2.

## September–December 1943

*General Comments*: The tension between the Guomindang and the Communist Party increased. In the newspaper it was marked by the proliferation of revolutionary rhetoric. Now called counterrevolutionary, the Guomindang army was accused of not fighting the Japanese. In November the first major labor hero/heroine meeting took place, and it dominated the news for November and December. There were also numerous articles on reducing rent and interest. Most war news from Europe focused on the Soviet Union.

### 1. General Page and Editorial Survey

| Subject of article/editorial | Location of article/editorial | | | | |
|---|---|---|---|---|---|
| | Editorial | Pg 1 | Pg 2 | Pg 3 | Pg 4 |
| Army | — | 8 | 9 | — | 6 |
| Arts and literature | — | 9 | 8 | — | — |
| Communist Party | — | 9 | — | — | — |
| Cooperatives | — | — | 4 | 8 | — |
| Economics | — | 5 | — | — | — |
| Education | — | — | 7 | — | — |
| Elections | — | — | 9 | — | — |
| Enemy | — | — | — | — | 7 |
| Essays | — | — | — | — | 1 |
| Factories | — | — | 7 | — | — |
| Guomindang | 3 | — | — | — | — |
| GMD/CCP fighting | — | — | 9 | — | — |
| GMD/CCP relations | 2 | 7 | — | — | — |
| Health | — | — | — | — | 4 |
| International affairs | — | — | — | 2 | — |
| Labor heroes/heroines | 3 | 2 | 2 | 3 | 3 |
| Media | — | — | — | — | 6 |
| Mutual aid | — | 9 | — | — | — |
| National affairs | — | 9 | — | — | — |
| New Democracy | 3 | — | — | — | — |
| 1911 Revolution anniversary | — | 9 | — | 5 | — |
| Organizing people | — | 8 | 6 | — | — |
| Production | — | 1 | 1 | 4 | — |
| Rectication | — | — | — | 8 | — |
| Reducing rents | 3 | 7 | 3 | — | — |
| Refugees | — | — | 8 | 8 | — |
| Russian revolution | — | 6 | — | 6 | 5 |
| Self-defense | — | 8 | 6 | — | — |
| Short stories | — | — | — | — | 2 |
| Ten-ten commemoration | — | — | — | — | 8 |
| Textiles | — | — | 5 | — | — |

| Subject of article/editorial | Location of article/editorial | | | | |
|---|---|---|---|---|---|
| | Editorial | Pg 1 | Pg 2 | Pg 3 | Pg 4 |
| Village life | — | — | 6 | — | — |
| War in China | 3 | 3 | — | — | — |
| War in Europe and Asia | 1 | 4 | — | 1 | — |
| Women | — | — | 4 | 7 | — |
| Youth | — | 9 | — | — | — |

## 2. Important Editorials

"Fandui Guomindang de fandong xinwen zhengce" (Oppose the Guomindang's reactionary news policy), September 1, 1943.

"Zhi you xinminzhu zhuyi cai neng jiu Zhongguo" (If only we had New Democracy then we can save China), October 10, 1943.

"Kaizhan qunzhong jianzu yundong" (Expanding the mass movement to reduce rent), November 15, 1943.

"Bianqu laoding yingxiong biaodahui gei women zhichule shemma?" (To what does the Border Region labor hero/model worker assembly point us?), December 26, 1943.

## 3. Columns Replacing Editorials

"Banyue junshi dongtai" (Semimonthly military reports), September 5, 19; October 6, 17; November 2, 17; December 3.

"Dongtiao de dongxiang" (Eastern line movements), November 10, 1943 (Pingshi).

"Du Sudalin baogao" (Reading Stalin's report), November 12, 1943 (Pingshi).

"Kailuo huiyi yu Deheilan huiyi" (The meetings in Cairo and Tehran), December 10, 1943 (Pingshi).

## 4. Major Page 1 Articles

"Guomindang cuican xinwen shiye" (The Guomindang destroys news enterprises), September 1, 1943.

"Shei aihu qingnian, shei qianghai qingnian?" (Who takes good care of youth? Who kills and harms them?), by Deng Fa, September 6, 1943 (continued page 2).

"Gongshen shouyao tewu hanjian, da hanjian sanren tongdi panguo panchu sixing" (The public investigation of spies and special agents, the three biggest who colluded with the enemy and betrayed the country receive the death sentence), September 7, 1943.

"Duiyu Zhongguo zhengfu zhi piping" (Regarding criticisms of the Chinese government), by Luo Guofu, September 14, 1943.

"Yanxian zhankai fangjian yundong" (Yan'an *xian* launches the stop-the-spies movement), September 21, 1943.

"Gao Gang tongzhi zai, Yan'an xian minjia fandui Rite, guote dongyuan dahuishang jiangci" (Comrade Gao Gang here for a mobilization speech to the people of Yan'an *xian* to oppose Japanese spies and Nationalist spies), September 22, 1943.

"Bianqu minzhong ziwei dongyuan zongjie" (Border Region's mass self-defense mobilization summary), by Liu Yingfan, September 29, 1943, (continued p. 4).

"Zhonggong Zhongying zhengzhiju, guanyu jianzu shengchan yongzheng aimin ji xuanchuan shida zhengce de zhishi" (The CCP's Central Committee Politburo's directive regarding reducing rent, production, supporting the government, loving the people and propagandizing important government policy), October 1, 1943.

"Yanshu diwei guanyu dang bao tongxun gongzuo de zhishi" (Directive of the Yan'an neighborhood committees regarding the Party report on communication work), October 2, 1943.

"Mizhi renmin fangjian rechao" (The stop-the-spies fervor among the masses of Mizhi), October 3, 1943.

"Ping Guomindang shiyi Zhongquanhui ji sanjie erci guomin canzhenghui" (Criticizing the third session, second meeting of the Guomindang's 11th national people's assembly), October 5, 1943 (continued p. 2, editorial).

" 'Zai Yan'an wenyi zuotanhuishang de jianghuo' " ("Talks at the Yan'an conference on literature and art"), by Mao Zedong, October 19, 1943, all of pp. 1, 2, and 4.

"Guanyu zhixing dang de wenyi zhengce de jueding" (Regarding the decision to implement the Party's policy in literature and art), November 8, 1943.

"Nanqu hezuoshe banlixin yong hezuo de jingyan" (The experience of a cooperative in Nanqu who managed a credit cooperative), December 12, 1943 (continued page 2).

"Kouhao kaizhan yongzheng aimin yundong" (Slogans to open the support the government, cherish the people movement), December 14, 1943.

### Page 1 Articles on Labor Heroes

"Bianqu laodong yingxiong dahui" (Border Region labor hero/ model worker assembly), November 25, 1943.

"Gao Gang tongzhi zai bianqu laodong yingxiong daibiao dahui yu shengchan zhanlanhui kaimu dianli shang de jianghui" (Comrade Gao Gang's talk at the Border Region labor hero/model worker representative assembly and the opening ceremonies of the production display meeting), November 27, 1943.

"Zuzhiqilai" (Get organized), by Mao Zedong, December 2, 1943, p. 1 all.

*Note:* Originally a speech at a November 29, 1943, Border Region Labor Hero meeting.

"Wu Manyou chuangzao mufan xiang" (Wu Manyou created a model *xiang*), December 11, 1943.

"Gao Gang tongzhi zai xibei ju zhaodai laodong yingxiong dahuishang de jianghuo" (Comrade Gao Gang's talks at the reception for Northwest labor heroes and model workers), December 11, 1943.

"Laodong yingxiong daibiao dahui xuanyan" (Manifesto of the labor hero/model worker assembly), December 17, 1943.

"Bianqu laoding yingxiong daibiao dahui gei women zhichuli shemma?" (What does the Border Region labor hero/model worker assembly point out to us?), December 26, 1943.

### 5. Major Page 4 Articles

"Women duiyu xinwenxue de jiben guandian" (My basic viewpoint regarding journalism), by Lu Dingyi, September 1, 1943.

"Zhongguo faxisi zhuyi zhi mingyun" (The fate of Chinese fascism), September 13, 1943.

"Sannianlai Guomindang jiuci yingzhan de yanjiu" (The research in the past three years on the Guomindang's nine responses to enemy attack), September 23, 1943.

"Mizhi xian Yindouba xiang jianzu diaocha" (Mizhi *xian* Yindouba *xiang* investigates rent reduction), October 30, 1943, all p. 4.

"Yimin wenti" (Immigrant problem), November 15, 1943.

"Lun fandui tongyi zhanxianzhong de jihuizhuyi" (Discussing opposition to opportunism in the United Front), November 25, 1943.

"Wu Manyou gushi" (Wu Manyou's story), by Kong Jue, December 14–17, 1943.

"Du Mao Zedong tongzhi 'Zai Yan'an yishu tanhuishang de jianghua' biji" (Notes on reading Comrade Mao Zedong's "The talks at the Yan'an Forum"), by Liu Bairuo, December 26, 1943.

### 6. Regular Page 4 Columns

*News and Communication* (September 1, 26; November 18, December 14).

*Army* (September 12; October 27; November 20; December 2).

*Enemy* (September 27, 28; December 1).

*Health* (October 9, 20, 29; November 14, 30; December 17, 30).

### 7. Other Significant Articles

"Yan'an qinggong shenghuo de yiyue" (A month in the life of a young Yan'an worker), by Li Ping, September 6, 1943, p. 3.

"Yanchuan funü relie laojun" (Yan River women enthusiastically greet the army), November 1, 1943, p. 2.

*Note:* Examples of "Support the government, cherish the people campaign."

"Mao Zedong tongzhi shi Zhongguo renmin de jiuxing" (Comrade Mao Zedong is the savior of the Chinese people), November 21, 1943, p. 2.

### January–April 1944

*General Comments:* Production articles dominated the Border Region news for this four-month period as the area sought to achieve economic self-sufficiency. Although news of the war in Europe, the Pacific, and China remained the lead page 1 story, articles on production were third and outnumbered those on pages 2 and 4 (page 3 remained devoted to war news). Beginning in January, many page 1 articles dealt with supporting the army. As the page survey illustrates, however, the *Liberation Daily*'s content became more diverse. Beginning in January, articles on individual labor heroes/heroines appeared in a column entitled "The Border Region Production Movement." First seen on page 2, it moved to page 4 where it remained with other news of production. Readers began to see an emphasis on men and women working together in agriculture, in competition among villagers and between mutual-aid teams, and on increasing production. Finally, beginning in April, there were numerous articles on reforms in education.

## 1. General Page and Editorial Survey

| Subject of article/editorial | Location of article/editorial | | | | |
|---|---|---|---|---|---|
| | Editorial | Pg 1 | Pg 2 | Pg 3 | Pg 4 |
| Antishaman movement | 2 | — | — | — | — |
| Army | — | 4 | 5 | — | 2 |
| B.R. Assembly | — | 7 | — | — | — |
| B.R. Government | — | 7 | 8 | 5 | — |
| Cadres | — | 8 | — | — | — |
| Children | — | — | 10 | — | — |
| Cooperatives | — | — | 7 | — | — |
| Culture | — | 8 | — | — | — |
| Economics | 2 | — | 10 | — | — |
| Education | 2 | 6 | 6 | — | — |
| Enemy | — | — | — | — | 4 |
| Essays | — | — | — | — | 1 |
| Factories | — | — | 9 | 5 | — |
| Health | — | 7 | — | 5 | 3 |
| International affairs | — | — | — | 2 | — |
| Labor heroes/heroines | 2 | 5 | 2 | 4 | 2 |
| March 8 | — | 8 | 10 | 5 | — |
| Media | — | — | — | — | 5 |
| Mutual aid | — | 8 | 9 | — | — |
| Organizing people | — | — | 10 | — | — |
| Politics (domestic) | — | 7 | — | — | — |
| Production | 1 | 3 | 1 | 3 | — |
| Reducing rents | — | 8 | — | 5 | — |
| Reform in work | — | 8 | — | — | — |
| Refugees | — | — | 8 | 5 | 5 |
| Self-criticism | 2 | — | — | — | — |
| Self-defense | — | — | 7 | — | — |
| Short stories | — | — | — | — | 3 |
| Soviet Union | 2 | — | — | — | — |
| Sun Yat-sen | — | 8 | — | — | — |
| Textiles | — | — | 4 | — | — |
| Village (model) | — | 7 | — | — | — |
| War in China | 1 | 2 | 8 | — | — |
| War in Europe and Asia | — | 1 | — | 1 | — |
| Women | — | 7 | 3 | 5 | — |

## 2. *Important Editorials*

"Benbao chuangkan yiqianqi" (The newspaper's initial 1000 issues), February 16, 1944.

"Ma Xiwu tongzhi de Shenpan fangshi" (The trial of Comrade Ma Kiuri), March 13, 1944.

"Genjudi putong jiaoyu de gaige wenti" (Problems in the reform of popular education in the base areas), April 7, 1944. (Mao Zedong edited.)

"Jiancha gongzu ju ziwo piping" (Investigation work and self-criticism), April 22, 1944.

"Kaizhan fandui wushen de donzheng" (Expand the struggle to oppose Shamans), April 29, 1944.

## 3. *Columns Replacing Editorials*

"Banyue junshi dongtai" (Semimonthly military report), March 31.

"Hongjun jin di xin guojie" (Red armies advance to reach national boundaries), March 29, 1944 (Pingshi).

"Ridou zuijin de dongtai" (The most advanced trends of the Japanese bandits), April 18, 1944 (Pingshi).

## 4. *Major Page 1 Articles*

"Zhankai yongzheng, aimin yundong" (Expand the support the government, cherish the people movement), by Zhu De, January 4, 1944.

"Yinianlai de yongzheng aimin gongzuo" (A year's work in supporting the government, cherishing the people), January 19, 1944 (continued page 4).

"Yinianlai de yongjun gongzuo" (A year's work in supporting the army), January 24, 1944 (continued page 2).

"Ban hezuoshe de jige jingyan" (A few experiences in managing a cooperative), by Liu Jianzhang, February 4, 1944 (continued page 2).

"Shixing yongzheng aimin de banfa" (Methods to implement supporting the government, cherishing the people), by Zhang Yunyi, February 5, 1944 (continued page 2).

"Bianqu zhengfu yinian gongzuo zongjie" (A summary of the year's Border Region's government work), February 8, 1944 (continued page 2; related articles page 3).

"Laoli wuli jieheqilai" (Labor and army unite), February 12, 1944, all page 1.

"Laodong jiushi zhengfeng" (Work that is rectification), by Ai Siqi, February 19, 1944.

"Shengying Mao zhuxi haohao, ganbu jiashu ye yao zuzhiqilai" (Response to Chairman Mao's summons, neighborhood cadre must also begin organizing), February 21, 1944.

"Guanyu jundui zhengzhi gongzuo wenti" (Concerning the army's political work problems), April 15, 1944 (continued page 3 and all page 4).

"Bianfu fachu zhishi, tichang xiaoxue minban gongzhu" (The Border Region government issues a directive, promote locally run subsidized elementary education), April 23, 1944.

"Benshi Bai Jiaping wushen Yang Hanzhu" (This city's Bai Jiaping and shaman Yang Hanzhu), by Mu Qing, April 29, 1944.

*Note:* This was the first "society news" (*shewen*). Shamanism became controversial because the editors could not agree if it was the place of the newspaper to publish this kind of article. It began the antishaman campaign. See Lu Dingyi's accompanying editorial.

### 5. Significant Page 4 Articles

"Bianqu laodong huzhu de fazhan" (The expansion of mutual-aid in Border Region's labor), February 10, 1944.

"Bianqu zuzhi laodong huzhu de zhuyao jingyan he jinhou gongzuo" (The important experience and future work of Border Region labor mutual-aid organizing), February 11, 1944.

"Xibei ju jiguan gongzuo renyuan geren shengchan jihua" (The Northwest organization workers' individual production plans), February 24, 1944.

"Biaoxian xin de qunzhong de shidai" (Manifesting the new mass period), by Zhou Yang, March 21, 1944.

"Makesi zhuyi yu wenyi" (Marxism and literature and art), by Zhou Yang, April 8, 1944.

"Liangge yue de xiaxiang xuexi" (Two months of going down to the villages to study), April 11, 1944.

"Xuexi mofanban" (Study the model class), April 20, 1944.

### 6. Regular Page 4 Columns

*Immigrants* (January 10).

*Health* (January 15; February 16; March 1, 16, 28; April 16).
*Enemy* (January 24; February 29; March 27; April 25).
*News and Communication* (March 18).

## 7. Other Significant Articles

"Bianqu shengchan yundong" (Border Region production movement), January 1, 1944, p. 2.
*Note:* For the next three months this column summarized the accomplishments of various labor heroes/heroines.
"Sanyan liangyu" (In a few words), February 21–24, 28, 29; March 1–2, 4–5, 11, 17, 23–24, 26–27; April 2, 4–6, 8, 10, 15, 17–18, 20–21, 29, p. 2.

## May–August 1944

*General Comments*: Production and the war were again the lead stories. Production articles focused on production competitions, spring plowing, labor heroes/heroines, improving the quality of goods, especially textiles, and building factories. Changes in education were also a popular topic. The major news from Europe was the Russian front, while in China the emphasis was on talks between the Communist Party and the Guomindang and the arrival in Yan'an of the U.S. observer mission. Editorials appeared more frequently than in the recent past, and page 4 usually contained only one long article. At the end of May, the government initiated a health campaign along with its mass education program already in progress.

## 1. General Page Survey

| Subject of article/editorial | Location of article/editorial | | | | |
|---|---|---|---|---|---|
| | Editorial | Pg 1 | Pg 2 | Pg 3 | Pg 4 |
| Anniversary | 2 | 7 | — | — | — |
| Army | — | — | 7 | 2 | 5 |
| B.R. Assembly | — | 4 | 7 | — | — |
| Cooperatives | — | — | 6 | — | — |
| Education | 2 | 6 | 2 | — | 6 |
| Essays | — | — | — | — | 1 |
| Factories | — | 7 | — | — | — |

| Subject of article/editorial | Location of article/editorial | | | | |
|---|---|---|---|---|---|
| | Editorial | Pg 1 | Pg 2 | Pg 3 | Pg 4 |
| GMD/CCP talks | — | 8 | — | — | — |
| Health | 2 | 5 | — | — | 7 |
| Japan | — | — | — | 5 | — |
| Labor heroes/heroines | — | 5 | 3 | 4 | — |
| Politics (national) | — | 5 | 4 | 3 | 4 |
| Production | 2 | 3 | 1 | 5 | 3 |
| Sino-British treaty | — | 7 | — | — | — |
| Textiles | — | — | — | — | 7 |
| United Nations | 2 | 7 | — | — | — |
| War in China | 1 | 2 | 5 | 1 | 2 |
| War in Europe and Asia | — | 1 | — | 1 | 2 |
| Women | — | 7 | — | — | — |

## 2. Editorials

"Bianqu qingnian yundongzhong de yige jiben wenti" (The Border Region youth movement's basic problem), May 5, 1944.

"Dihou genjudi shengchan yundong de kaizhan" (The expansion of the production movement in the base areas behind enemy lines), May 26, 1944.

"Lun putong jiaoyuzhong de xuezhi yu kecheng" (Systems and courses in general education), May 27, 1944 (continued page 2).

"Dier zhanchang kaipi yu Zhongguo kangzhan" (The second battlefront opens in the Chinese war of resistance), June 8, 1944.

"Jinian lianheguori, baowei Xi'an yu xibei" (Commemorating United Nations day, protect Xi'an and the Northwest), by Mao Zedong, June 14, 1944.

"Zhongguo gongchandang chuangli niansan zhounian" (The 23rd anniversary of the founding of the Chinese Communist Party), July 1, 1944.

"Balujun xinsijun de yingxiong zhuyi" (Labor heroism in the 8th Route Army and New 4th Army), by Zhu De, July 7, 1944.

"Zai minzhu yu tuanjie jichu shang jiaqiang kangzhan zhengqu zuihou shengli!" (Based on democracy and unity, strengthen the anti-Japanese war, strive for the final victory!), July 7, 1944.

"Kaizhan quan bianqu weisheng yundong de sange jiben wenti" (Three basic problems of launching the Border Region health movement), July 10, 1944.

"Jin-Cha-Ji xin wenyi yundong fazhan de daolu" (The road of

expanding the Jin-Cha-Ji new literature and art movement), by Sha Kefu, July 24, 1944.

"Hengyang shishou hou Guomindang jiang ruhe?" (How is the GMD general after the fall of Hengyang?), August 12, 1944. (Mao edited.)

"Huanying Meijun guanchazu de zhanyoumen" (Welcome the wartime friends of the American army observer group), August 15, 1944. (Mao edited.)

"Shandong jiebao" (Reports of success in Shandong), August 28, 1944. (Mao edited.)

### 3. Columns Replacing Editorials

"Ping Taipingyang zhanju" (Criticize the Pacific War situation), July 5, 1944 (Pingshi).

"Mengbang renshi zhengyan" (Allied soldiers debate), July 6, 1944 (Pingshi).

"Deguo de neizhan" (Germany's civil war), July 24, 1944 (Pingshi).

"Diguo de zhengbian he xiaoji neige de chuxian" (The coup of the enemy and the appearance of the small cabinet), July 25, 1944 (Pingshi).

### 4. Major Page 1 Articles

"Benshi gequ jiji choujian qunzhong weisheng hezuoshe" (The city's various districts positively prepare to build mass health cooperatives), May 12, 1944.

"Jishu renyuan zuotanhui, haohao yiqie gongye jishu renyuan huidao gongye zhanxian shanglai" (The discussion meeting of professionals summons a segment of industrial professionals to return to the industrial battlefront), June 4, 1944.

"Bianqu wenjiaohuiyi shiyue juxing ge gongzuozu xiaxiang diaocha yanjiu" (The October Border Region cultural education meeting convenes, various work groups go to the villages to advance investigation and research), July 17, 1944.

"Guanyu xuexi wenti gei zhun beiqu dangwei" (Regarding the study problem in accordance with the letter of the northern district Party committee), July 27, 1944 (continued page 4).

"Shaan-Gan-Ning bianqu gongchang zhigong dahui xuanyan"

(Proclamation from the factory staff and workers meeting), July 30, 1944.

## 5. Major Page 4 Articles

"Liangzhong zuzhi biangongdui banfa de jieshao" (Introducing two ways of reforming the work troops), May 5, 1944.

"Qiqiling tuan de dierlian" (The second company of the 770th regiment), May 7, 1944.

"Diyige shengchan de chengji" (The first production successes), May 17, 1944.

"Shixing dengji anlao fenpei de yijian" (Implementing opinions on several levels of distributing work points), May 26, 1944.

"Xuanchuan gongzuo zuotanhui" (Propagandizing the work discussion meeting), June 5, 1944.

"Ershi ba banfu" (Twenty grasp the broad ax), by Ding Ling, June 13, 1944.

"Qing kan shijie de xinmianmao" (Please look at the new view of the world), June 14, 1944.

"Wushen de pianshu" (The shaman's hoax), by Mu Qing, June 18, 1944.

"Wushen zicong Hai de tanbai" (The shaman since Hai's frankness), June 18, 1944.

"Weisheng hezuoshe" (Health cooperatives), June 23, 1944.

"Tian bao lin" (The fields preserved by the continuous rain), by Ding Ling, June 30, 1944.

"Huo zai xin shehuili" (Life in the new society), by Ouyang Shan, June 30, 1944.

"Mao Zedong tongzhi de chuqi geming shenghuo" (The beginning stages of Comrade Mao Zedong's revolutionary life), July 1 and 2, 1944.

"Tan zonghe baodao" (Discussing comprehensive news coverage), by Mu Qing, July 23, 1944.

"Zai laodongzhong gaizao sixiang" (Reform thinking in labor), by Shi Ping, August 4, 1944.

## 6. Regular Page 4 Columns

Enemy (May 10, 27; June 11, 26, 27; July 12, 28; August 11, 26).

*Literature and Art* (May 14, 15, 20–26, 30, 31).
*Health* (May 18; June 1, 24; August 13).
*News and Communication* (July 23).

## 7. Other Significant Articles

"Sanyan liangyu" (In a few words), May 4–5, 8, 11, 14, 16, 19, 31; June 10, 26; July 17; August 15, page 2.
June 4, 1944, all page 2 dealt with education.
"Guoji yulun" (International opinion), June 24, 1944, p. 3.

## September–December 1944

*General Comments*: Production and the literacy campaign were the most important domestic issues of the late fall. On October 21 an advertisement appeared announcing new books available at the Xinhua Bookstore. During these four months, the *Liberation Daily* also printed an occasional photograph. Although these were grainy and blurred, the images were decipherable. National and domestic political issues dominated the remainder of the newspaper as the Guomindang and Communist Party turned their attention from the war with Japan to the impending civil war. More articles appeared on government and self-government, and expansion of Party-held territory outside of the Border Region.

## 1. General Page Survey

| Subject of article/editorial | Location of article/editorial | | | | |
|---|---|---|---|---|---|
| | Editorial | Pg 1 | Pg 2 | Pg 3 | Pg 4 |
| Army | — | — | 8 | — | — |
| B.R. Assembly | 3 | 5 | — | — | — |
| B.R. Government | — | 7 | — | — | — |
| Cadres | — | 8 | — | — | — |
| Communist Party | — | 8 | — | — | — |
| Cooperatives | — | — | 6 | — | — |
| December 9th anniversary | — | 8 | — | — | — |
| Education | — | 4 | — | — | — |
| Elections | — | 8 | 8 | — | — |
| Enemy | — | — | — | — | 6 |

| Subject of article/editorial | Location of article/editorial | | | | |
|---|---|---|---|---|---|
| | Editorial | Pg 1 | Pg 2 | Pg 3 | Pg 4 |
| Essays | — | — | — | — | 1 |
| Expanding liberated areas | — | 7 | 7 | 4 | — |
| GMD/CCP relations | — | 8 | — | — | — |
| Health | — | 8 | 8 | — | 5 |
| Internal conditions | — | — | 3 | — | 6 |
| International affairs | — | — | 7 | 1 | — |
| Labor heroes/heroines | 2 | 7 | 4 | — | 5 |
| Letters to *Liberation Daily* | — | — | — | — | 6 |
| Literacy campaign | — | 7 | 2 | — | 2 |
| Media | — | — | 7 | — | — |
| 1911 Revolution anniv. | 3 | 8 | — | — | 4 |
| Observer mission | — | — | 5 | — | — |
| Politics (national) | — | — | 3 | 7 | 5 |
| Production | — | — | 6 | 1 | — |
| Russian revolution | — | 7 | — | — | — |
| Short stories | — | — | — | — | 3 |
| Soviet Union | — | — | — | — | 4 |
| Taxes | — | — | 8 | — | — |
| U.S. elections | — | 8 | — | 3 | — |
| Villages (reform in) | — | — | — | — | 5 |
| War in China | 1 | 1 | 5 | — | — |
| War in Europe and Asia | — | 2 | — | 2 | — |

## 2. Editorials

"Caiyong xin de zuzhi xingshi yu gongzuo fangshi" (Adopt the new organizational form and work model), September 5, 1944. (Mao edited.)

"Yanlun 'ziyou' yihou" (After "freedom" of speech), September 12, 1944 (continued page 2).

"Cong haishang dadao Riben, cong lushang dadao Dongbei—jinian 'jiuyiba' shisan zhounian" (Overthrow Japan from the sea, overthrow the Northeast from the land—commemorating the 13th anniversary of September 18), September 18, 1944. (Mao edited.)

"Ping cici guomin canzhenghui" (Criticizing the National Assembly), September 24, 1944. (Mao edited.)

"Xinsijun de shengli chuji yu Zhongguo de jiuguo shiye" (The victorious attack of the New Fourth Army and the save-the-nation enterprise), October 1, 1944, editorial. (Mao edited.)

"Jintian he Xinhai" (Today and the 1911 revolution), October 10, 1944. (Mao edited.)

"Zai tan laodong yingxiong yundong" (Again discuss the labor hero/model worker movement), November 20, 1944.

### 3. Columns Replacing Editorials

"Faguo renmin de liliang" (The power of the French people), September 14, 1944 (Pingshi).

"Yan'an you zige rentu pinglun, mengguo yuanzhu wuzi fenpei wenti" (Yan'an has discussions on people, land qualifications, allies support materials distribution problems), September 15, 1944 (Pinglun). (Mao edited.)

"Yan'an guanchajia pinglun Jiang Jieshi yanshuo juyou weixiansheng" (Yan'an observers criticize Chiang Kai-shek's speech for possessing a dangerous nature), by Mao Zedong, October 12, 1944 (Pinglun).

"Ying jiandui qianlai yuandong" (The British squadron advances in the Far East), October 14, 1944 (Pingshi).

"Meijun xi Taiwan zhi yi" (The American army's campaign to invade Taiwan), October 21, 1944 (Pingshi).

" 'Dadong ya gongcequan' de chedi huimiao" (Thorough destruction of the "East Asian Co-prosperity sphere"), October 24, 1944 (Pingshi).

"Feidao haimian Mei jiandui dajie" (Great American victory in the Philippine Islands), October 30, 1944 (Pingshi).

### 4. Major Page 1 Articles

"Zhonggong zhongying xiang guomin zhengfu tichu zhi yijianshu" (The ideas of the CCP's Central Committee about putting forward a national government), September 20, 1944.

"Lin Zuhan tongzhi baogao quanwan" (The full text of Comrade Lin Zuhan's report), September 22, 1944.

"Liji gaizu zhengfu yu tongshuaibu" (Reform the government and the supreme command immediately), September 23, 1944.

"Xibeiju guanyu yu dongji quxiang ganbu xunlian wenti de zhishi" (The directive of the Northwest bureau regarding the winter training problems of district and village cadres), October 8, 1944.

"Wenjiao dahui weishengzu lianri shangtao" (Daily cultural and education meetings discuss health organization), October 21, 1944.

"Mao zhuxi zai bianqu wenjiao dahui jiangyan" (Chairman Mao's speech at the Border Region culture and education meeting), November 1, 1944.

"Gao Gang tongzhi zai wenjiao dahui jiangyan" (Comrade Gao Gang's speech at the culture and education meeting), November 11, 1944.

"Wenjiao dahui shengli bimu" (The curtain falls on the victorious culture and education meeting), November 20, 1944.

"Jindong zhongxin gongzuo" (This winter's core work), by Gao Gang, November 29, 1944.

"Bianqu minzhu zhengzhi de xin jieduan" (The new stage of Border Region democratic politics), December 8, 1944.

"Wenjiao gongzuo de fangxiang" (The direction of culture and education work), December 10, 1944.

"Yijiusiwunian de renwu" (The duties of 1945), by Mao Zedong, December 16, 1944.

"Qunying dahui fenzu taolun Chen Defa baogao huode haoping" (Small groups in the heroes' meeting discuss the positive comments obtained by Chen Defa's report), December 26, 1944.

## 5. Major Page 4 Articles

"Guanyu lingdao zuofeng wenti" (Regarding the leadership's workstyle problem), September 14 and 15, 1944.

"Ji zhuanyaowanlu dahui" (Recording Brick kiln cove's assembly), by Ding Ling, September 17, 1944.

"Tangui shuomeng de shijie" (The world of talking ghosts and dreams), by Ding Ling, October 21, 1944.

"Gaibian mianmu gaibian naojin" (Reform appearances, reform the mind), by Ai Siqi, November 6, 1944.

"Nuoerman Baiqiuen duanpien" (Fragments about Norman Bethune), by Zhou Erfu, November 12 and 13, 1944.

"Kaizhan da guimo de qunzhong wenjiao yundong" (Developing a large-scale cultural education movement), November 20, 1944.

"Guanyu budui de baozhi gongzuo" (Regarding the army's newspaper work), December 21, 1944.

## 6. Regular Page 4 Columns

*Health* (September 16, 30; October 28; November 11).
*Enemy* (September 13, 27; October 14, 27; November 15).
*News and Communication* (September 1, 18).

### 7. *Other Significant Articles*

"Sanyan liangyu" (In a few words), September 5, 7, 19; November 1, 3; December 22, p. 2.

"Zhu bianqu budui mofan xuexizhe daibiao huiyi" (Warm wishes to the Border Region's troops' model students representative meeting), September 21, 1944, p. 2.

"Kaizhan qunzhong xin wenyi yundong" (Launching the new literature and art mass movement), by Zhou Yang, November 21, 1944, p. 2.

"Zongjie jiguan xuexiao gongchan wenjiao gongzuo" (Summarizing official cultural education work in schools and factories), November 22, 1944, p. 2.

"Zongjie budui wenjiao gongzuo" (Summarizing cultural education work among the troops), November 22, 1944, p. 2.

## January–April 1945

*General Comments*: Although victory was in the air, war news still dominated pages 1 and 3. However, the *Liberation Daily* turned increasingly to national and domestic political issues. Party-held territory expanded and another campaign for reform began, although not as yet a page 1 story. As tension grew between the Guomindang and the Party, more articles appeared on political work and the army's role in it. Spring plowing was the major production item, with news of labor heroes/heroines running second. The important Seventh Party Congress convened on April 23, 1945.

### 1. *General Page Survey*

| Subject of article/editorial | Location of article/editorial | | | | |
|---|---|---|---|---|---|
| | Editorial | Pg 1 | Pg 2 | Pg 3 | Pg 4 |
| Army | — | 7 | 7 | 3 | — |
| B.R. Assembly | — | 7 | — | — | — |
| B.R. Government | — | 6 | 4 | — | — |
| Building new China | — | 7 | — | — | — |
| Cooperatives | — | — | 3 | — | — |
| Culture | — | 7 | 8 | — | — |
| Economics | — | — | 6 | — | — |

| Subject of article/editorial | Location of article/editorial | | | | |
|---|---|---|---|---|---|
| | Editorial | Pg 1 | Pg 2 | Pg 3 | Pg 4 |
| Education | — | — | 7 | 5 | — |
| Elections | — | — | 8 | — | — |
| Essays | — | — | — | — | 1 |
| Expanding liberated areas | — | 6 | — | — | — |
| Health | — | — | 5 | — | — |
| "How to" articles | — | — | — | — | 2 |
| International affairs | — | — | 5 | 2 | — |
| Labor heroes/heroines | — | — | 3 | 8 | — |
| Liberated areas (other) | — | — | — | 8 | 5 |
| New Year | — | — | — | 8 | — |
| Politics (national) | — | — | 5 | 8 | 4 |
| Postwar China | — | — | 6 | — | — |
| Production | — | 1 | 4 | 1 | 5 |
| Rectification campaign | — | — | 7 | 2 | — |
| Reducing rent & interest | — | — | — | 7 | 5 |
| Transportation | — | — | — | 8 | — |
| U.S. (politics) | — | — | 7 | — | — |
| War in China | — | — | 2 | — | — |
| War in Europe and Asia | — | — | 1 | 8 | 1 |
| Women's federation | — | — | 7 | — | — |
| Workers' associations | — | — | 6 | — | — |

## 2. Editorials

"Youjiqu ye chenggou shengchan" (Guerrilla areas can also be sufficient in production), by Mao Zedong, January 31, 1945.

"Zhangrui de hezuozhe daolu" (The Zhangrui Cooperative Road), February 22, 1945.

"Xinwen bixu wanquan zhenshi" (The news must be completely accurate), March 23, 1945.

## 3. Columns Replacing Editorials

None.

## 4. Major Page 1 Articles

"Bianqu gongyejie xin chuangzao" (New production in the Border Region's industrial world), January 8, 1945.

*Note:* One of a series of articles concerning the use of the word "new."

"Guanyu laodong yingxiong mofan gongzuozhe wenti" (Regarding the labor hero/model worker problem), January 9, 1945 (continued page 4).

"Mofan quxiang ganbu youliang zuofeng" (The exemplary work styles of the area's model cadres), January 9, 1945.

"Liangsanniannei wanquan xuehui jingji gongzuo" (We have completely mastered economic work in the past two or three years), by Mao Zedong, January 12, 1945.

"Guanyu gongzuo zuofeng wenti" (Regarding the problem of workers' work styles), by Gao Gang, February 5, 1945 (continued page 2).

"Dihou jiefangqu yiyue dongtai" (A month's developments in the liberated areas behind enemy lines), April 7, 1945.

### 5. Major Page 4 Articles

"Guanyu kaizhan qunzhong weisheng yiyao gongzuo de jueyi" (The resolution regarding launching health and medical work), January 8, 1945.

"Yuan Guanghua—bianqu tedeng laodong yingxiong" (Yuan Guanghua—the Border Region's top notch labor hero), by Ding Ling, January 12, 1945.

*Note:* An example of propaganda concerning labor heroes written by literary people.

"Jinlu buduan qiannian hou—ji Tong Yuxin" (The golden furnace has a continuous fire for 1000 years—remembering Tong Yuxin), by Ai Qing, January 15, 1945.

*Note:* An example of propaganda concerning labor heroes written by literary people.

"Zhang Desheng" (Zheng Desheng), by Yang Shuo, January 16, 1945.

*Note:* An example of propaganda concerning labor heroes written by literary people.

"Zhong chuangzao" (Important creations), by Shi Tianshou, January 19, 1945.

*Note:* An example of propaganda concerning labor heroes written by literary people.

"Suweiai shehuizhuyi gongheguo lianming quantu" (A total picture of the Soviet Socialist Republic's coalition), February 23, 1945.

"Gaizao budui de wenhua xuexi" (Reform the troops' cultural study), March 6, 1945.

"Didao" (The tunnel), by Zhou Erfu, April 8 and 9, 1945.

"Zhishifenzi yu qunzhong jiehe de haodianxing" (A good example of worker-intellectual unity), April 24, 1945.

## 6. Regular Page 4 Columns

*Enemy* (January 31; March 31).

*News and Communication* (March 23).

*Health* (January 20, 21; February 2–3, 7; March 22, 30; April 2, 8, 11, 24, 27, 30).

*Note:* This is different from earlier column and initiated during the antishaman campaign.

## 7. Other Significant Articles

"Mofan xiangchang Liu Chengtong" (Model xiang leader Liu Chengtong), by Feng Mu, January 14, 1945, p. 2.

*Note:* An example of propaganda concerning labor heroes written by literary people.

"Sanyan liangyu" (In a few words), January 14, 16–17, 19; March 4, 6, 25; April 21.

## May–August 1945

*General Comments*: The war with Japan ended in August 1945 but, although news of it continued to be the *Liberation Daily*'s top priority, the impending civil war with the Guomindang assumed an increasingly important position. When Japan surrendered, victory was met with news of Chinese armies positioning themselves for the upcoming battle. In addition, more and more space was devoted to speculation about postwar China and to reports on conditions in the liberated areas. Instead of viewing the Shaan-Gan-Ning Border Region as separate from the others, these articles referred to one Communist Party-held entity. The importance placed on the political situation is evident in two issues. The May 2, 1945, edition contained eight pages, with pages 1–6 devoted to essays on the subject. Pages 1–4 of the May 9, 1945, edition contained another essay on politics by Zhu De (see number 4 below). Equal in importance to the end of the war was the crucial Seventh

Party Congress (April 23 to June 11, 1945). Because it was late spring and summer, production also held a predominant place. Articles emphasized students and soldiers cooperating with peasants to clear land. Textile work continued to be a popular topic. On the international scene, numerous articles appeared on conditions in the Soviet Union; these generally appeared on page 2. Another topic of interest was the establishment of the United Nations.

## 1. General Page Survey

| Subject of article/editorial | Location of article/editorial | | | | |
|---|---|---|---|---|---|
| | Editorial | Pg 1 | Pg 2 | Pg 3 | Pg 4 |
| Anniversary of war | — | 8 | 5 | — | — |
| Army | — | — | 6 | — | — |
| Art and literature | — | — | — | — | 3 |
| Cadres | — | — | 6 | — | — |
| Civil war, impending | — | 4 | 5 | — | — |
| Cooperatives | — | — | 6 | 7 | — |
| Culture | — | — | 4 | 7 | — |
| Education | — | — | 5 | — | — |
| Elections | — | — | 5 | — | — |
| Essays | — | — | — | — | 1 |
| Factories | — | — | 3 | 7 | — |
| Great Britain (politics) | — | 8 | — | — | — |
| Guomindang | — | 8 | — | — | — |
| Health | — | — | 4 | — | — |
| "How to" articles | — | — | — | — | 2 |
| Hurley, criticisms of | — | 8 | — | — | — |
| Internal conditions | — | — | 5 | 5 | — |
| International affairs | — | — | — | 1 | — |
| Japan, surrender demands | — | 7 | — | — | — |
| Land, opening new | — | — | 1 | — | — |
| Liberated areas | — | 2 | 4 | — | — |
| Mao in Chongqing | — | 6 | — | — | — |
| May 4th commemoration | — | — | 8 | — | — |
| Politics (national) | — | 1 | 5 | — | — |
| Postwar Asia | — | — | — | 6 | 4 |
| Postwar Europe | — | — | 6 | — | 2 |
| Postwar Japan | — | — | 7 | — | — |
| Production | — | 2 | — | 2 | — |
| 7th Party Congress | — | 2 | 7 | — | — |
| USSR/Japan war | — | — | 6 | — | — |
| U.S. aid to CCP | — | — | 8 | — | — |
| War in Asia | — | — | 8 | — | 3 |
| War in China | — | — | 1 | 5 | — |
| War in Europe and Asia | — | — | 8 | — | — |
| War in Europe, victory | — | — | 3 | — | 6 |

## 2. Editorials

"Zhongguo renmin shengli de zhinan" (A guide to the Chinese people's victory), May 5, 1945
*Note*: This article concerns "On coalition government."
"Lun zifang zizhi" (Discussing individual spinning and weaving), May 13, 1945.
"Yingjie xin jumian" (Welcome the new situation), May 15, 1945.
"Tigao yibu" (Rising one step), May 16, 1945.
"Tuanjie de dahui, shengli de dahui" (A united congress, a victorious congress), June 14, 1945.

## 3. Columns Replacing Editorials

"Cong liuren beibuan, kan Meiguo dui Hua zhengce de liangtiao luxian" (From the cases of six arrested people, seeing the U.S. regard the two lines of Chinese political policy), June 25, 1945 (Pingshi).
"He'erli zhengce de weixian" (The danger of the Hurley policy), by Mao Zedong, July 13, 1945 (Pinglun).
"Xinhuashe jizhe zai ping He'erli zhengce" (New China News Agency reporter again criticizes the Hurley policy), July 20, 1945 (Pinglun). (Mao edited.)
"Yingguo renmin de shengli" (The English victory), July 28, 1945 (Pingshi).

## 4. Major Page 1 Articles

"Zhonggong gongchandang juxing, diqici quanguo daibiao dahui, tuanjie quandang—tuanjie quanminzu—dabai Riben—jianli xin Zhongguo" (CCP holds a meeting, 7th National Congress, unite the whole Party—unite all the people—defeat Japan—build a new China), May 1, 1945.
"Lun lianhe zhengfu" (On coalition government), by Mao Zedong, May 2, 1945, pp. 1–6.
*Note:* Publication of Mao's April 24, 1945 speech.
"Lun jiefangqu zhanchang" (On the battlefields of the liberated areas), by Zhu De, May 9, 1945, pp. 1–4.
"Guomindang diliuci quanguo daibiao dahui" (The Guomindang's 6th national congress meets), May 30, 1945.

"Zhongguo gongchandang diqici dahui shengli bimu" (The curtain falls on the victorious Seventh Party Congress), June 14, 1945.

"Jiwen" (Funeral oration), June 19, 1945.

"Zhaokai jiefangqu renmin daibiao huiyi" (Convening the liberated areas' people's assembly), June 23, 1945.

" 'Guanyu Zhongguo jiefangqu renmin daibiaohuiyi xuanju shixiang de jueyi' caoan de shuoming" (Draft explanation of "Regarding the resolution of the Chinese liberated areas people's assembly's discussion of election items"), by Zhou Enlai, July 16, 1945.

"Zai ping He'erli zhengce" (Again criticize the Hurley policy), July 20, 1945. (Mao edited.)

"Xinhuashe jizhe lun shiju—neizhan weixian kongqian yanzhong" (New China News Agency reporters discuss the current politial situation—the danger of civil war is unprecedentedly grave), by Mao Zedong, July 28, 1945.

"Kefu touxiangzhuyi zhongjian gongchandang" (Overcome capitulationism, lay stress on building the Communist Party), by Mao Zedong, July 31, 1945.

"Jiangjun guangfan shiyong Meiguo wuqi" (Jiang's army uses American weapons extensively), August 7, 1945.

"Zhanzheng jishushang de geming yuanzidan xi di Guangdao" (War-time technological revolution, atom bomb surprise attack on the enemy's Hiroshima), August 9, 1945. See related articles pages 1 and 3.

*Note:* The *Liberation Daily*'s headline for the day did not concern the bomb but was "Sulian duiRi xuanzhan" (Soviet Union declares war on Japan).

"Mao Zedong fabiao shengming, duiRi zhanzheng jinru zuihou jieduan" (Mao Zedong publishes an announcement that the war against Japan enters the final stage), August 10, 1945. See related editorial and articles on page 1.

"Xin Huashe jizhe bochi Jiang Jieshi mingling" (New China News Agency reporter denounces Chiang Kai-shek's command), August 13, 1945. (Mao edited.)

"Mei-Su-Ying-Zhong siguo xuanbu Ri jourang shou wutiaojian touxiang" (The U.S., USSR, Great Britain, and China proclaim the unconditional surrender of the Japanese bandits), August 15, 1945.

"Zhong-Su youyi tongmeng tiaoyue quanwen" (The full text of the Sino-Soviet friendship alliance treaty), August 27, 1945.

## 5. Major Page 4 Articles

"Sanri zaji" (Three days' jottings), by Ding Ling, May 19, 1945.

"Guanyu zhengce yu yishu—'Tongzhi, ni zuo cuole lu' xuyan" (Concerning politics and art—the preface to "Comrade you are taking the wrong road"), by Zhou Yang, June 2, 1945.

"Yinggai pizhun 'Lun lianhe zhengfu' " ("On coalition government" should be ratified), July 5, 1945.

"Guanyu xiaoxue jiaoyu de jige wenti" (Regarding several problems of elementary education), by Hu Yisheng, July 20, 1945.

"Yu duzhe jianmian" (Meeting with the readers), July 23, 1945.

"Dui" (Opposition), by Ai Siqi, July 25, 1945.

"Taixing liuqu yu zaihuangzuo douzheng de jingyan" (The experience of Taixing's 6th district with famine struggle), August 9, 1945, all page 4.

"Cong xuanchuan beihuang yundong tan difangbao dui yige yundong de xuanchuan" (From propagandizing preparation for a natural disaster movement to discussing a local newspaper's propaganda regarding that movement), by Hu Jiwei, August 24, 1945.

## 6. Regular Page 4 Columns

*Health* (May 3, 10–15, 22; June 3; July 18, 19).
*News and Communication* (April 25).

## 7. Other Significant Articles

"Sanyan liangyu" (In a few words) May 21, 25–26; June 4, p. 2.

"Yige yuanzidan weili de guji" (An appraisal of the atom bomb's power), August 10, 1945, p. 3.

*Note:* An article composed of foreign wire service reports.

"Yuanzidan you zha Changqi" (Atom bomb also explodes in Nagasaki), August 10, 1945, p. 3.

*Note:* Mao charged *Liberation Daily* reporters with "grave political mistakes" for using a combination of foreign wire service reports to write these articles. See Wang Jing, p. 121.

## September–December 1945

*General Comments:* With the war over, the Communist Party turned its attention to "building a peaceful and democratic China" and, given that goal's inevitable failure, to preparing for war with the Guomin-dang. The newspaper now included class terminology and revolution-ary rhetoric in its articles; references were made frequently to the impending civil war. Moreover, there are more articles on all the liber-ated areas as the Party concentrated on uniting people behind it. Never-theless, the new emphasis on revolution meant that cadres had to tow the revolutionary line; therefore, a second rectification campaign began. On the international scene, pages 3 and 4 carried news of the elections in France and the relationship between the Chinese Commu-nist Party and the USSR.

## 1. *General Page Survey*

| Subject of article/editorial | Location of article/editorial | | | | |
|---|---|---|---|---|---|
| | Editorial | Pg 1 | Pg 2 | Pg 3 | Pg 4 |
| Army | — | — | 7 | — | — |
| Art and literature | — | — | — | — | 2 |
| B.R. Government | — | — | 6 | — | — |
| Cadres | — | — | 3 | — | — |
| Civil war, impending | — | 1 | 3 | 4 | — |
| Clearing land | — | — | 4 | — | — |
| Economics | — | — | 5 | — | — |
| Education | — | — | 5 | — | — |
| Elections | — | 2 | 1 | 3 | — |
| Essays | — | — | — | — | 1 |
| Expanding liberated areas | — | 6 | — | — | — |
| GMD/CCP relations | — | 2 | — | — | — |
| Harvest | — | — | 5 | — | — |
| Health | — | 6 | — | — | 3 |
| "How to" articles | — | — | — | 1 | — |
| Irrigation | — | — | 7 | — | — |
| Japanese surrender | — | 4 | — | — | — |
| Liberated areas | — | — | 7 | — | — |
| Media | — | — | 5 | — | — |
| Mutual aid | — | — | 6 | — | — |
| 1911 Revolution anniversary | — | 6 | — | — | — |
| Peace in China | — | 5 | 6 | — | — |
| Postwar Japan | — | 4 | 6 | 2 | — |
| Postwar world | — | — | — | 3 | — |
| Production | — | 4 | 2 | — | — |
| Reducing rent and interest | — | 5 | 5 | 4 | — |
| Sino-Soviet treaty | — | — | 7 | — | — |
| U.S. aid to GMD | — | 3 | — | — | — |

## 2. Editorials

None.

## 3. Columns Replacing Editorials

"Qingzhu Menggu renmin gongheguo duli" (Celebrating the independence of the Mongolian People's Republic), October 29, 1945 (Pingshi).

"Zhongguo renmin gongyi de biaoxian" (The expression of the Chinese people's will), October 29, 1945 (Pingshi).

"Chaban He Yingqin Yan Shanhe siyuan" (Investigate the thought of He Yingqin and Yan Shanhe and deal with it accordingly), November 1, 1945 (Pingzhuan).

## 4. Major Page 1 Articles

"Xiangxuan zhishi" (Election directive), October 6, 1945.

## 5. Major Page 4 Articles

"Baowei hezuoshe" (Defend cooperatives), September 19–21, 1945.

"Guanyu diguan de jige wenti" (Regarding a few problems of land ownership), October 6, 1945.

"Ruhe jinxing ziyou xuanju" (How to carry out free elections), by Liu Zhinong, October 7, 1945.

"Zhe jiushi Mao Zedong—Zhongguo gongchandang de lingdui" (This is Mao Zedong—leader of the Chinese Communist Party), October 10, 1945.

Under heading "Guangbo XNCR" (Broadcasting XNCR), October 21, 25; November 4, 7, 11, 23, 25–27, 30, 1945.

"Zhongguo jindai dizu gaishuo" (A general explanation of China's recent land tax), by Chen Boda, October 26, 27, 28, 1945.

"Sulian hongjun jiefang dongbei xingshi tuan" (A map of the Soviet red army's liberation of the Northeast), November 9, 1945.

"Xiangxuan sange jingtou" (Three scenes from village elections), November 14, 1945.

"Xuanju yu jianzu jieheqilai" (Combining elections and reducing rent), by Shi Lin, November 14, 1945.

"Fadong fangshi de jieshao" (An introduction to methods of mobilization), by He Zai, November 16, 1945.

### 6. Regular Page 4 Columns

*Health* (October 30; November 12, 22).

### 7. Other Significant Articles

"Sanyan liangyu" (In a few words), October 25; November 29.

## January–April 1946

*General Comments*: Many of the editions at this time were two pages. The war was over, prospects for a coalition government with the Guomindang dim, and civil war seemingly inevitable. In various forms, land reform and reducing rent and interest along with the rectification movement were the dominant themes of the *Liberation Daily* as the Party worked to consolidate support and implement the revolution in areas under its control. Along with this were village elections and questions of self-rule, not only in the Shaan-Gan-Ning Border Region but in all liberated areas. Jin-Cha-Ji became an area of particular interest. It is clear that the *Liberation Daily* was no longer a newspaper of one area but the primary medium for all Communist Party-controlled territory.

### 1. General Page Survey

| Subject of article/editorial | Location of article/editorial | | | | |
|---|---|---|---|---|---|
| | Editorial | Pg 1 | Pg 2 | Pg 3 | Pg 4 |
| Army | — | 6 | 6 | — | — |
| Art and literature | — | — | — | — | 4 |
| B.R. Assembly | — | 7 | 4 | 4 | — |
| Capitalism | — | — | 6 | 4 | — |
| Civil war | — | 1 | 2 | — | — |
| Clearing land | — | 9 | — | — | — |
| Commerce | — | — | 5 | — | — |
| Conditions in Northeast | 3 | 6 | 4 | — | — |

| Subject of article/editorial | Location of article/editorial | | | | |
|---|---|---|---|---|---|
| | Editorial | Pg 1 | Pg 2 | Pg 3 | Pg 4 |
| Conditions in SE Asia | — | — | — | 4 | — |
| Cooperatives | — | — | 6 | — | — |
| Economics | — | — | — | 2 | — |
| Education | — | — | 5 | — | — |
| Elections | — | 8 | 5 | — | — |
| Essays | — | — | — | — | 1 |
| Guomindang | 1 | — | 6 | — | — |
| Health | — | — | — | — | 2 |
| International affairs | — | — | — | 1 | — |
| Labor heroes/heroines | — | — | 6 | — | — |
| Land reform | — | — | — | 2 | — |
| Liberated areas (other) | 3 | 5 | 5 | — | — |
| Marshall visit | 3 | 9 | — | — | — |
| May 1 celebration | — | — | 6 | — | — |
| Media | — | — | 6 | — | 3 |
| National affairs | — | 9 | — | — | — |
| Organizing people | — | 9 | 6 | — | — |
| Peace in China | 2 | 5 | 5 | 4 | — |
| Peace talks | — | — | — | 3 | — |
| Political Consultative Conf. | — | 2 | 6 | — | — |
| Politics (national) | — | — | 6 | 4 | — |
| Production | — | 2 | 1 | 4 | — |
| Rectification campaign | — | 9 | 4 | — | — |
| Reducing rent and interest | — | 4 | 3 | — | — |
| Sino-Soviet relations | — | — | 6 | — | — |
| Soviet Union | — | 8 | — | — | — |
| Stalin | — | 9 | — | — | — |
| Textiles | — | — | 6 | — | — |
| Troop demobilization | — | — | 5 | — | — |
| U.S. army in China | — | — | — | 4 | — |
| Women's day | 3 | 8 | 6 | 4 | — |

## 2. Editorials

"Jiang Jieshi yuandan yanshuo yu zhengzhi xieshanghuiyi" (The New Year's Day speech of Chiang Kai-shek and the Political Consultative Conference), January 7, 1946 (all page 1, continued page 2).

"Heping shixian" (Bringing about peace), January 12, 1946.

"Jianchi heping, baohu heping" (Persist in peace, protect peace), January 27, 1946.

"Qianjin yibu" (Advance a step), February 10, 1946.

*Note:* This is about production.

"Zhongguo faxisipai de gangling" (The guiding principles of the Chinese fascist clique), February 28, 1946.

"Zhongguo faxisipai xiang Sun Zhongshan minzhuzhuyi tiao-zhan" (China's fascist clique challenges Sun Yat-sen's democracy to battle), March 1, 1946.

"Zhongguo faxisipai shixing kongbu de ziyou" (China's fascist clique implements terror freely), March 2, 1946.

"Huanying Maxie'er jiangjun" (Welcome General Marshall), March 4, 1946.

"Zhongguo funü jinhou de renwu" (The future responsibility of China's women), March 8, 1946.

"Guomindang gaige wenti de liangge daolu" (The two roads of the Guomindang reform problem), March 12, 1946.

"Ping Guomindang erzhong quanhui" (Criticizing the Guomindang's second plenary session), March 19, 1946.

"Pochan de zhengzhi lilun" (The bankrupt government theory), March 22, 1946.

"Jianzu-jianxi shi yiqie gongzuo de jichu" (Reducing rent and interest is the foundation of all work), March 26, 1946 (continued page 2).

"Bo Jiang Jieshi" (Contradicting Chiang Kaishek), April 7, 1946 (continued page 2).

"Zai ping pochan de zhengzhi lilun" (Again criticize bankrupt political theory), April 10, 1946. (Mao edited.)

"Dongbei ying wutiaojian tingzhan" (The Northeast should unconditionally stop fighting), April 12, 1946. (Mao edited.)

"Jiefangqu zhigong yundong de renwu" (The responsibility of the labor movement in liberated areas), April 30, 1946.

### 3. *Columns Replacing Editorials*

"Shixing maoyi ziyou, jiefang chengshi jimin" (Implement free trade, liberate the city's hungry), March 17, 1946 (Pingzhuan).

"Shei zai pohuai zhengjun xieding?" (Who destroyed the whole army agreement?), March 25, 1946 (Pingzhuan).

### 4. *Major Page 1 Articles*

"Baogao ting zhan shangtan jingguo" (Reports that the truce talks continue), January 13, 1946.

"Guomindang jun xu xiang wo jingong" (Guomindang army continuously attacks us), January 13, 1946.

"Tingzhan shangtan jingyan jiaoxun" (Lessons from the experience of truce discussions), January 13, 1946.

"Heping jianguo gangling caoan" (Draft program for peacefully building the country), January 24, 1946.

"Bianqu funü zai xuanju yundong zhong" (Border Region women in the election movement), by Qin Sa, March 8, 1946.

"Dongbei kangzhan lishi yu xianshi" (The history of resistance in the Northeast and reality), March 12, 1946 (continued page 2).

"Jiefangqu shengchan lingdao de jige wenti" (A few problems with the liberated areas' production leadership), April 8, 1946.

"Bianqu jianshe de xin jieduan" (The new stage of Border Region construction), April 9, 1946 (continued page 4).

"Zhonggong zhongying yi jida beitong xuanbu, Wang Shiwei deng yunan" (The CCP's Central Committee announces in extreme grief, Wang Shiwei and others die in an accident), April 12, 1946.

"Zhou Enlai tongzhi baogao, tingzhan shangtan jingyan jiaoxun" (Comrade Zhou Enlai reports the experiences and lessons of the conference to stop the war), April 13, 1946.

"Shaan-Gan-Ning bianqu fuyuan fangan" (Shan-Gan-Ning Border Region demobilization scheme), April 25, 1946.

"Wo jun jianshou Sipingjie" (Our army holds fast to Sipingjie), April 29, 1946.

*Note:* One of several articles propagandizing major battles.

## 5. Major Page 4 Articles

Under heading "Guangbo XNCR" (Broadcasting XNCR), January 7, 8, 10, 11, 28, 1946.

"Ba women de xinwen shiye geng tigao yibu" (Taking our journalistic matters and then raising them a step), January 15, 1946.

"Zhongguo zibenzhuyi jingji fazhan de qiantu" (The future of China's capitalist economic expansion), by Wang Xuewan, January 22, 1946.

"Jiulian lingdao zuofeng gaijin" (Reforming the 9th Company's leadership work), January 29, 1946.

"Dijia" (Land value), by Chen Boda, February 9, 1946.

"Jin-Cha-Ji bianqu de yingyeshui yu suodeshui" (The business tax and income tax of Jin-Cha-Ji), March 10, 1946.

"He wei 'diyiqi jingji jianshe yuanze'?" (What is the meaning of "the principles of the first stages of economic construction"?), March 14, 1946.

"Dongbei kangRi lianjun douzheng shilüe" (Brief history of the resistance struggle of the allies in the Northeast), by Mu Qing, March 17–18, 1946.

"Nongye gongye ji duiwai jingji hezuo zhengce" (The policy of agricultural, industrial, and foreign economic cooperation), by Xu Fanglüe, March 21, 1946.

"Jianzu yundong de ruogan jingyan" (A number of experiences in the reducing rent movement), March 25, 1946.

"Zhongguo gongchandang yu jiefangqu" (The CCP and the liberated areas), April 5, 1946.

"Jiang Jieshi yanshuo yaodian" (The main points of Chiang Kai-shek's speech), April 7, 1946.

"Bianqu renmin de weida shengli" (The great victory of the Border Region's people), April 12, 1946.

"CC pai daguanliao ziben" (CC clique officials' capital), by Xu Fanglüe, April 18, 1946.

## 6. Regular Page 4 Columns

*Health* (January 11, 12, 18, 19, 26–28; February 9, 12, 15, 18; March 14, April 1).

## 7. Other Significant Articles

"Guangbo XNCR" (Broadcasting XNCR), January 2, 1946, p. 2.
"Sanyan liangyu" (In a few words), April 8.

## May–August 1946

*General Comments*: Politics dominated the *Liberation Daily* during its final year of publication. Almost every article focused on building a new democratic China, and that meant implementing a thorough revolution. With class unity no longer essential to fight the Japanese, the Party radicalized its policies in the rapidly expanding areas under its control. This is reflected best in the number of articles on land reform.

## 1. General Page Survey

| Subject of article/editorial | Location of article/editorial | | | | |
|---|---|---|---|---|---|
| | Editorial | Pg 1 | Pg 2 | Pg 3 | Pg 4 |
| Army | — | — | 7 | — | — |
| Art and literature | — | — | 7 | — | 2 |
| B.R. Government | — | — | 7 | — | — |
| Cadres | — | 9 | — | — | — |
| CCP and 3 People's Principles | — | — | 7 | — | — |
| Chiang Kai-shek | 2 | 9 | — | — | — |
| Civil war | 1 | 1 | 3 | 3 | — |
| Conditions in Northeast | — | 5 | — | — | — |
| Cooperatives | — | — | 7 | — | — |
| Democracy | — | — | 6 | — | — |
| Economics | — | — | — | 4 | — |
| Elections | — | 9 | 7 | — | — |
| Essays | — | — | — | — | 1 |
| Factories | — | — | 7 | — | — |
| Health | — | — | — | — | 3 |
| Internal conditions | — | — | 6 | — | — |
| International affairs | — | — | — | 1 | — |
| International role in civil war | — | 7 | — | 2 | — |
| Irrigation | — | 8 | 7 | — | — |
| Liberation Daily's anniversary | — | — | 7 | — | — |
| July 7 commemoration | — | 9 | — | — | — |
| Labor heroes/heroines | — | — | 6 | — | — |
| Land reform | — | — | 4 | 6 | — |
| Liberated areas (other) | — | 3 | 2 | — | — |
| May 4 commemoration | — | 9 | — | — | 5 |
| Media | — | — | — | — | 4 |
| Peace talks | — | 4 | — | 5 | — |
| Politics (national) | 2 | 6 | — | — | — |
| Production | 2 | 2 | 1 | — | — |
| Rectification campaign | — | — | 5 | — | — |
| Refugees | — | — | 7 | — | — |
| Soviet Union | — | — | 7 | — | — |
| Textiles | — | — | 6 | — | — |
| Troop demobilization | — | — | 7 | — | — |
| Women's federation | — | — | — | 6 | — |
| Workers | — | 9 | 7 | — | — |

## 2. Editorials

"Guangrong de Sipingjie baowei zhan" (Honoring the battle for Sipingjie), May 21, 1946.

*Note:* One of several articles propagandizing major battles.

"Nuli shengchan zhengqu fengshou" (Put forth effort in production, strive for a bumper harvest), May 24, 1946.

"Meiguo ying ji tingzhi zhuzhang Zhongguo neizhan" (The United States should immediately stop fostering China's civil war), June 5, 1946.

"Zhongguo gongchandang yu Zhongguo" (The CCP and China), July 1, 1946.

"Qige yue zongjie" (A seven month summary), August 14, 1946. (Mao edited.)

"Riben touxiang yizhounian" (First anniversary of Japan's surrender), August 15, 1946.

*Note:* Problems in the Northeast.

"Fensui Jiang Jieshi de jingong!" (Smash Chiang Kai-shek's offensive), August 16, 1946.

"Yinian de jiaoxun" (A year's lesson), August 29, 1946. (Mao edited.)

### 3. Columns Replacing Editorials

"Kangyi Xi'an xinwenjie xuean" (Protesting Xi'an journalistic circle's murder case), May 8, 1946 (Pingzhuan).

"Sipingjie baowei zhan" (The defensive battle for Sipingjie), May 19, 1946 (Pingshi).

"Jiang Fang junshi wuda ruodian" (The five great weaknesses of General Fang's military affairs), August 21, 1946 (Pinglun).

### 4. Major Page 1 Articles

None.

### 5. Major Page 4 Articles

"Benbao chuangban wuzhounian fang duzhe" (Asking the readers on the newspaper's fifth anniversary), May 16, 1946.

"Shaan-Gan-Ning bianqu yijiusiliunian zhi yijiusibanian jianshe jihua fangan" (The scheme for the 1946–48 construction plan for the Shaan-Gan-Ning Border Region), May 25, 1946.

"Riben touxiang yihou de Zhongguo" (China after Japan's surrender), June 3, 1946.

"Guanyu xianshi zhuji" (Concerning realism), by He Qifang, June 10–11, 1946.

"Ruci Nanjing" (Nanjing like this), June 22, 1946.

"Yige heping de jianyi" (A peace proposal), June 29, 1946.

"Women zai Zhongguo gan shemme?" (What are we in China to do?), July 3 and 4, 1946.

"Guangbo XNCR" (Broadcasting XNCR), July 9; August 1, 13.

"Binxian qunzhong gongzuo jingyan zongjie" (Summary of the people's work experiences in Bin *xian*), July 14, 1946.

"Fandui neizhan fandui ansha" (Oppose civil war, oppose assassination), July 26, 1946.

"Women gongchandangyuan shi tezhong cailiao zuo chengde" (Our Communist Party members are those made from special material), by Li Zonglin, August 6, 1946.

"Zaixiang Meiguo jiang jijuhua" (Saying a few more words to the United States), August 8, 1946.

### 6. Regular Page 4 Columns

*Health* (May 10, 13, 27; June 9, 11, 17).

### 7. Other Significant Articles

None.

## September–December 1946

*General Comments*: As fighting intensified between the Guomindang and the Communist Party, all news concentrated on the civil war. Page 1 was devoted almost exclusively to war news. But the enemy was not the Guomindang per se but rather Chiang Kai-shek, with references not to the Guomindang army but to "Chiang's army." Also, beginning in November 1946, editions of the newspaper were two pages.

### 1. General Page Survey

| Subject of article/editorial | Location of article/editorial | | | | |
|---|---|---|---|---|---|
| | Editorial | Pg 1 | Pg 2 | Pg 3 | Pg 4 |
| Art and literature | — | — | — | — | 2 |
| B.R. Assembly | — | 3 | — | — | — |
| Cadres | — | — | — | 4 | — |
| CC Clique | — | — | — | 4 | — |
| Civil war | 1 | 1 | 3 | 2 | — |
| Conditions in Northeast | — | 3 | — | — | — |
| December 9 commemoration | — | 4 | — | — | — |
| Economics | — | — | 7 | — | — |

| Subject of article/editorial | Location of article/editorial | | | | |
|---|---|---|---|---|---|
| | Editorial | Pg 1 | Pg 2 | Pg 3 | Pg 4 |
| Education | — | — | 7 | — | — |
| Essays | — | — | — | — | 1 |
| Harvest | — | 4 | — | — | — |
| International affairs | — | 4 | 1 | 1 | — |
| International role in civil war | — | 2 | 6 | 3 | — |
| Labor heroes/heroines | — | — | — | 4 | — |
| Land reform | — | 2 | 4 | — | — |
| Liberated areas (other) | — | 4 | 6 | — | — |
| Media | — | — | — | — | 3 |
| Politics (national) | — | 4 | — | — | — |
| Production | — | 4 | 2 | 3 | — |
| Rectification campaign | — | 4 | 5 | — | — |
| Troop demobilization | — | — | 7 | — | — |
| U.S. workers' movement | — | — | 7 | — | — |
| Women | — | — | 7 | — | — |

## 2. Editorials

"Gaijin women de tongxunshe he baozhi" (Reforming the press and the newspaper), September 1, 1946.

"Jiangjun bi bai" (Chiang's army must be defeated), September 12, 1946.

"Wei shixian yiyue tingzhan xieding ju zhengxie jueyi er dou-zheng" (Fighting to realize a month's truce agreement and the resolution of the Political Consultative Conference), October 3, 1946. (Mao edited.)

"Bianqu renmin jingtiqilai fandui tewu pohuai" (People of the Border Region are being vigilant about destroying counterrevolutionary spies), October 4, 1946.

"Haohao jinxing fulu gongzuo" (Conduct the prisoner of war work well), October 7, 1946.

"Wancheng minzu yundong de zuihou yibu" (Complete the last step of the national movement), October 10, 1946.

"Lun zhanju" (Discussing the war department), November 4, 1946. (Mao edited.)

"Ping Jiang-Mei shangyue" (Criticize the commercial treaty between Chiang and the United States), November 26, 1946.

"Zhanju zai kaishi biandong" (The war situation begins to change), December 6, 1946.

### 3. Columns Replacing Editorials

"Zhang Yuan yinmou baodongan de pohuo" (Discovery and arrest in the Zhang Yuan conspiracy riot case), September 25, 1946 (Pingzhuan).

"Jiang Jieshi xiang renmin gongkai xuanzhan" (Chiang Kai-shek's public propaganda war toward the people), September 26, 1946 (Pingshi).

"Xiangying 'Meijun tuichu Zhongguo' yundong" (Response to the "U.S. withdraw-from-China" movement), September 29, 1946 (Pingshi).

"Huazhong minzhu lianjun, chushi huojie" (Central China's people's allied forces, military expedition obtains a victory), October 7, 1946 (Pingzhuan).

"Dao jinfan Jiang jun de houfang qu" (Invading the rear areas of Chiang's army), October 18, 1946 (Pingshi).

"Jiang Jieshi de heping zhengshi" (Chiang Kai-shek's power of peace), October 21, 1946 (Pingshi).

"He xin shiyi lüqiyi zhounian" (Celebrating the New 11th army uprising), October 25, 1946 (Pingzhuan).

"Jiang Jieshi he pingyanmu de pomiao" (Chiang Kai-shek and the destruction of the peace smoke screen), October 25, 1946 (Pingshi).

"Hao zhanpai bi jiang zishiqili" (The Hao army clique must reap what they have sown), October 29, 1946 (Pingshi).

"Kanyi Rilun shi Hu" (Protest the Japanese ships sailing into Shanghai), November 8, 1946 (Pingzhuan).

"Ping Meiguo guohui xuanju" (Criticize the American congressional elections), November 9, 1946 (Pingshi).

"Haohao putong xiangying" (Summons for a popular response), November 11, 1946 (Pingshi).

"Zhanfan de pengyou" (Friends of the war criminals), December 8, 1946 (Pingshi).

"Daonian tui zhi Wan jiaoshou" (Mourn Professor Wan who has retired), December 21, 1946 (Pingshi).

### 4. Major Page 1 Articles

"Zhonggong zhongying fabiao shiju shengming" (The CCP's Central Committee's publishes an announcement on the current situation), October 18, 1946.

*Note:* Problems in the Northeast.

## 5. Major Page 4 Articles

"Yige xuanchuan shishi de hao banfa" (A good method of propagandizing current affairs), September 9, 1946.

Under heading "Guangbo XNCR" (Broadcasting XNCR), September 15; October 14, 15, 18, 22, 23, 25, 26, 29; November 1, 1946.

"Gongchandangyuan yu yewu" (Communist Party members and professional work), by Bo Lite, September 29, 1946.

"Xibeijun de lishi he xianzhuang" (The history and present situation of the army in the Northwest), October 10, 1946.

"Zhongguo sida jiazu" (China's four big families), by Chen Boda, November 13–18, 1946 (November 18 has a page 5).

## 6. Regular Page 4 Columns

None.

## 7. Other Significant Articles

None.

## January–March 1947

*General Comments*: During the last two months of its publication, the now two-page paper was dominated by civil war and revolution news. A Sunday supplement appeared beginning on February 2, 1947. The *Liberation Daily* ended publication on March 27 when the Guomindang army attacked Yan'an.

## 1. General Page Survey

| Subject of article/editorial | Location of article/editorial | | | | |
|---|---|---|---|---|---|
| | Editorial | Pg 1 | Pg 2 | Pg 3 | Pg 4 |
| B.R. finances | — | — | 3 | — | — |
| Civil war | — | 1 | 2 | — | — |
| Cooperatives | — | — | 3 | — | — |
| Democracy | — | — | 3 | — | — |

| Subject of article/editorial | Location of article/editorial | | | | |
| --- | --- | --- | --- | --- | --- |
| | Editorial | Pg 1 | Pg 2 | Pg 3 | Pg 4 |
| Essays | — | — | — | 1 | — |
| International affairs | — | — | 2 | — | — |
| Land reform | — | 3 | 1 | — | — |
| New Year | — | 4 | 3 | 1 | — |
| Peace proposals | — | 4 | — | — | — |
| Production | — | — | 3 | — | — |
| Youth patriotism | — | 2 | — | — | — |

## 2. Editorials

None.

## 3. Columns Replacing Editorials

"Ping Jiang Jieshi de yuandan yanshuo" (Criticize Chiang Kai-shek's New Year's speech), January 4, 1947 (Pingshi).

"Huo Qi jiangjun de wengao" (Message from General Huo Qi), January 31, 1947 (Pingshi).

## 4. Major Page 1 Articles

"Duiyu zhanhou guoji xingshizhong jige jiben wenti de jieshi" (An explanation of several basic problems in the postwar international situation), by Lu Dingyi, January 4–5, 1947.

"Meijun yiri busan, yundong yiri buting—Nanjing wuqian daxuesheng youxing suxie" (Each day American troops don't disperse, each day movements don't stop—5,000 Nanjing University students demonstrate), January 7, 1947.

## 5. Major Page 4 Articles

None.

## 6. Regular Page 4 Columns

None.

## 7. Other Significant Articles

None.

# FOUR

# The Medium: A Topical Survey

The following is a survey of the *Liberation Daily* according to topic. It lists articles, editorials, columns replacing editorials, and regular page 4 columns cited in chapters 2 and 3. No specific titles are given; rather, dates and page numbers are listed so that the researcher can find the title easily in the earlier surveys or in the newspaper itself. Citations from chapter 2 are listed under "Rectification," or under the appropriate column title.

*Agriculture* (see also production): **1942:** December 22 (p. 4); **1943:** January 23 (p. 4), April 17 (dailun), May 29 (dailun); **1945:** February 14 (editorial), June 18 (editorial), June 29 (editorial); **1946:** May 24 (editorial).

*Ai Siqi* (as author): **1941:** September 19–20 (p. 3), October 14 (p. 3); **1942:** March 11 (p. 4), April 22 (p. 4), May 5 (p. 4), May 15 (p. 4), May 21 (p. 4), June 24 (p. 4), September 17 (p. 4), December 26–27 (p. 4); **1943:** January 21 (p. 4); **1944:** February 19 (p. 4), November 6 (p. 4); **1945:** July 25 (p. 4).

*American Observer Mission:* **1944:** August 15 (editorial), October 12 (pinglun).

*Anti-Japanese War:* **1941:** July 7 (p. 2), July 30–31 (dailun), August 3 (dailun); **1942:** May 1 (dailun), July 7 (p. 1); **1943:** July 2–8 (p. 4), July 2 (p. 1); **1944:** July 7 (editorial), September 18 (editorial), October 1 (editorial); **1945:** July 7 (editorial).

*Antisubversive movement:* **1943:** September 7 (p. 1), September 21 (p. 1), September 22 (p. 1), October 3 (p. 1); **1946:** September 25 (pingzhuan).

*Army, Communist Party:* **1941:** June 14 (dailun); **1942:** February 23 (p. 1), July 10 (dailun), October 12 (editorial), December 25 (pingshi); **1943:** January 9 (pingshi), January 24 (pingshi), February 8 (pingshi), February 17 (pingshi), February 19 (pingshi), June 22

(p. 1); **1944:** January 24 (p. 1), March 29 (pingshi), April 15 (p. 1), May 7 (p. 4), August 28 (editorial), September 18 (editorial), October 1 (editorial), December 21 (p. 4); **1945:** May 9 (p. 1); **1946:** January 9 (editorial), January 27 (editorial), January 29 (p. 4), March 25 (pingzhuan), April 12 (editorial), April 29 (p. 1), October 10 (p. 4).

*Army, page 4 column:* **1941:** October 29, November 12, 16, December 12, 26; **1942:** January 9, 23, February 6, 20, March 6, 20; **1943:** April 1, 16, May 3, 17, June 2, 19, July 1, 31, August 18, September 12, October 27, November 20, December 2.

*Assembly, Border Region:* **1941:** October 12 (editorial), October 25–31 (p. 4), November 2, 4–5, 10–12, 16 (p. 4), November 22 (p. 1).

*Bethune, Norman:* **1944:** November 12, 13 (p. 4).

*Bo Gu* (as author): **1943:** July 13 (p. 1); July 17 (p. 1).

*Cadres:* **1942:** May 21 (editorial); **1943:** January 4 (p. 1), March 4 (editorial); **1944:** May 5 (p. 4), September 14, 15 (p. 4), October 8 (p. 1).

*Cai Chang* (as author): **1943:** March 8 (dailun).

*Capitalism:* **1946:** January 22 (p. 4), March 14 (p. 4).

*Chen Boda* (as author): **1942:** February 4–5, 7–9 (p. 3), June 9, 10 (p. 4), June 15 (p. 4), June 27 (p. 4), July 3–4 (p. 4), July 23 (p. 4), August 28 (p. 4); **1943:** January 10 (p. 4), March 27 (p. 4), July 21 (pp. 1–4); **1945:** October 26, 27, 28 (p. 4); **1946:** February 9 (p. 4), November 13–18 (pp. 4–5).

*Chen Duxiu:* **1942:** May 8 (p. 3).

*Chen Yun:* (as author): **1942:** April 12 (p. 4); **1943:** March 29 (p. 4).

*Chiang Kai-shek:* **1943:** August 9 (p. 4), August 10 (p. 4); **1945:** August 13 (p. 1); **1946:** January 7 (editorial, p. 1), April 7 (editorial, p. 4), September 26 (pingshi), October 21 (pingshi), October 25 (pingshi); **1947:** January 4 (pingshi).

*Children:* **1942:** April 4 (p. 4).

*"China's Destiny":* **1943:** July 21 (pp. 1–4), August 11 (p. 1).

*Chinese Communist Party:* **1941:** July 1 (editorial, p. 2—founding of), December 10 (p. 1—war, Asia), December 13 (p. 1—war, Asia); **1942:** July 1 (p. 1—anniversary of); **1943:** January 4 (p. 1—party life), June 4 (p. 1—leadership), June 5 (p. 1—leadership), June 10 (p. 4—red and expert), July 1 (editorial—relations with the people), July 2–8 (p. 4—anniversary of), July 6 (p. 1—Menshevik thought), July 8 (pp. 1–4—national liberation), July 13 (p. 1—defending the

CCP), August 25 (editorial—new China); **1944:** July 1 (editorial—
23d anniversary of); **1945:** May 1 (p. 1—7th Party Congress), June
14 (editorial—7th Party Congress), July 31 (p. 1—strengthening the
CCP); **1946:** July 1 (editorial—relations with remainder of China),
August 6 (p. 4—membership in the CCP), September 29 (p. 4—
work of).

*Civil war* (see also Northeast, struggle for): **1943:** July 9 (editorial),
July 18 (editorial); **1945:** July 28 (p. 1), August 7 (p. 1), September
14 (editorial), November 14 (editorial), November 17 (editorial);
**1946:** January 12 (editorial), January 13 (p. 1), January 27 (editorial), April 10 (editorial), April 13 (p. 1), April 29 (p. 1), May 21
(editorial), June 5 (editorial), June 29 (p. 4), July 26 (p. 4), August 8
(p. 4), August 14 (editorial), August 16 (editorial), August 29 (editorial), September 12 (editorial), September 28 (pingshi), October 3
(editorial), October 4 (editorial), October 7 (editorial, pingzhuan),
October 10 (editorial), October 25 (pingzhuan), October 29
(pingshi), November 4 (editorial), December 6 (editorial).

*Civil war, U.S. involvement in:* **1946:** June 5 (editorial), August 8
(p. 4), September 29 (pingshi).

*Communist International:* **1943:** May 27 (p. 1), May 28 (editorial, p. 1),
June 27 (editorial).

*Cooperatives* (see also Nanqu cooperative): **1943:** January 25 (editorial), June 12 (p. 1); **1944:** February 4 (p. 1), May 12 (p. 1), June 23
(p. 4); **1945:** September 19, 20, 21 (p. 4).

*"Crack troops and simple administration":* **1941:** December 6 (editorial); **1942:** January 9 (p. 4), February 1 (p. 4), February 20 (editorial), April 9 (editorial), June 23 (editorial), July 3 (p. 1), July 13
(dailun), August 3 (editorial), August 19 (p. 2), August 23 (editorial), October 21 (editorial), December 14 (p. 1).

*Dailun [opinions]:* **1941:** June 14, July 30, 31; **1942:** April 22, May 1,
13, June 4, 13, July 10, 30, August 8, September 2, 16, 18, October
4, November 5, December 24; **1943:** January 16, February 1, 7,
March 8, April 17, 24, 28, May 7, 9, 29.

*Deng Fa* (as author): **1942:** May 1 (dailun); **1943:** February 7 (dailun),
May 7 (dailun).

*Ding Ling* (as author): **1941:** October 23 (p. 1); **1942:** March 9 (p. 4),
March 12 (p. 4), June 16 (p. 4); **1944:** June 13 (p. 4), June 30 (p. 4),
September 17 (p. 4), October 21 (p. 4); **1945:** January 12 (p. 4), May
19 (p. 4).

*Economics, Border Region:* **1941:** August 1 (editorial); **1942:** January 20–21 (p. 4).

*Education:* **1941:** June 4 (editorial), October 4 (editorial), November 26 (p. 4); **1942:** January 13 (editorial), January 14 (editorial), January 28 (p. 4), February 5 (editorial), June 2 (editorial); **1943:** January 4 (p. 1), June 13 (p. 4); **1944:** April 7 (editorial), April 23 (p. 1), May 27 (editorial), June 4 (p. 2), July 17 (p. 1), November 1 (p. 1), November 11 (p. 1), November 20 (p. 1), November 23 (editorial), December 10 (p. 1); **1945:** July 20 (p. 4).

*Enemy page 4 column:* **1941:** September 27, October 11, 25, November 8, 22, December 6, 20; **1942:** January 15, 17, 31, February 14, 28, March 28, April 21, May 6, 17, June 7, 21, July 6, 21, August 6, 21, September 6, 21, October 7, 22, November 6, 21, December 8, 21; **1943:** January 6, 22, February 9, 25, March 11, 25, April 7, May 25, June 25, August 28, September 27, 28, December 1; **1944:** January 24, February 29, March 27, April 25, May 10, 27, June 11, 26, 27, July 12, 28, August 11, 26, September 13, 27, October 14, 27, November 15; **1945:** January 31, March 31.

*Epidemics, prevention of:* **1943:** May 31 (pingshi).

*Factories* (see also Production): **1943:** May 1 (p. 4); **1944:** July 30 (p. 1).

*Fan Wenlan* (as author): **1942:** June 9 (p. 4), June 29 (p. 4).

*Gao Gang:* **1943:** April 17 (dailun), April 24 (dailun), September 22 (p. 1); **1944:** November 11 (p. 1), November 29 (p. 1); **1945:** February 5 (p. 1),

*Government, China:* **1942:** March 13 (editorial), May 25 (editorial); **1943:** September 14 (p. 1); **1944:** September 23 (p. 1), September 24 (editorial); **1945:** November 7 (editorial); **1946:** March 22 (editorial), April 7 (editorial).

*Government, postwar China:* **1945:** May 2 (pp. 1–6), May 5 (editorial), May 9 (pp. 1–4), July 5 (p. 4), October 3 (editorial), October 7 (p. 4), October 11 (editorial), October 13 (editorial), October 19 (editorial); **1946:** January 24 (p. 1), June 3 (p. 4).

*Government, Shaan-Gan-Ning Border Region:* **1941:** May 21 (editorial), August 1 (editorial), August 29 (editorial), October 13–14 (p. 4); **1942:** September 11 (p. 1) **1943:** March 6 (p. 4); **1944:** February 8 (pp. 1, 3), September 21 (editorial), December 5 (editorial); **1945:** June 26 (editorial), October 6 (p. 1); **1946:** April 9 (p. 1).

*Guomindang:* **1941:** June 9 (editorial); **1943:** July 12 (editorial), August 7 (pp. 1, 4), August 21 (editorial), August 24 (p. 1), September 13 (p. 4), October 5 (p. 1); **1944:** August 12 (editorial); **1945:** May 31 (editorial); **1946:** February 28 (editorial), March 1 (editorial), March 2 (editorial), March 12 (editorial), March 19 (editorial), April 18 (p. 4), August 16 (editorial), November 13–18 (pp. 4, 5).

*He Long* (as author): **1943:** February 1 (dailun).

*He Qifang* (as author): **1942:** April 3 (p. 4), May 19 (p. 4), May 21 (p. 4); **1943:** April 3 (p. 4).

*Health:* **1944:** June 23 (p. 4), July 10 (editorial), October 21 (p. 1); **1945:** January 8 (p. 4).

*Health, page 4 column:* **1941:** November 24, December 22; **1942:** January 19, February 23, March 22, 31, April 19, 29, May 18, 29, June 14, July 22, 30, August 14, September 2, 15, 29, October 15, 29, November 15, 29, December 14, 29; **1943:** January 15, 31, February 3, 16, 27, March 15, 21, 22, April 10, 29, May 15, 31, June 17, 28, 29, August 14, October 9, 20, 29, November 14, 30, December 17, 30; **1944:** January 15, February 16, March 1, 16, 28, April 16, May 18, June 1, 24, August 13, September 16, 30, October 28, November 11.

*Health* (under heading of "Weishang" p. 4): **1945:** January 20, 21, February 2–3, 7, March 22, 30, April 2, 8, 11, 24, 27, 30, May 3, 10, 15, 22, June 3, July 18, 19, October 30, November 12, 22; **1946:** January 11, 12, 18, 19, 26, 27–28, February 9, 12, 15, 18, March 14, April 1, May 10, 13, 27, June 9, 11, 17.

*Hiroshima, bombing of:* **1945:** August 9 (pp. 1, 3), August 10 (pp. 1, 3, editorial).

*Hurley, Patrick J.:* **1945:** July 13 (pinglun), July 20 (pinglun).

*In a Few Words, page 2 column:* **1944:** February 21–24, 28, 29, March 1–2, 4–5, 11, 17, 23–24, 26–27, April 2, 4–6, 8, 10, 15, 17–18, 20–21, 29, May 4–5, 8, 11, 14, 16, 19, 31, June 10, 26, July 19, August 15, September 5, 7, 19, October 28, November 1, 3, December 22; **1945:** January 14, 16–17, 19, March 4, 6, 25, April 21, May 21, 25–26, June 4, October 25, November 29; **1946:** April 8.

*Industry:* **1945:** January 8 (p. 1).

*International conditions:* **1943:** January 14 (pingshi—Sino-American treaties); **1944:** June 14 (p. 4), July 4 (editorial—United States), November 10 (editorial—United States' elections); **1945:** February 23 (p. 4—Soviet Union), August 1 (editorial—Communist Party in the United States).

*International opinion column:* **1944:** June 24 (p. 3).
*International treaties:* **1943:** January 14 (p. 1—China/United States and Great Britain); **1945:** August 20 (editorial—Sino-Soviet), August 27 (p. 1—Sino-Soviet); **1946:** November 26 (editorial—Sino-American commercial).
*Irrigation:* **1944:** October 3 (editorial).
*Japan, surrender of:* **1945:** September 17 (editorial).
*Jiang Jieshi:* See Chiang Kai-shek.
*Jin-Cha-Ji Border Region:* **1943:** April 11 (p. 3); **1944:** July 24 (editorial); **1946:** March 10 (p. 4).
*Kai Feng* (as author): **1942:** May 13 (dailun), June 11 (p. 4); **1943:** March 28 (p. 4).
*Kang Sheng* (as author): **1942:** April 22 (p. 1), August 11 (p. 4).
*Kang Youwei:* **1942:** January 19–21 (p. 3).
*Labor* (see also *Workers* page 4 column): **1944:** February 12 (p. 1), May 26 (p. 4), June 4 (p. 1), June 5 (p. 4), August 4 (p. 4), September 5 (editorial); **1945:** February 7 (editorial), April 24 (p. 4); **1946:** April 30 (editorial).
*Labor heroes/heroines* (see also Wu Manyou, Zhao Zhankui): **1942:** April 22 (p. 2); **1943:** January 25 (p. 4), February 3 (p. 1), November 26 (p. 1), November 27 (p. 1), November 29 (p. 1), December 2 (p. 1), December 11 (p. 1), December 17 (p. 1), December 26 (editorial, p. 1); **1944:** January 1 (p. 2), July 7 (p. 2), July 31 (p. 2), September 21 (p. 2), November 30 (editorial); **1945:** January 9 (p. 1), January 12 (p. 4), January 14 (p. 2), January 15 (p. 4), January 16 (p. 4), January 19 (p. 4).
*Land policy:* **1942:** February 6 (pp. 1, 3), December 30 (pp. 1, 2); **1943:** January 23 (p. 1); **1945:** August 24 (p. 4), October 6 (p. 4); **1946:** February 9 (p. 4).
*Lenin* (as author): **1942:** May 14 (p. 4).
*Liberated areas:* **1945:** April 7 (p. 1), May 9 (pp. 1–4), June 23 (editorial), July 16 (p. 1), September 25 (editorial); **1946:** January 14 (editorial), March 4 (p. 4), March 10 (p. 4), April 5 (p. 4).
*Liberation Daily* (see also Media): **1942:** April 2 (p. 4), July 20 (p. 4), August 4 (editorial), September 22 (editorial); **1943:** March 30 (p. 1), April 8 (p. 4), June 10 (p. 1); **1944:** February 16 (editorial); **1945:** July 23 (p. 4).
*Literature and art:* **1941:** May 19 (p. 2), June 10 (editorial); **1942:** March 25 (editorial), May 15 (p. 4), May 19 (p. 4), June 9 (p. 4),

September 30 (p. 2), November 18 (p. 2); **1943:** January 16 (p. 4), March 28 (p. 4), March 29 (editorial, p. 4), April 3 (p. 4), April 25 (editorial), October 19 (pp. 1, 2, 4), November 8 (p. 1), November 24 (p. 2), June 13 (p. 4), June 30 (p. 4), July 24 (p. 4), July 31 (p. 4), September 17 (p. 4), October 21 (p. 4), November 22 (p. 2); **1945:** March 6 (p. 4), April 8–9 (p. 4), May 19 (p. 4), June 2 (p. 4).

*Literature and art, page 4 columns:* **1941:** September 16–20, 22, 23, 25, 26, 29, 30, October 1–3, 6, 15–18, 19, 21, 23, 24, 27, 28, 30, 31, November 3–4, 6, 7, 11, 13–16, 18, 20, 22, 25, 27, 28, December 1, 2, 4, 5, 8–11, 15–18, 23–25, 29–31; **1942:** January 1, 7, 8, 10, 13–15, 20–22, 24, 27, 29, February 2–5, 9–12, 15, 17, 19, 21, 25–26, March 2–5, 9–12, 17–19, 23–26, 29, 30; **1944:** May 14, 15, 20–26, 30, 31.

*Liu Shaoqi* (as author): **1942:** April 13–14 (p. 4), October 9 (pp. 1–2); **1943:** July 6 (p. 1).

*Lu Dingyi* (as author): **1942:** May 13 (p. 4), May 28 (p. 4); **1947:** January 4–5 (p. 1).

*Lu Xun:* **1941:** August 12–14 (p. 2); **1942:** October 18 (p. 4), October 19 (editorial).

*Lunzhuan [essays]:* **1942:** December 20, 22; **1943:** January 18.

*Luo Feng* (as author): **1942:** March 12 (p. 4).

*Mao Zedong:* **1943:** November 21 (p. 2); **1944:** July 1, 2 (p. 4), November 1 (p. 1); **1945:** October 10 (p. 4).

*Mao Zedong* (as author or editor): **1941:** May 18 (editorial); **1942:** February 23 (p. 1), April 10 (p. 4), April 27 (p. 1), June 18 (pp. 1–2), September 7 (p. 1), October 12 (editorial), October 14 (editorial), October 16 (editorial), October 19 (pp. 1, 2, 4), November 7 (editorial); **1943:** July 12 (p. 1), July 13 (p. 1), October 5 (editorial), December 2 (p. 1); **1944:** April 7 (editorial), June 1 (editorial), June 14 (editorial), June 23 (editorial), July 24 (pingshi), August 12 (editorial), August 13 (editorial), August 15 (editorial), August 16 (p. 1), August 28 (editorial), September 5 (editorial), September 15 (pinglun), September 18 (editorial), September 20 (pinglun), September 24 (editorial), October 1 (editorial), October 9 (editorial), October 10 (editorial), October 11 (editorial), October 12 (pinglun), December 16 (editorial); **1945:** January 31 (editorial), March 9 (editorial), July 13 (pinglun), July 20 (pinglun), July 23 (p. 1); **1946:** February 28 (editorial), March 19 (editorial), March 26 (editorial), April 10 (editorial), April 12 (editorial), August 14 (editorial), August 29 (editorial), October 8 (editorial), November 4 (editorial), November 11 (editorial), November 25 (editorial).

*Marshall, George:* **1946:** March 4 (editorial).

*Media* (see also *Liberation Daily*): **1942:** August 25 (editorial), September 1 (p. 2), November 17 (editorial); **1943:** August 25 (editorial), September 1 (pp. 1, 4, editorial), October 2 (p. 1); **1944:** July 23 (p. 4), December 21 (p. 4); **1945:** March 23 (editorial), August 24 (p. 4); **1946:** January 15 (p. 4), September 1 (editorial), September 9 (p. 4).

*Mongolian People's Republic:* **1945:** October 29 (pingshi).

*Mutual aid:* **1944:** February 10 (p. 4), February 11 (p. 4).

*Nanniwan:* **1942:** December 12 (editorial); **1943:** May 19 (p. 2).

*Nanqu cooperative* (see also *Cooperatives*): **1941:** May 25 (p. 2); **1943:** December 12 (pp. 1, 2).

*News and Communication, page 4 column:* **1942:** October 28; **1943:** January 26, March 5, April 8, August 8, September 1, 26, November 18, December 14; **1944:** March 18, July 23, September 1, 26, November 18; **1945:** March 23, April 25.

*1911 Revolution:* **1941:** October 10 (p. 3); **1942:** November 7 (editorial), October 10 (editorial).

*Northeast, struggle for* (see also Civil war): **1942:** September 18 (dailun); **1945:** September 18 (editorial), October 30 (editorial), November 9 (p. 4); **1946:** February 25 (editorial), March 12 (p. 1), March 17–18 (p. 4), April 12 (editorial), August 15 (editorial), October 18 (p. 1).

*October Revolution:* **1944:** November 7 (editorial).

*"On Coalition Government":* **1945:** May 2 (entire issue).

*Party committees, local:* **1944:** July 27 (p. 1).

*Party life, page 2 column:* **1942:** September 15, October 3, 7, 12, 15, 18, 22, 29, November 2, 4, 11, 28, 30, December 5, 9, 12, 19, 22, 25, 27, 31; **1943:** January 6, 9, 13, 25, 28, February 2, 8, 11, 18, 26, March 2, 4, 6–8, 16–17, 22–23.

*Peng Zhen* (as author): **1942:** May 14 (dailun), May 16 (p. 4), November 9 (p. 4); **1943:** January 16 (p. 4).

*Pingshi [comments]:* **1942:** December 7; **1943:** January 9, 13, 14, 24, 27, February 8, 17, 19, March 7, 19, 25, April 2, 3, 19, 26, May 10, 31, June 13, 24, November 10, 12, December 10; **1944:** March 29, April 18, July 5, 6, 24, 25, September 13, 14, October 14, 21, 24, 27, 30; **1945:** January 19, April 10, October 29, November 21;

**1946:** May 19, September 29, October 16, 18, 25, 29, December 8; **1947:** January 4, 8.

*Pingzhuan [critical comments]:* **1945:** November 1; **1946:** March 17, 25, May 8, September 25, October 7, November 8.

*Postwar world:* **1941:** May 18 (editorial); **1947:** January 4–5 (p. 1).

*Production* (see also Agriculture, Factories, and Textiles): **1942:** December 14 (p. 1); **1943:** January 4 (p. 1), January 25 (editorial), March 3 (editorial), April 28 (dailun), June 13 (p. 4); **1944:** February 24 (p. 4), May 17 (p. 4), May 26 (editorial), June 30 (editorial), September 29 (editorial); **1945:** January 12 (p. 1), January 31 (editorial); **1946:** February 10 (editorial), April 8 (p. 1), May 25 (p. 4).

*Rear areas:* **1943:** April 15 (pp. 3, 4).

*Rectification, 1941:* **1941:** May 19 (p. 2), July 1 (p. 2), July 17–19 (p. 2), September 1 (editorial), September 2 (editorial), September 6 (editorial), September 19–20 (p. 3), October 14 (p. 3), November 8 (p. 3), November 29 (p. 3), December 1 (p. 3), December 14 (p. 4), December 20 (p. 1).

*Rectification, communications:* **1941:** September 1 (p. 2).

*Rectification, crackdown on critical essays:* **1942:** April 7 (p. 4), May 14 (p. 4), May 15 (p. 4), May 21 (p. 4), May 26 (p. 4), June 9 (p. 4), June 10 (p. 4), June 13 (p. 4), June 15 (p. 4), June 16 (p. 4), June 17 (p. 4), June 19 (p. 4), June 20 (p. 4), June 24 (p. 4), June 28 (p. 4), June 29 (p. 4), July 3, 4 (p. 4), July 28, 29 (p. 4); **1943:** October 19 (pp. 1, 2, 4).

*Rectification, critical essays:* **1941:** October 23 (p. 4); **1942:** March 9 (p. 4), March 11 (p. 4), March 12 (p. 4), March 13, 23 (p. 4), March 25 (p. 4), April 3 (p. 4), April 8 (p. 4).

*Rectification, cult of Mao Zedong:* **1941:** December 14 (p. 4); **1943:** February 18, 19 (p. 3), July 1 (p. 1), July 13 (p. 1), July 17 (p. 2).

*Rectification, education of cadres:* **1941:** December 20 (p. 1); **1942:** February 5 (editorial), February 15 (editorial), February 22 (p. 3), March 2 (p. 1), March 7 (editorial), March 8 (p. 1), April 1 (p. 2), June 24 (p. 2).

*Rectification, Liberation Daily:* **1942:** March 30 (p. 1), April 2 (p. 1), July 20 (p. 4).

*Rectification, Northwest Branch of the CCP:* **1942:** January 31 (p. 4), April 24 (p. 1), June 16 (p. 2), August 21 (p. 2); **1943:** January 31 (p. 1); **1944:** July 31 (p. 2).

*Rectification, official documents for:* **1941:** December 20 (p. 1); **1942:**

March 2 (p. 1), March 27 (p. 1), April 7 (p. 1), April 10 (p. 4), April 12 (p. 4), April 13, 14 (p. 4), April 18 (p. 4), April 27 (p. 1), June 18 (pp. 1, 2); **1943:** June 4 (p. 1), July 6 (p. 1).

*Rectification, other areas:* **1942:** November 15 (p. 2); **1943:** April 11 (p. 3), June 5 (p. 1), August 2 (p. 1), October 24 (p. 3); **1944:** July 24 (p. 4).

*Rectification of styles campaign, articles:* **1942:** January 6 (p. 3), February 2 (p. 4), February 4, 5, 7–9 (p. 3), February 10 (pp. 3, 4), February 12 (p. 3), February 18, 19 (p. 3); February 22 (p. 3), March 2 (p. 1), March 3 (p. 1), March 8 (pp. 1, 3), March 23 (p. 4), March 24 (p. 1), March 27 (pp. 1, 4), March 28 (p. 3), April 1 (p. 1), April 2 (p. 1), April 4 (p. 4), April 6 (p. 2), April 7 (p. 1), April 8 (p. 2), April 10 (p. 4), April 11 (p. 2), April 12 (p. 4), April 13, 14 (p. 4), April 14 (p. 2), April 16 (p. 2), April 17–19 (p. 2), April 18 (p. 4), April 19 (p. 2), April 20 (pp. 1, 4), April 22 (pp. 1, 4), April 23 (p. 2), April 27 (p. 1), April 30 (p. 2), May 3 (p. 2), May 5 (p. 4), May 6 (p. 1), May 13 (dailun), May 14 (dailun), May 19 (p. 4), June 1 (pp. 1, 2), June 12 (p. 1), June 13 (dailun), June 16 (p. 2), June 18 (pp. 1, 2), June 27 (p. 4), July 1 (p. 1), July 10 (p. 1), July 23 (p. 4), July 26 (p. 2), July 31 (p. 2), August 7 (p. 2), August 8 (p. 2, dailun), August 10 (p. 1), September 13 (p. 2), September 17 (p. 4), September 24 (p. 2), September 30 (p. 2), October 3 (p. 1), October 9 (pp. 1, 2), October 16 (p. 4), October 17 (p. 2), October 28 (p. 2), October 31 (p. 4), November 1 (p. 4), December 26, 27 (p. 4); **1943:** January 16 (p. 4), January 21 (p. 4), January 26 (p. 4), January 31 (p. 1), March 29 (p. 4), April 2 (p. 3), April 24, 25 (p. 2), April 26 (p. 1), May 6 (pp. 1, 2), May 22 (p. 2), June 4 (p. 1), June 5 (p. 1), July 6 (p. 1), July 8 (pp. 1, 2).

*Rectification of styles campaign, editorials:* **1941:** June 2, 7, September 6, 9; **1942:** January 13, February 2, 5, 11, 13, 15, 17, March 7, 10, 19, 21, April 1, 4, 6, 8, 9, 11, 15, 17, 18, 20, 23, 28, May 5, 9, 11, 14, 23, June 5, 10, July 2, 3, 18, August 4, 16, 25, September 4, 9, 17, 22, 24, October 30, November 10, 17, December 18; **1943:** January 25, March 4.

*Reducing rent and interest:* **1943:** October 30 (p. 4), November 15 (editorial); **1945:** February 9 (editorial), September 23 (editorial), November 14 (p. 4); **1946:** March 25 (p. 4), March 26 (editorial).

*Refugees:* **1943:** November 15 (p. 4).

*Self-defense:* **1943:** September 29 (pp. 1, 4).

*Senior Cadre Conference:* **1943:** January 25 (editorial), January 31 (p. 1), March 4 (editorial).

*Science, page 4 column:* **1941:** October 4, 18, November 1, 10, 29, December 13, 27; **1942:** January 12, 26, February 7, 24, March 7, 21, May 3, 30, July 1, 31, August 30, September 30, October 30, November 30, December 30; **1943:** January 30, March 2–4.

*Semimonthly military developments, page 1 column:* **1942:** May 15, 31, June 16, 30, July 15, 31, August 15, 31, September 15, 30, October 17, 31, November 15, December 1, 17, 31; **1943:** January 15, February 2, 16, March 1, 16, April 1, 15, May 2, 15, June 1, 17, July 19, August 5, 17, September 5, 19, October 6, 17, November 2, 17, December 3.

*Shamans:* **1944:** April 29 (p. 1, editorial), June 18 (p. 4).

*Stalin, Joseph:* **1942:** April 10 (p. 4), April 18 (p. 4), April 20 (p. 4).

*Study, page 4 column:* **1942:** May 13, 16, 21, 24, 28, June 1, 8, 11, 15, 17, 20, 27, 30, July 13, 23, August 5, 11, 23, 28, September 8, 25, October 6, November 9; **1943:** January 16.

*"Support the government, cherish the people" movement:* **1943:** February 1 (dailun, p. 1), November 1 (p. 2), December 14 (p. 1); **1944:** January 4 (p. 1), January 19 (p. 1), February 5 (p. 1).

*Taxes:* **1942:** November 10 (p. 4), December 6 (p. 4), December 30 (pingshi); **1945:** October 26–28 (p. 4); **1946:** March 10 (p. 4).

*Textiles* (see also Production): **1945:** May 13 (editorial).

*359th Brigade:* **1943:** May 6 (p. 4).

*"To the Villages":* **1942:** March 15 (p. 2), November 19 (editorial); **1943:** November 24 (p. 2); **1945:** January 9 (p. 1).

*Treaties, unequal:* **1943:** February 4 (editorial), February 4–8 (p. 4).

*United front:* **1943:** November 25 (p. 4).

*Wang Jiaxiang* (as author): **1943:** July 8 (pp. 1–2).

*Wang Shiwei* (as author): **1942:** March 13, 23 (p. 4).

*Wang Shiwei, attacks on:* **1942:** April 7 (p. 4), May 19 (p. 4), May 26 (p. 4), June 9 (p. 4), June 9, 10 (p. 4), June 10 (p. 4), June 17 (p. 4), June 20 (p. 4), June 28 (p. 4), June 29 (p. 4),

*Wang Shiwei, death of:* **1946:** April 12 (p. 1).

*War, Asia:* **1941:** December 10 (p. 1), December 11 (editorial), December 13 (p. 1); **1943:** June 13 (pingshi); **1944:** July 5 (pingshi), October 14 (pingshi), October 21 (pingshi), October 24 (pingshi), December 8 (editorial); **1945:** April 8 (editorial).

*War, Europe:* **1941:** June 23 (p. 1), June 26 (editorial), June 29 (editorial), July 26 (editorial), August 20 (p. 1); **1942:** October 14 (editorial), October 16 (editorial); **1943:** July 14 (p. 1), December 10 (pingshi); **1944:** June 22 (editorial), July 24 (pingshi), July 25 (pingshi), September 14 (pingshi), November 22 (editorial); **1945:** May 10 (editorial), July 28 (pingshi).

*Women:* **1942:** March 8 (editorial, p. 4), March 9 (p. 4); **1943:** February 26 (p. 1), March 8 (dailun), November 1 (p. 2); **1945:** April 9 (editorial); **1946:** March 8 (editorial, p. 1).

*Women, page 4 column:* **1941:** September 28, October 12, 26, November 9, 13, December 7, 21; **1942:** January 6, 18, February 1, 16.

*Workers, page 4 column* (see also Labor): **1941:** September 24, October 8, 22, November 5, 19, December 2, 19; **1942:** January 16, 30, February 13, 27, March 27.

*Wu Manyou:* **1942:** April 30 (p. 1, editorial, p. 2), May 6 (editorial); **1943:** January 11 (editorial), March 15 (pp. 1, 2, editorial), December 11 (p. 1), December 14–17 (p. 4).

*Xiao Jun* (as author): **1942:** March 25 (p. 4), April 8 (p. 4), May 14 (p. 4), June 13 (p. 4),

*Xie Juezai* (as author): **1942:** June 4 (dailun), June 13 (dailun), August 8 (dailun).

*XNCR:* **1946:** January 2 (p. 2).

*XNCR, page 4 column:* **1945:** October 21, 25, November 4, 7, 11, 23, 25–27, 30; **1946:** January 7–8, 10–11, 28, July 9, August 1, 13, September 15, October 14, 15, 18, 22–23, 25–26, 29, November 1.

*Yan'an Forum:* **1943:** October 19 (pp. 1, 2, 4), December 26 (p. 4).

*Yangko:* **1943:** April 25 (p. 4).

*Youth, page 4 column:* **1941:** September 21, October 5, 20, November 2, 17, 30, December 14, 28; **1942:** January 11, 25, February 8, 22, March 1.

*Zhang Ruxin* (as author): **1942:** March 8 (p. 3), May 28 (p. 4), June 17 (p. 4), October 31–November 1 (p. 4).

*Zhao Zhankui:* **1942:** September 13–14 (p. 4), September 29 (p. 2), December 22 (lunzhuan); **1943:** February 7 (dailun), May 7 (dailun).

*Zhou Enlai* (as author): **1941:** June 14 (dailun), July 13 (dailun), July 30, 31 (dailun); **1942:** July 30 (dailun); **1945:** July 16 (p. 1).

*Zhou Erfu* (as author): **1944:** November 12, 13 (p. 4); **1945:** April 8, 9 (p. 4), May 1 (p. 1); **1946:** March 4 (p. 4).

*Zhou Wen* (as author): **1942:** June 16 (p. 4).

*Zhou Yang* (as author): **1941:** July 17–19 (p. 2), August 12–14 (p. 2), October 30–31 (p. 3); **1942:** July 28–29 (p. 4); **1944:** March 21 (p. 4), April 8 (p. 4), November 21 (p. 2); **1945:** June 2 (p. 4).

*Zhu De* (as author): **1941:** July 7 (p. 2); **1942:** July 1 (p. 1), September 18 (dailun); **1944:** January 4 (p. 1), July 7 (p. 1); **1945:** May 9 (pp. 1–4).

# The Medium and Its Legacy

A study of the *Liberation Daily* reaches beyond the world of the Shaan-Gan-Ning Border Region and the Communist Party during and after the Anti-Japanese war. Because the newspaper laid the foundation for journalistic policy in post-1949 China, its legacy cannot be overlooked. After the Maoists took control in 1942, the *Liberation Daily* became the means through which Party leaders tried to make people see the value of their programs and the personal benefits of supporting them. It propagandized the official line in a general way while simultaneously providing concrete guidelines for cadres implementing that line. Truth mattered less than ideological correctness as articles became the horns through which the Party sounded its message. There was no place for opposition since it implied a lack of unified belief in the message. The standards set by the postreform *Liberation Daily* dominated China's press until the death of Mao and the demise of his domination of the Party.

The *People's Daily* (*Renmin ribao*), more than any other newspaper, inherited the mantle of the *Liberation Daily*. Both publications dealt in what Jacques Marcuse calls "prefabricated public opinion," fulfilling their roles as the Party's principal propaganda organ by doggedly relaying the Party line.[1] This is well illustrated in the six categories of news found in the *People's Daily* during the 1950s. Although they reflected the concerns of a national, not a regional, government, the categories could have come right out of a 1943 edition of the *Liberation Daily*. They included articles and columns that (1) aided Marxist education; (2) related the experiences of various enterprises and government offices and described the activities of exceptional Party members under the heading of "Party Life"; (3) mobilized people to resist America and aid Korea; (4) promoted the socialist transformation of the nation; (5) publicized rural policies and those who successfully followed them; and (6) maintained close contact with readers.[2] The newspaper, like its predecessor, played the education, mobilization, and promotion role so dear to Mao's heart.

Articles appeared in a layout that showed priorities had not changed greatly over time. In 1972, the makeup of the *People's Daily* looked like this: page 1, important news and commentaries; page 2, economic news; page 3, politics, art and literature; page 4, academic and theoretical topics; pages 5 and 6, international news.[3] The similarities to the postreform *Liberation Daily*, with its page 1, important news and commentaries; page 2, news of the liberated areas; page 3, national politics, art and literature; and page 4, international news, are unmistakable.

Other similarities existed as well. Like its predecessor, the *People's Daily* was intended for an elite audience. In the early 1960s, each edition ran around 700,000 copies, 150,000 of which were sold in Beijing (with a population of 6 million).[4] By 1972 circulation had increased to 3.4 million copies with 1.5 million sold in Beijing.[5] The size of its circulation did not really matter because the *People's Daily*, with its vocabulary of more than 5,000 characters (as compared to the 2,000–2,500 of the *Liberation Daily*) was unintelligible to the average Chinese. Most people learned the contents of the China's primary propaganda organ from distillations of *People's Daily* articles published in other newspapers.[6]

Even if the population had access to or could read it, the *People's Daily* was not meant for a general readership. Like the *Liberation Daily*, it functioned as a textbook. Through the newspaper, cadres learned what the leadership wanted them to know about current policies. Their job in turn was to make sure the message reached the masses. That usually occurred through ubiquitous loudspeakers or in compulsory political study sessions. More than being a source of information, the *People's Daily*'s contents became the framework through which people lived their lives. As it did in the Shaan-Gan-Ning Border Region, the newspaper took on an importance unmatched by anything found in the West.

The *People's Daily* continued in the tradition of the *Liberation Daily* when it underwent a major reform during the Cultural Revolution. Although carrying the mantle of the postreform *Liberation Daily*, it did not avoid the pitfalls of the prereform publication. In the early 1960s, the editor-in-chief of the *People's Daily*, Wu Lengxi, also served, as did Bo Gu, as the director of the NCNA. As a member of the original staff of the *Liberation Daily*, Wu was well acquainted with the newspaper during its first year. Wu's *People's Daily*, like the prereform *Liberation Daily*, had little contact with the masses. Instead it concentrated on interpreting documents and bulletins issued by the Party. Long-winded editorials and secondhand reports dominated the news. The Chinese incursion into India in October 1963 is a good illustration of the lack of original reporting. No Chinese war correspondents (and no foreign correspondents) reported directly from the field. Information came in daily NCNA bulletins and generally focused on Indian prisoners of war testifying to their humane treatment at the hands of the Chinese. This is not to say that the *People's Daily* revealed nothing about daily life in China. It contained, as the *Liberation Daily* had before it, a variety of short articles and commentaries that painted a fairly accurate portrait of daily life and political trends at the local level.[7] But for the most part, the newspaper remained a bulletin board for Central Committee notices.

That aloofness did not go unnoticed. The *People's Daily* of the early 1960s fared no better than did the equally dry *Liberation Daily* of early 1942. Each suffered for their "sins" by falling victim to inner-Party struggle. Mao's frustration over the media's inability to rouse the countryside during the Great Leap Forward harkened back to his anger over *Liberation Daily*'s failure to mobilize the masses to overcome the crises of 1941. He targeted the media and purged it as he had done some twenty years earlier. Moreover, because it was under the direct control of the Central Committee, the *People's Daily* lost additional prestige and authority when Central Committee members came under attack during the first years of the Cultural Revolution. By April 1966 it had stopped printing independent editorials, relying instead on reprinted and joint ones.[8]

While the reform of the *Liberation Daily* in 1942 cannot be compared to the destruction of China's press during the Cultural Revolution, the goal was the same. Mao sought to bring a wandering media under his firm control and through it implement a mass campaign. Throughout China, newspaper readers gathered peasants together in fields, homes, and meeting halls to read and discuss the day's *People's Daily*. Peasants responded to this no better than they did to similar efforts in the Shaan-Gan-Ning Border Region. As it did then, this enforced newspaper study imposed upon peasants' precious time and concerned things that had little meaning to their everyday lives.

Like rectification, the Cultural Revolution made journalists all too aware of the penalties paid for independent thinking. By 1970, the

*People's Daily* was thoroughly cowed. Relying upon a pedagogic-utilitarian style, reporters hid safely in turgid and dull writing.

To insure uniformity, the Central Committee became as actively involved in determining the editorial policy of the newspaper as it had been in theory after the 1942 reform. MacFarquhar reported that while the Central Committee had no formally defined relationship with the *People's Daily*, it interfered freely in newspaper affairs. According to his personal observations, a month before National Day in 1972, senior staff members, along with their counterparts from *Red Flag* and *Liberation Army News*, attended a joint briefing by members of the Central Committee. They received instructions about the major points to be made in editorials commemorating the occasions. Editors then collectively drafted editorials, consulted a second time with the Central Committee, and reworked their drafts until Committee members approved their National Day messages.[9]

Although the Central Committee appointed the *People's Daily*'s editors and exercised enormous control over it, no Central Committee members served on the newspaper's staff. The *People's Daily* also never had a PLA work team or a revolutionary committee, as did many other newspapers. Seven people collectively exercised leadership in the immediate post–Cultural Revolution years. Like his *Liberation Daily* predecessor after 1942, former *People's Daily* editor-in-chief Wu Lengxi was a part of that group.[10] As happened when Lu Dingyi joined the *Liberation Daily*'s staff and ended Bo Gu's dominance, collective leadership in the *People's Daily* ended any trace of independent ideological positions.

The Cultural Revolution did revive the populist legacy of the post-reform *Liberation Daily*, however. Reporters from the *People's Daily*, like their colleagues thirty years before, found themselves out gaining "real" experience living and working among the people. In 1972 approximately three hundred people belonged to the editorial department. Of those, two hundred actively engaged in journalism while the remainder worked the farm at the newspaper's May 7th cadre school. Half of the two hundred active staff members worked in Beijing, spending the majority of their time helping officials and others to write their own articles for the newspaper. The remaining staff members traveled the country collecting materials on specific themes.[11] Journalists were once again engaging "mass line" reporting.

The *Liberation Daily*'s legacy ended with Mao Zedong's death in

1976. Certainly, many of the Maoist era trappings remain. Officials continue to rely on word-of-mouth dissemination of news, for example. To this day, loudspeakers blare it forth, and it remains the subject of compulsory political study. Nevertheless, when Deng Xiaoping and his bureaucratic wing of the Party took control, they instituted a more conventional propaganda system. That meant a large structure of professional newspapers, an active press service, and a bureaucracy to administer it. By 1979, the government vowed to "seek truth from facts" through the press. Newspapers rushed to confess that they had taken factual liberties for years to get the Party line across. The new goal was to report China's problems objectively so that the people could decide for themselves.[12]

Party leaders maintained the need for propaganda, but they sought to redefine it to fit the changing role of journalism in China. A 1985 textbook, *An Introduction to Journalism*, used at Shanghai's Fudan University makes a clear distinction between news and propaganda.

> The purpose of propaganda is to persuade people, to make [them] accept the view of the propagandist and thereby to make the object of propaganda consciously act in accord with the intentions of the propagandist. . . .
>
> But, news only gives people one kind of information, [and] what people decide to do after receiving such information is up to the individual.[13]

While the above definition may be subscribed to more in theory than in practice, its very existence shows a sharp divergence with the *Liberation Daily*.

One Chinese newspaper that has broken markedly with the past is the English-language *China Daily*. Originally intended for foreign businessmen, tourists, and diplomats, *China Daily* is widely read by academics and bureaucrats alike. Its popularity grew so fast that it tripled its circulation within nine months. Because it is backed by the State Council, it has become in its own way an official propaganda organ. That is about the only similarity it shares with either the *Liberation Daily* or the *People's Daily*. It is a Western-style newspaper in content, design, and managerial structure. In theory, censorship and political content are not dictated from above but are the responsibility of individual page editors. National and international news dominates page 1; page 2 contains economic news, complete with closing stock quotations from New York, Tokyo, London, and Hong Kong; page 3 has domestic news; page 4, opinions; page 5, features; page 6, entertainment; page 7, international sports; and page 8, the Third World. The NCNA provides national news but, like the *Liberation Daily* during its first years, augments its international reporting with Reuter, Associated Press, and United Press International wire service stories.[14]

Although China's current leadership has promoted seeking "truth from facts" and has allowed a degree of freedom within the Party propaganda system not seen before, it has also been the architect of a massive breakdown of the system. This failure brings up an important point in relation to the study of the *Liberation Daily*. In the preceding pages, I argued that after the 1942 reform, the *Liberation Daily* served its propaganda function well under a unified leadership. It reinforced the Party's viewpoints and affirmed its programs and policies allowing little deviation from the accepted Party line. The newspaper disseminated information from the top levels down and gathered the kinds of information at the mass level necessary for policy making decisions. In its postreform state, the *Liberation Daily* made an excellent conduit for Party propaganda.

This analysis has focused upon a viable propaganda system. The question that remains, however, is: What happens when the system fails? The blatant disregard for the truth following the government's suppression of student demonstrators in Tiananmen Square in June 1989 is a good illustration of failure. The propaganda system broke down under the duress of the hard-liners' attempt to justify their actions. What Westerners witnessed at that time was a distortion of the system described in this study. They saw instead a system that reflected panic at the top levels of a severely divided leadership.

To understand why breakdowns occur, it is appropriate to return to Frederick Teiwes's conclusions regarding rectification campaigns cited in chapter 2. Teiwes argues that consensus at the top level of Party leadership generates clearly articulated policies easily conveyed through the propaganda system to their targets. Absence of consensus creates the opposite effect. Unclear or frequently reversed policy signals complicate and erode the propaganda system. In such a situation, it becomes impossible for the system to play the education, mobilization, and promotion roles expected of it. Unable to achieve the desired response through persuasion, the leadership resorts, as it did in June 1989, to coercion.[15]

In other words, when the leadership is united as it was in Yan'an after 1942, the propaganda system functions well. When the leadership is divided as it was in June 1989, the system loses its effectiveness and becomes a tool of repression. The message sent out through the propaganda system is mixed, underlining the division at the top. Without clear direction, the media breaks down, often becoming a target of inner-Party struggle. Unable to carry out its role, Party leaders will bypass a disfunctioning propaganda sytem and attempt to implement their policies through coercion. Mao Zedong succeeded in bringing a disfunctioning media under his control in 1942 and using it to implement an effective mass campaign. Deng Xiaoping and his supporters were not so successful. This is not the only example of the system's breakdown under a divided leadership; the Cultural Revolution and the campaign against Right Opportunism of 1959–1960 are others.

Nevertheless, it is safe to say that whether functioning under a united or a divided leadership, the relationship between the Communist Party and the press has changed greatly since the days of the Shaan-Gan-Ning Border Region. What lies ahead will reflect the politics and practices of the group in power. No matter who they are, however, one thing is certain: the Party's domination of its principal propaganda organs will never be as total as it was in Yan'an. The *Liberation Daily* was a creation of the Party and, after 1942, a tool of the Maoists. Its pages became a living history of the period. But the legacy of the *Liberation Daily* extends beyond that. The doctrines that dominated this small, four-page newspaper governed journalism in China for the next thirty years.

# Notes

## Introduction

1. Will Irwin, *Propaganda and the News* (New York, 1936), pp. 47, 49; Gaye Tuchman, *Making News: A Study in the Construction of Reality* (New York, 1978), pp. 2, 4, 12, 104, 177, 183–88.

2. According to Alan Liu, "It is the ambition of Chinese leaders and other contemporary nation-builders, to use the mass media 'to alter reality by influencing the perspective of the observer' so to realize his vision of a 'good society.'" See Alan P. L. Liu, "People's Republic of China," in *Newspapers in Asia*, ed. John A. Lent (Hong Kong, 1982) p. 48.

3. Ibid., p. 39. In his book *The Challenge of Red China*, Gunther Stein gives a good example of how Mao Zedong perceived the pedagogic-utilitarian function of the press. "Mao [Zedong] showed me a copy of the *Liberation Daily*. 'Take the example in tonight's newspaper. Here is a long article covering a whole page which describes in detail the ways in which one of the companies of the Eighth Route Army got rid of its shortcomings and became one of the best units. The cadres and fighters of every company in our armies will read and study and discuss this article. This is the simple way in which the positive experiences of one company will be taught as policy to five thousand companies. On the other days you may find similar articles about a cooperative, a school, a hospital, or a local administrative unit.'" See Gunther Stein, *The Challenge of Red China* (New York, 1945), p. 117.

4. This process of reform in the *Liberation Daily* is discussed in chapter 1.

5. Tuchman, *Making News*, pp. 31, 41, 46. The quotation is from p. 38.

6. Ibid., p. 174.

7. The structure and organization of the *Liberation Daily* will be discussed in detail in the next chapter.

8. For example, see "Zhanzheng jishushang de geming yuanzidan xi di Guangdao" (Wartime technological revolution, atom bomb surprise attack on the enemy's Hiroshima), August 9, 1945, p. 1.

9. Tuchman, *Making News*, p. 25.

10. Ibid., pp. 36, 97f.

11. Liu argues that in Communist governments, state-controlled presses are not uncommon; party-controlled ones are. See Alan P. L. Liu, *Communication and National Integration in Communist China* (Berkeley, 1971), p. 35.

12. Garth S. Jowett and Victoria O'Donnell, *Propaganda and Persuasion* (Newbury Park, 1986), p. 16.

13. Ibid., pp. 19, 20, 23.

14. Yi-tsi Feuerwerker, *Ding Ling's Fiction* (Cambridge: Harvard University Press, 1982), p. 95; Peter Kenez, *The Birth of the Propaganda State: Soviet*

*Methods of Mass Mobilization, 1917–1929* (Cambridge, 1985), p. 4.

15. Even such prominent leaders as Zhu De, Zhou Enlai, and Liu Shaoqi bided their time before jumping on the Mao bandwagon. Wang Ming later asserted that an "absolute majority of Party cadres" were against rectification and claimed that Mao told him as much in April 1944. See Wang Ming, *Mao's Betrayal* (Moscow, 1979), p. 45.

16. Mao Tse-tung (Mao Zedong), "A Talk to the Editorial Staff of the *Shansi-Suiyuan Daily*," in *Selected Works* (Beijing, 1969), 4:241.

17. Ibid., p. 242.

18. Liu, *Communication and National Integration*, p. 135; John A. Lent, "Freedom of the Press in East Asia," in *Newspapers in Asia*, ed. Lent, p. 20.

19. Chapter 3 cites articles on these topics.

20. Liu cites a similar lack of knowledge for the Propaganda Department at the time of the Cultural Revolution. See Liu, *Communication and National Integration*, p. 40.

21. The entire discussion of the press in Guomindang-controlled China is taken from Lee-hsia Hsu Ting, *Government Control of the Press in Modern China, 1900–1949* (Cambridge, 1974), pp. 85–139.

22. People turned instead to "mosquito" newspapers for information and enjoyment. Printed in small printing shops with the most primitive equipment, these publications could change their titles, dismantle their plants, and move whenever the authorities got too close. They enjoyed much greater freedom than their larger, more respectable, contemporaries.

23. The puppet government under Wang Qingwei passed a publication law on January 24, 1941, similar to that of the 1937 Guomindang law. It had already taken drastic steps to quiet the press. In May 1940, most Chinese-language papers received anonymous letters warning them not to publish materials detrimental to Wang or they might be executed. From the number of kidnapings, assassinations, and bombings, the Wang Qingwei government meant what it said.

24. Theodore White and Annalee Jacoby, *Thunder Out of China* (New York, 1984), p. 232.

25. I examine this process of evaluation and revision concerning policy for women in my book *Yan'an Women and the Communist Party* (Berkeley, 1983).

26. White and Jacoby, *Thunder Out of China*, p. 229.

27. Liu, *Communication and National Integration*, pp. 6, 10; Liu, "PRC," p. 49.

28. This is not to say that outside forces do not try to influence the press. A good example is the harassment the *New York Times* experienced after the publication of the Pentagon Papers.

29. Leonard L. Chiu, "Press Criticism and Self-Criticism in Communist China: An Analysis of Its Ideology, Structure and Operation," *Gazette* 31 (1983): 47, 49, 57, 58.

30. The Internationalists were a group of Chinese Communist Party members who were sent to Moscow to study at Sun Yat-sen University in the late 1920s. Led by Wang Ming and Bo Gu, they were known at the University as the "Internationalist faction" because of their loyalty to the Comintern and the Communist Party of the Soviet Union rather than to the Chinese Communist Party. (Western scholars sometimes refer to them as the "Returned Students Clique" or the

"Twenty-eight Bolsheviks.") Stalin sent Wang Ming to China in 1931 to take control of the faltering Party from Li Lisan. He was a perfect vehicle for the Comintern line in China. He had spent his young adult life in the Soviet Union except for two brief visits to China in mid-1927 and 1930–31.

It is interesting to note that Chen Boda, who later became Mao's must enthusiastic supporter, was also studying at Sun Yat-sen University at this time. He belonged to the "Branch faction," which remained loyal to the Chinese Communist Party. When Stalin launched a purge of the Communist Party of the Soviet Union in 1930 following his victory over Trotsky and Bukharin, Wang Ming and Bo Gu launched a purge of the Chinese Party. Part of that purge was a warning to Chen about sectarianism. Chen never forgot the incident, which was one of the reasons why he supported Mao as strongly as he did during the rectification campaign. See Raymond F. Wylie, *The Emergence of Maoism* (Stanford, 1980), p. 12.

31. See, for example, Gregor Benton, "The 'Second Wang Ming Line' (1935–38)," *China Quarterly* 61 (March 1975): 61–94; Kui-kwong Shum, *The Chinese Communists' Road to Power: The Anti-Japanese National United Front 1935–1945* (New York, 1988); John W. Garver, *Chinese-Soviet Relations 1937–1945* (New York, 1988); James Pinckney Harrison, *The Long March to Power* (New York, 1972); Wang Ming, *Mao's Betrayal* (Moscow, 1979); Raymond F. Wylie, *The Emergence of Maoism* (Stanford, 1980); John W. Garver, "The Origins of the Second United Front: the Comintern and the Chinese Communist Party," *China Quarterly* 113 (March 1988): 29–59; S. Bernard Thomas, *Labor and the Chinese Revolution* (Ann Arbor, 1983).

32. Peter Seybolt argues persuasively that Wang Ming capitulated to Mao publicly in a speech entitled "Learn from Mao Zedong" at the opening of the Zedong Youth Cadre School on May 3, 1940. Although Wang Ming may have acknowledged Mao's leadership in 1940, the Internationalists retained control of the Party's primary propaganda organ until the spring of 1942. See Peter J. Seybolt, "Tribute to a 'Crane Among Chickens': Wang Ming's Capitulation to Mao Zedong," *East Asia Insight*, pp. 93–95.

33. Ibid.

34. Wang Ming claims that under Mao's orders he was poisoned for a time in 1942 and 1943. According to Wang, he received large doses of a mercury preparation that slowly poisoned him. Only when he complained in 1943 did the Central Committee send consultants from the Yan'an Central Hospital, the Norman Bethune Peace Hospital, and the Yan'an Medical Institute to investigate. They apparently found evidence supporting Wang's claim. See Wang, *Mao's Betrayal*, p. 40–42.

35. Wylie, *The Emergence of Maoism*, pp. 152f, 234.

36. "*Kaiho nippo*" *kiji mokuroku* (Index to the *Jiefang ribao*) (Tokyo, 1967), 3 vols.

37. Lucien Pye, *Communication and Political Development* (Princeton, 1963), p. 10.

## Chapter One

1. Lynn T. White, III, "Local Newspapers and Community Change, 1949–1969," in *Moving a Mountain: Cultural Change in China*, ed. Godwin C. Chu and Francis L. K. Hsu (Honolulu, 1979), p. 78.

2. Frederick T. C. Yu, "China's Mass Communication in Historical Perspective," in ibid., p. 31.

3. "Yan'an 'Jiefang ribao shi' dagang" (An outline of the history of Yan'an's *Liberation Daily*), *Xinwen yanjiu ziliao* (News research materials) 17 (1983): 7. Hereafter Dagang 17.

4. "Zhonggong zhongying guanyu chuban 'Jiefang ribao' deng wenti de tongzhi" (The Party's Central Committee notification regarding several questions in publishing the *Liberation Daily*), *Zhongguo gongchandang xinwen gongzuo wenjian huibian* (Compilation of documents on journalism in the Chinese Communist Party) (Beijing, 1980), 1:97.

5. Jia Shaoqin, "1936 nian Xi'an faxing de Jiefang ribao" (The *Liberation Daily* published in Xi'an in 1936), *Xinwen yanjiu ziliao* 24 (1984): 204; Dagang 17, p. 7; Wang Jing, "Chen Kehan tongzhi tan Yan'an 'Jiefang ribao' " (Comrade Chen Kehan discusses Yan'an's *Liberation Daily*), *Xinwen yanjiu ziliao* 26 (1984): 118.

6. Dagang 17, p. 8; Wang Fengchao and Yue Songdong, comps. "Yan'an 'Jiefang ribao' dashiji" (Important events of Yan'an's *Liberation Daily*), *Xinwen yanjiu ziliao* 26 (1984): 126. Hereafter "Dashiji."

7. Wang Jing, "Chen Kehan," p. 118.

8. Yu, "China's Mass Communication," p. 31; Harrison, *Long March to Power*, p. 319.

9. Harrison, *Long March to Power*, p. 319.

10. A native of Ningpo, Zhejiang, Bo Gu was active in the student movement during the early 1920s. He attended Shanghai University in the mid-1920s where he was influenced by Qu Qiubai, Chen Duxiu, and others. In November 1926 he began studying at Sun Yat-sen University in Moscow with others who later became known as the Internationalists. He stayed in Moscow for three and a half years, returning to Shanghai in May 1930 where he served as editor of *Red Flag*, the central organ of the Communist Party, and *Shanghai Worker*, a trade union newspaper. In 1931 he was promoted to the Central Committee, and in September the twenty-four-year-old Bo became the acting general secretary of the Central Committee of the Chinese Communist Party.

By the end of 1932 the political situation in Shanghai was so precarious that Bo Gu and other members of the Provisional Politburo decided to move the Central Committee apparatus to Ruijin, the capital of the Jiangxi Soviet. Once there, he was elected head of the Provisional Politburo of the Central Committee and officially became general secretary of the Central Committee in January 1934. When Mao Zedong asserted his power at the Zunyi Conference in 1935, Bo Gu's eclipsed. He was not out of the picture entirely, however. He served as the mediator in the negotiations among Chiang Kai-shek, Zhang Xueliang, and Yang Huchen after the Xi'an Incident and represented the Party on the National Political Council in Wuhan and Chongqing.

Soon after he arrived in Yan'an from Chongqing, he was named editor-in-chief of the *Liberation Daily* and head of the NCNA. As such, he controlled all information and propaganda in the Border Region. Although under attack as an Internationalist from 1942 on, he retained his editorship until 1944. At the Seventh Plenum of the Party (held prior to the Seventh Congress [April–June 1945]) he was named with Wang Ming as having committed "leftist dogmatist errors." Lu

Dingyi replaced him as head of the propaganda department and, while his name remained on the list of forty-four full members of the Central Committee in 1945, it appeared last. In 1946 he was again in Chongqing, negotiating with the Guomindang over the democratization of China. He died on April 8, 1946, in a plane crash traveling back to Yan'an. See Benton, "The 'Second Wang Ming Line' "; A. Pantsov, "Life Given to the Struggle for Freedom," *Far Eastern Affairs* 1 (1983): 122–29; and Donald W. Klein and Anne B. Clark, *Biographic Dictionary of Chinese Communism, 1921–1965* (Cambridge, 1971), p. 199f.

11. Wang Jing, "Chen Kehan," p. 118.

12. Harrison, *Long March to Power*, p. 318.

13. Timothy C. Cheek, "Orthodoxy and Dissent in People's China: The Life and Death of Deng Tuo (1912–1966)," Ph.D. Harvard University, 1986, pp. 100, 113, 115.

14. Yu, "China's Mass Communication," p. 36f.

15. Chen Dan, "Huiyi Jiefang ribao she de gongzuo" (Recollections of the work at the *Liberation Daily* ), *Xinwen yanjiu ziliao* 22 (1983): 18.

16. Dagang 17, p. 8.

17. Ibid., p. 9.

18. To illustrate how expensive a subscription to the *Liberation Daily* was, one can compare it to the salary of a staff reporter. They received one to three yuan a month.

19. Claire and William Band, *Two Years with the Chinese Communists* (New Haven, 1948), p. 256; *Jiefang ribao* (hereafter *JFRB*), May 16, 1941, p. 1.

20. Stein, *The Challenge of Red China*, p. 228.

21. I found that while news of the war in Europe and Asia were the lead stories on page 3, national news occupied the remainder of the page.

22. Dagang 17, p. 10; "Dashiji," p. 133.

23. After the reform, "Letters" were almost a daily feature on page 2.

24. "Dashiji," p. 166.

25. Later page 4 sections included "Comprehensive Reports" (April 1, 1942–November 19, 1946) and "Sunday Supplements" (November 20, 1946–March 15, 1947).

26. "Yan'an 'jiefang ribao' dagang" (An outline of Yan'an's *Liberation Daily*), *Xinwen yanjiu ziliao*, 18 (1983): 24. Hereafter Dagang 18.

27. Ibid., p. 26.

28. Ibid., p. 25.

29. Lu Dingyi, "Women duiyu xinwenxue de jiben guandian," *Zhongguo gongchandang xinwen gongzuo wenjian huibian*, 3:187–96. For a full translation of this article, see Womack, ed. *Media and the Chinese Public* (Armonk, NY, 1986), pp. 164–73. See also "Lu Dingyi tongzhi tan Yan'an Jiefang ribao gaiban" (Comrade Lu Dingyi discusses reform in Yan'an's *Liberation Daily*), *Xinwen yanjiu ziliao* 9 (1981): 1–8.

30. Chen, "Huiyi Jiefang ribao she de gongzuo," p. 15.

31. Dagang 18, pp. 44f, 47.

32. Ibid., p. 47.

33. Peter Seybolt argues that up to the time of Wang's speech at the Zedong School for Young Cadre, no one had so clearly and systematically set out Mao's claim to legitimacy. This was an odd capitulation from a man who had mounted

the most serious challenge to Mao's power in his 1932 tract. Ironically, "Further Bolshevization" was republished in 1940 at a time when Mao appeared to have prevailed over Wang Ming. According to Seybolt, at the Sixth Plenary Session of the Sixth Central Committee (October 1938), Mao called for a study campaign, saying "theoretical study is a condition of victory." Wang Ming and members of the Internationalists, many of whom had studied Marxist theory in Moscow, seized the initiative by creating a number of research associations to provide study materials. Wang Ming directed the Marxist-Leninist Research Association, which was probably responsible for republishing his 1932 tract. Two months after its reappearance, Wang repudiated "Further Bolshevization" and affirmed Mao's views in his speech at the cadre school. See Seybolt, "Tribute to a 'Crane Among Chickens,' " pp. 93–95.

34. Li Rui, a prominent journalist and an original staff member of the *Liberation Daily*, believes that Wang Ming and Bo Gu were not of the same mold even though they were members of a loosely defined group called the Internationalists. Li Rui interview with Christina Gilmartin, January 13, 1989, Harvard University.

35. "Dashiji," p. 133. For an example of Bo Gu's assessment of the newspaper made in 1944, see Bo Gu, "Dangbao jizhe yao zhuyi xie shemma wenti?" (To what problems should Party newspaper reporters pay attention?), *Zhongguo gongchandang xinwen gongzuo wenjian huibian*, 3:203–205. In it, Bo Gu said that the newspaper was the eyes and ears of the masses. Through it, Party leaders could understand conditions in the lower levels. The newspaper had two responsibilities: It received, analyzed, and criticized opinions for Party use, and it passed Party resolutions down to the masses (p. 203).

36. See "Zhongying dangxiao longzhong kaixue" (Central Committee's Party school ceremoniously begins study), February 2, 1942, p. 3.

37. The March 13, 1942, edition published a list of those writing editorials. They were Xie Juezai, Lin Zhe, Ye Jianying, Wang Jiaxiang, Kai Feng, Lu Dingyi, Kang Sheng, Peng Zhen, Ren Bishi, Qiao Mu, and Yao Tuofu. Chances of this illustrious group producing what Yang wanted were slim. Their other duties undoubtedly occupied the majority of their time. See "Dashiji," p. 142; Wang, *Mao's Betrayal*, pp. 55, 122–23, 147.

38. "Dashiji," p. 139; Chen, "Huiyi Jiefang ribao she de gongzuo," p. 14.

39. Wylie, *The Emergence of Maoism*, p. 180f.

40. Dagang 17, p. 15.

41. "Zhong xuanbu wei gaizao dangbao de tongzhi" (Notification of reform in the party's newspaper from the central propaganda bureau), *Zhongguo gongchandang xinwen gongzuo wenjian huibian*, 1:126–27.

42. "Dashiji," p. 144.

43. Li Rui believes that Bo Gu's self-criticism was heartfelt. Li Rui interview.

44. "Dashiji," p. 144f.

45. Articles on reforms in the *Liberation Daily* ran for two years. Examples: (1) "Lun women de baozhi" (Our newspaper), by Lenin, July 20, 1942, p. 4; (2) "Baozhi he xin de wenfeng" (The newspaper and the new style of writing), August 4, 1942, editorial; (3) "Zhankai tongxunyuan de gongzuo" (Expanding communications workers' work), August 25, 1942, editorial [Note: Page 1 of this edition is missing]; (4)"Jianquan women de tongxunwang" (Perfecting our communication network), by Yang Pingzhen, September 1, 1942, p. 2 [Note:

Page 2 of this edition is missing]; (5) "Dang yu dangbao" (The Party and the Party's newspaper), September 22, 1942, editorial; (6) "Gei dangbao de jizhe he tongxunyuan" (For the benefit of reporters and communication workers), November 17, 1942, editorial; (7) "Zhengzhi yu jishu-dangbao gongzuozhong de yige zhongyao wenti" (Politics and technique—a serious problem in newspaper work), June 10, 1943, p. 1; (8)"Benbao chuangkan yiqianqi" (Newspaper's first 1,000 issues), February 16, 1944, editorial.

46. Cheek, "Orthodoxy and Dissent," p. 103.

47. Ibid., pp. 104, 116. Quotation is from p. 104.

48. Wang Jing, "Chen Kehan," p. 120.

59. Dagang 18, p. 35.

50. The Topical Survey lists Mao, Zhou Enlai, and Zhu De as authors. Liu Shaoqi's articles are cited in chapter 2. Only Mao and Liu remained above criticism during rectification. Both Zhou and Zhu (along with Ren Bishi, Deng Fa, and Peng Dehuai) were charged with "empiricism and dogmatism" during rectification. See Wang, *Mao's Betrayal*, p. 147.

51. Yue Songdong and Wang Fengchao, comps., "Yan'an 'Jiefang ribao' dashiji" (continued), *Xinwen yanjiu ziliao* 27 (1984): 84. Hereafter "Dashiji, cont."

52. "Zhonggong zhongying xibeiju guanyu 'Jiefang ribao' gongzuo wenti de jueding" (pp. 132–34) and "Zhonggong zhongying xibeiju guanyu 'Jiefang ribao' jige wenti de tongzhi" (pp. 141–44), both in *Zhongong gongchandang xinwen gongzuo wenjian huibian*, vol. 1.

53. Lu had worked in propaganda since the mid-1920s when he headed the Communist Youth League's propaganda office and edited the League's magazine. He continued that work in the Jiangxi Soviet and during the Long March before becoming director of the Red Army's propaganda department in 1936. When the Eighth Route Army was formed in 1937, he took charge of its propaganda work. He became director of the Party's propaganda department after 1949 and had the distinction of publicly announcing the Hundred Flowers Campaign in May 1956. See Howard L. Boorman, ed. *Biographical Dictionary of Republican China* (New York, 1967), 2:453; Wang, *Mao's Betrayal*, p. 137.

54. Chen, "Huiyi Jiefang ribao she de gongzuo," p. 13.

55. "Dashiji," p. 162f.

56. Chen, "Huiyi Jiefang ribao she de gongzuo," p. 14.

57. Dagang 18, p. 39.

58. "Dashiji," pp. 141, 150.

59. Dagang 18, p. 44.

60. "Dashiji," p. 159.

61. Mao Tse-tung, "A Talk to the Editorial Staff of the *Shansi [Shanxi]-Suiyuan Daily*," 4:243. This idea saw a comeback in the Cultural Revolution. See Liu, "PRC," p. 38.

62. Wang Ming claims that between 50 and 60,000 people were killed during rectification. See Wang, *Mao's Betrayal*, p. 150.

63. Dagang 18, p. 44.

64. Ibid., p. 45f. I found no record of such meetings or how many of the resident staff were Party members.

65. "Zhong xuanbu wei gaizao dangbao de tongzhi" (Notification that the

central propaganda bureau is reforming the Party newspaper), *Zhonguo gong-chandang xinwen gongzuo wenjian huibian*, 1:126–27.

66. Dagang 17, p. 18.

67. Dagang 18, p. 41.

68. "Benbao chuangkan yiqianqi" (The newspaper's initial 1,000 issues), February 16, 1944, editorial.

69. Communications workers criticized management, arguing that *Liberation Daily* editors failed to return submitted manuscripts and paid no attention to helping young writers prepare or revise their contributions. They only directed them to write. See Dagang 18, p. 36.

70. Lu Dingyi, "Women duiyu xinwenxue de jiben guandian," pp. 187–96. For examples see articles by Hu Jiwei on editors (August 24, 1945), Wang Yi on international news (March 5, 1943), Ji Cang on 1942 misprints (April 8, 1943), Mu Qing on style and form (July 23, 1944), and Liu Wenyi on transmissions (January 26, 1943, March 5, 1943).

71. My own survey found that with generous exceptions, war news continued to take first place on pages 1 and 3.

72. Dagang 17, p. 17f.

73. Ibid., p. 18; "Dashiji," p. 105.

74. "Dashiji," pp. 165–68.

75. Dagang 18, p. 27.

76. Feuerwerker, *Ding Ling's Fiction*, pp. 10, 107.

77. For a translation of that speech see Andrew Watson, *Mao Zedong and the Political Economy of the Border Region* (Cambridge, 1980).

78. Dagang 17, p. 27.

79. See Patricia Stranahan, "Labor Heroines of Yan'an," *Modern China* 9, 2 (April 1983): 228–52.

80. Mao, "A Talk to the Editorial Staff," p. 245.

81. This issue is missing from the *Liberation Daily*, so the article could not be checked. However, because several sources cite the date and discuss the contents, I use it as an example.

82. Wang Jing, "Chen Kehan," p. 120.

83. Wang Fengchao, "Yan'an 'Jiefang ribao' de diyipian shehui tiwen ji qi yingxiang" (Yan'an's *Liberation Daily*'s first social news and its influence], *Xinwen yanjiu ziliao* 11 (1982): 84. See "Benshi Bai Jiaping wushen Yang Hanzhu" (This city's Bai Jiaping and shaman Yang Hanzhu), by Mu Qing, April 29, 1944, p. 1; and "Kaizhan fandui wushen de douzheng" (Launch the struggle to oppose shamans), by Lu Dingyi, April 29, 1944, editorial.

84. Examples include Gunther Steins's *The Challenge of Red China*, Harrison Forman's *Report from Red China*, Huang Yanpei's *Yan'an guilai* (Return to Yan'an), Jin Dongping's *Yan'an jianwen lu* (Report from Yan'an), and Zhao Chaoyou's *Yan'an yi yue* (A month in Yan'an).

85. See, for example, the two editorials by Mao Zedong on July 12, 1943, and October 5, 1943.

86. Dagang 18, p. 42; "Dashiji, cont.," p. 113. The departure of Lu did not mean that Mao lost his representative on the *Liberation Daily*. Ai Siqi was the leading member of Mao's personal "think tank," which included Ai Siqi, Zhou Yang, Zhang Ruxin, and Chen Boda. See Wylie, *The Emergence of Maoism*, p. 7. For an analysis

of Ai Siqi's contribution to Maoism see Joshua A. Fogel, *Ai Ssu-ch'i's [Ai Siqi] Contribution to the Development of Marxism* (Cambridge, 1987).

87. Dagang 18, p. 42.

88. Ibid.

89. "Dashiji," continued, p. 102; Zhou Disheng, "Jiefang ribao cheli Yan'an qianhou" (The entire story of the *Liberation Daily*'s evacuation of Yan'an), *Xinwen yanjiu ziliao* 27 (1984): 122.

90. Bo Gu died in the crash of an American transport plane carrying him, Deng Fa, Ye Ting (and family), Wang Ruofei, and several Americans from Chongqing to Yan'an on April 8, 1946. See Pantsov, "Life Given to the Struggle for Freedom," p. 129.

91. Dagang 18, p. 43.

92. Ibid., p. 21; "Dashiji, cont.," p. 118.

93. Dagang 18, pp. 21–23.

## Chapter Two

1. Terms commonly used for purge are "qingchu" (weed out), "qingxi" (get rid of), and "suqing" (eradicate). All are terms of retribution and punishment, which generally resulted in expulsion from cadre ranking. Frederick C. Teiwes, *Politics and Purges in China* (White Plains, 1979), pp. 10–11, 16–17.

2. Warren Kuo, *Analytical History of the Chinese Communist Party*, Book 4 (Taipei, 1971), p. 563.

3. Wylie, *The Emergence of Maoism*, p. 164.

4. Wang, *Mao's Betrayal*, p. 55.

5. Timothy Cheek, "The Fading of Wild Lilies: Wang Shiwei and Mao Zedong's 'Yan'an Talks' in the First [CCP] Rectification Movement," *The Australian Journal of Chinese Affairs* 11(1984), p. 37.

6. Teiwes, *Politics and Purges*, pp. 59, 66.

7. Ibid., pp. 60–63.

8. Ibid., pp. 64, 66; Wylie, *The Emergence of Maoism*, p. 59f.

9. Wylie, *The Emergence of Maoism*, pp. 160, 164.

10. By "foreign formalism" opponents of the Internationalists meant that they continually wrote about their experiences in the Soviet Union rather than illustrating points with Chinese examples understandable to native audiences. See Teiwes, *Politics and Purges*, p. 68.

11. The full text of the February 1 speech is found in the April 27, 1942, *Liberation Daily*, p. 1; the February 2, 1942 editorial discusses the speech. Boyd Compton, in *Mao's China: Party Reform Documents, 1942–1944* (Seattle, 1966), pp. 9–32, translates the speech. The full text of the second speech is found in the June 18, 1942, *Liberation Daily*, pp. 1 and 2; translated in Compton, pp. 33–53. On April 3, 1942, the Central Committee announced rectification would begin at all levels of the Party. A full text of that announcement is found in the April 7, 1942, *Liberation Daily*; translated in Compton, pp. 3–8.

Boyd Compton's *Mao's China* is a translation of twenty-one of the twenty-seven documents found in *Zhengfeng wenxian* (Zhengfeng documents) (N.p.: Jiefang, 1944). *Zhengfeng wenxian* was the official handbook for study and discussion.

12. Cheek, "The Fading of Wild Lilies," pp. 26, 30–33.

13. After the fall of the Gang of Four, the government sought advice from intellectuals, the scientific community, etc., in a similar manner. These writers used the critical essay, which was then praised for playing a positive role. It was still a method for criticizing the shortcomings of the Party. See Merle Goldman, *China's Intellectuals: Advise and Dissent* (Cambridge, 1981), p. 234.

14. Timothy Cheek argues that Deng Tuo, not Mao, argued these same ideas as early as February 1939. See Cheek, "Orthodoxy and Dissent," p. 106.

Mao's May 1942 speeches were not published in the *Liberation Daily* until October 19, 1943, in commemoration of Lu Xun's death. See "Zai Yan'an wenyi zuotanhuishang de jianghua" (Talks at the Yan'an conference on literature and art), October 19, 1943, pp. 1, 2, 4. For a translation see Bonnie S. McDougall, *Mao Zedong's "Talks at the Yan'an Conference on Literature and Art": A Translation of the 1943 Text and Commentary* (Ann Arbor, 1980), pp. 55–86.

15. Wang Ming later accused Mao of trying to convert the Chinese revolutionary writers into "court scribes singing the praises of 'Maoism' and Mao's person, into trumpeters and drummers who could create a cult of his personality." See Wang, *Mao's Betrayal*, p. 114.

16. Cheek, "The Fading of Wild Lilies," p. 34.

17. Ibid., pp. 32, 37.

18. Wylie, *The Emergence of Maoism*, pp. 147–151; Cheek, "The Fading of Wild Lilies," p. 28; Dagang 18, p. 28.

19. Cheek, "The Fading of Wild Lilies," pp. 26, 39. The quote is from p. 26.

20. Ibid., p. 43f. Many believe that Wang's experience left him mentally unbalanced. Stricken from the Party rolls, he did reform through labor, apparently making match boxes. He was executed in 1946. See *Liberation Daily*, April 12, 1946, p. 1.

21. "Mao Zedong tongzhi kouhao zhengfeng sanfeng yao liyong baozhi" (Comrade Mao Zedong's slogan: We must use the newspaper to rectify the three styles). April 12, 1942, p. 1. See also *Zhongguo gongchandang diyici zhengfeng yundong de weida shengli* (Important victory of the Chinese Communist Party's first rectification movement) (hereafter *Weida Shengli*) (Changchun, 1957), p. 21; "Dao duzhe" (To the reader), April 1, 1942. See related articles, p. 2.

22. Teiwes, *Politics and Purges*, p. 71. For a full discussion of the counterrevolutionary campaign, see Peter J. Seybolt, "Terror and Conformity," *Modern China* 12, 1 (January 1986): 39–73.

23. Wang, *Mao's Betrayal*, p. 120.

24. Teiwes, *Politics and Purges*, p. 71. Liu Shaoqi was a leading force in this campaign. His key role cemented an alliance between him and Mao that had been developing since they joined forces in the united front discussions of 1937–38.

25. Ibid., p. 78.

26. *Weida Shengli*; "Dashiji"; *Yan'an zhengfeng yundong* (Beijing: Zhonggong zhongying dangxiao chubanshe, 1984.

27. Fogel, *Ai Ssu-chi*, p. 84; Wylie, *The Emergence of Maoism*, p. 7.

28. The special issues appeared on April 10, 11, 12, 13, 18, and 20.

29. Groups devised their own plans for studying the articles. See *Liberation Daily* articles on May 3, 1942 (p. 2), May 6, 1942 (p. 2), and June 16, 1942 (p. 2), for examples of various plans.

30. Klein and Clark, *Biographic Dictionary*, p. 425f. For a recent study of Kang Sheng see Roger Faligot and Remi Kauffer, *Kang Sheng et les services secrets Chinois* (Kang Sheng and the Chinese Secret Service) (Paris: Robert Laffont, 1987).

31. Lowell Dittmer, *Liu Shao-ch'i [Shaoqi] and the Chinese Cultural Revolution* (Berkeley, 1974), pp. 17–29.

32. Teiwes, *Politics and Purges*, p. 70; Wylie, *The Emergence of Maoism*, p. 228f; Andrew Watson, *Mao Zedong and the Political Economy of the Border Region* (Cambridge, 1980), p. 1f.; Mark Selden, *The Yenan Way in Revolutionary China* (Cambridge, 1971), pp. 237, 244.

33. Harrison, *The Long March to Power*, p. 340f.; quote from Klein and Clark, *Biographic Dictionary*, p. 432.

34. Wylie, *The Emergence of Maoism*, pp. 193f.; White and Jacoby, *Thunder Out of China*, p. 229f.

35. Wylie argues that Chen's research into economic matters was probably useful to Mao when he wrote on the political economy of the Border Region later that year. Chen's interest was more historical and theoretical than Mao's. See *The Emergence of Maoism*, pp. 177, 315. For a translation of Mao's writing on the economy of the Border Region, see Watson, *Mao Zedong*.

36. Klein and Clark, *Biographic Dictionary*, p. 122f.

37. For a discussion of this essay, see Feuerwerker, *Ding Ling's Fiction*, p. 101.

## Conclusion

1. Jacques Marcuse, The Peking Papers (New York, 1967), p. 109.

2. Liu, "PRC," p. 40.

3. MacFarquhar, "A Visit to the Chinese Press," *China Quarterly* 53 (January–March 1973): 146.

4. Marcuse, *The Peking Papers*, p. 109

5. MacFarquhar, "A Visit to the Chinese Press," p. 148. Once again a shortage of newsprint seems to be the culprit for the small print runs.

6. Marcuse, *The Peking Papers*, p. 109f.

7. Ibid., pp. 97, 102.

8. Liu, *Communications and National Integration*, pp. 33, 52; Womack, *Media and the Chinese Public*, p. 23.

9. MacFarquhar, "A Visit to the Chinese Press," p. 149.

10. Ibid., pp. 145, 149.

11. Ibid., p. 145f.

12. Liu, "PRC," p. 52; Liu, *Communications and National Integration*, p. xiii.

13. Quotation is from Timothy Cheek, "Redefining Propaganda: Debates on the Role of Journalism in Post-Mao China," *Issues and Studies* 25, 2 (February, 1989): 56. The author notes that this is a shockingly frank definition.

14. John Lawrence, "China Daily News," *The Australian Journal of Chinese Affairs* 8 (1982): 147–49.

15. Teiwes, *Politics and Purges*, p. 608. I am grateful to Timothy Cheek for his ideas on this subject in correspondence dated August 31, 1989.

# Bibliography

## Chinese and Japanese Sources

Chen Dan. "Huiyi Jiefang ribao she de gongzuo" (Recollections of the work at the *Liberation Daily* ), *Xinwen yanjiu ziliao* (News research materials) 22 (1983): 12–23.

Huang Yanpei. *Yan'an guilai* (Return to Yan'an). Dairen: Dazhong shudian, 1946.

Jia Shaoqin. "1936 nian Xi'an faxing de Jiefang ribao" (The 1936 *Liberation Daily* published in Xi'an), *Xinwen yanjiu ziliao* 24 (1984): 204–208.

*Jiefang ribao* (Liberation daily). Yan'an: n.p., 1941–1947.

Jin Dongpin. *Yan'an jianwen lu* (Report from Yan'an). Chongqing: Duli chubanshe, 1945.

"*Kaihō nippō*" *kiji mokuroku* (Index to the *Liberation Daily*). 3 vols. Tokyo: Kindai Chūgoku kenkyū i-inkai, 1967.

Li Rui. *Yaodong zashu* (Mixed narrations from a cave dwelling). Changsha: Remin chubanshe, 1981.

"Lu Dingyi tongzhi tan Yan'an Jiefang ribao gaiban" (Comrade Lu Dingyi discusses reform in the Yan'an *Liberation Daily*), *Xinwen yanjiu ziliao* 8 (1981): 1–8.

*Tantan baozhi gongzuo* (Discussing newspaper work). Beijing: Xinwen yanjiu-suo, 1978.

Wang Fengchao. "Yan'an 'Jiefang ribao' de diyipian shehui xinwen ji qi yingxiang" (Yan'an's *Liberation Daily*'s first social news and its influence), *Xinwen yanjiu ziliao* 11 (1982): 84–88.

Wang Fengchao and Yue Songdong, comps. "Yan'an 'Jiefang ribao' dashiji" (Great events in Yan'an's *Liberation Daily*), *Xinwen yanjiu ziliao* 26 (1984): 125–75.

Wang Jing. "Chen Kehan tongzhi tan Yan'an 'Jiefang ribao' " (Comrade Chen Kehan discusses Yan'an's *Liberation Daily*), *Xinwen yanjiu ziliao* 26 (1984): 115–24.

"Yan'an 'Jiefang ribao' dagang" (An outline of the *Liberation Daily*), *Xinwen yanjiu ziliao* 18 (1983): 18–47.

"Yan'an 'Jiefang ribao shi' dagang" (An outline of the history of Yan'an's *Liberation Daily*), *Xinwen yanjiu ziliao* 17 (1983): 5–47.

Yan'an zhengfeng yundong (Yan'an's rectification movement). Beijing: Zhonggong zhongying xuexiao chubanshe, 1984.

*Yan'an zhengfeng yundong jishi* (A chronology of the Yan'an rectification movement). Beijing: Qiushi chubanshe, 1982.

Yue Songdong and Wang Fengchao, comp. "Yan'an 'Jiefang ribao' dashiji," *Xinwen yanjiu ziliao* 26 (1984), 125–175.

———. "Yan'an 'Jiefang ribao' dashiji." (Great events in Yan'an's *Liberation Daily*), *Xinwen yanjiu ziliao* 27 (1984): 74–119.

Zhao Chaogou. *Yan'an yi yue* (A month in Yan'an). Nanjing: Xinmin baoshe, 1946.

Zhao Disheng. "Jiefang ribao cheli Yan'an qianhou" (The entire story of the *Liberation Daily*'s evacuation from Yan'an), *Xinwen yanjiu ziliao* 27 (1984): 121–27.

*Zhongguo gongchandang diyici zhengfeng yundong de weida shengli* (The great victory of the CCP's first rectification movement). Changchun: Jilin Renmin chubanshe, 1957.

*Zhongguo gongchandang xinwen gongzuo wenjian huibian* (Compilation of documents on journalism in the CCP). Vols. 1 and 3. Beijing: Xinhua chubanshe, 1980.

## English Sources

Band, Claire and William. *Two Years with the Chinese Communists*. New Haven: Yale University Press, 1948.

Benton, Gregor. "The 'Second Wang Ming Line' (1935–38)," *China Quarterly* 61 (March 1975): 93–106.

———. "The Yenan Opposition," *New Left Review* 92 (July–August 1975): 93–106.

Boorman, Howard L., ed. *Biographical Dictionary of Republican China*. Vol. 1. New York: Columbia University Press, 1967.

Cell, Charles P. *Revolution at Work: Mobilization Campaigns in China*. New York: Academic Press, 1977.

Chang Kuo-t'ao. *The Rise of the Chinese Communist Party, 1928–1938*. Vol. 2. Lawrence, Kansas: University Press of Kansas, 1972.

Cheek, Timothy. "The Fading of Wild Lilies: Wang Shiwei and Mao Zedong's 'Yan'an Talks' in the First CPC Rectification Movement," *The Australian Journal of Chinese Affairs* 11 (1984): 25–58.

———. "Orthodoxy and Dissent in People's China: The Life and Death of Deng Tuo (1912–1966)." Ph.D. Dissertation, Harvard University, 1986.

———. "Redefining Propaganda: Debates on the Role of Journalism in Post-Mao China," *Issues and Studies* 25, 2 (February 1989): 47–74.

Chiu, Leonard L. "Press Criticism and Self-criticism in Communist China: An Analysis of Its Ideology, Structure and Operation," *Gazette* 31 (1983): 47–61.

Chu, Godwin C. "Popular Media: A Glimpse of the New Chinese Culture." In *Popular Media in China: Shaping New Cultural Patterns*, edited by Godwin C. Chu. Honolulu: University Press of Hawaii, 1978.

———. *Radical Change Through Communication in Mao's China*. Honolulu: University Press of Hawaii, 1977.

Compton, Boyd. *Mao's China: Party Reform Documents, 1942–1944*. Seattle: University of Washington Press, 1966.

Curran, James, Michael Gurevitch, and Janet Woollacott, eds. *Mass Communication and Society*. Beverly Hills: Sage Publications, 1977.

Dittmer, Lowell. *Liu Shao-ch'i and the Chinese Revolution*. Berkeley: University of California Press, 1974.

Dorrill, William F. "Transfer of Legitimacy in the Chinese Communist Party:

Origins of the Maoist Myth." In *Party Leadership and Revolutionary Power in China*, edited by John Wilson Lewis. Cambridge: Cambridge University Press, 1970.

Engwall, Lars. *Newspapers as Organizations*. Westmead: Saxon House, 1978.

Feuerwerker, Yi-tsi Mei. *Ding Ling's Fiction*. Cambridge: Harvard University Press, 1982.

Fogel, Joshua A. *Ai Ssu-ch'i's Contribution to the Development of Marxism*. Cambridge: Harvard Contemporary China Series no. 4, 1987.

Forman, Harrison. *Report from Red China*. New York: Whittlesey House, 1945.

Gans, Herbert J. *Deciding What's News*. New York: Pantheon Books, 1979.

Garver, John W. *Chinese-Soviet Relations 1937–1945*. New York: Oxford University Press, 1988.

———. "The Origins of the Second United Front: the Comintern and the CCP," *China Quarterly* 113 (March 1988): 29–59.

George, Alexander L. *Propaganda Analysis*. White Plains: Row, Peterson and Co., 1959.

Goldman, Merle. *China's Intellectuals: Advise and Dissent*. Cambridge: Harvard University Press, 1981.

———. *Literary Dissent in Communist China*. New York: Atheneum, 1971.

Harrison, James Pinckney. *The Long March to Power*. New York: Praeger Publishers, 1972.

Inkeles, Alex. *Public Opinion in Soviet Russia*. Cambridge: Harvard University Press, 1967.

Irwin, Will. *Propaganda and the News*. New York: Whittlesey House, 1936.

Jowett, Garth S., and Victoria O'Donnell. *Propaganda and Persuasion*. Newbury Park: Sage Publications, 1986.

Kenez, Peter. *The Birth of the Propaganda State: Soviet Methods of Mass Mobilization, 1917–1929*. Cambridge: Cambridge University Press, 1985.

Klein, Donald W., and Anne B. Clark. *Biographic Dictionary of Chinese Communism, 1921–1965*. Cambridge: Harvard University Press, 1971.

Kuo, Warren. *Analytical History of the Chinese Communist Party*. Book 4. Taipei: Institute of International Relations, Republic of China, 1971.

Lawrence, John. "China Daily News," *The Australian Journal of Chinese Affairs* 8 (1982): 147–51.

Lent, John A. "Freedom of the Press in East Asia." In *Newspapers in Asia*, edited by John A. Lent. Hong Kong: Heinemann Educational Books, 1982.

———. "The Press Since Mao." In *Newspapers in Asia*, edited by John A. Lent. Hong Kong: Heinemann Educational Books, 1982.

Lerner, Daniel. "Effective Propaganda: Conditions and Evaluation." In *The Process and Effects of Mass Communications*, edited by Wilbur Schramm. Urbana: University of Illinois Press, 1954.

Li Rui. Interview with Christina Gilmartin, January 13, 1989, Harvard University.

Lindsay, Michael. *Notes on Educational Problems in Communist China, 1941–1947*. New York: Institute of Pacific Relations, 1950.

Liu, Alan P. L. *Communications and National Integration in Communist China*. Berkeley: University of California Press, 1971.

———. "People's Republic of China." In *Newspapers in Asia*, edited by John A. Lent. Hong Kong: Heinemann Educational Books, 1982.

————. "Problems in Communication in China's Modernization," *Asian Survey* 22, 5 (May 1982): 481–99.

Liu Shaoqi. *Three Essays on Party Building*. Beijing: Foreign Language Press, 1980.

McDougall, Bonnie S. *Mao Zedong's "Talks at the Yan'an Conference on Literature and Art": A Translation of the 1943 Text with Commentary*. Ann Arbor: Center for Chinese Studies, University of Michigan, 1980.

MacFarquhar, Roderick. "A Visit to the Chinese Press," *China Quarterly* 53 (January–March 1973): 144–52.

Mao Tse-tung (Zedong). "A Talk to the Editorial Staff of the *Shansi-Suiyuan Daily*." In *Selected Works*. Vol. 4. Peking: Foreign Language Press, 1969.

Marcuse, Jacques. *The Peking Papers*. New York: E. P. Dutton, 1967.

Pantsov, A. "Life Given to the Struggle for Freedom," *Far Eastern Affairs* 1 (1983): 122–29.

Pye, Lucien W., ed. *Communications and Political Development*. Princeton: Princeton University Press, 1963.

Schiller, Dan. *Objectivity and the News*. Philadelphia: University of Pennsylvania Press, 1981.

Schram, Stuart T. *The Political Thought of Mao Tse-tung*. New York: Praeger, 1963.

Schramm, Wilbur, ed. *Mass Communications*. Urbana: University of Illinois Press, 1960.

Schramm, Wilbur and Daniel Lerner, eds. *Communication and Change: The Last Ten Years and the Next*. Honolulu: The University Press of Hawaii, 1976.

Schurmann, Franz. *Ideology and Organization in Communist China*. Berkeley: University of California Press, 1968.

Selden, Mark. *The Yenan Way in Revolutionary China*. Cambridge: Harvard University Press, 1971.

Seybolt, Peter J. "Terror and Conformity," *Modern China* 12, 1 (January 1986): 39–73.

————. "Tribute to a 'Crane Among Chickens': Wang Ming's Capitulation to Mao Zedong," *East Asia Insight*, 93–106.

Shum, Kui-kwong. *The Chinese Communists' Road to Power: The Anti-Japanese National United Front 1935–1945*. New York: Oxford University Press, 1988.

Stein, Gunther. *The Challenge of Red China*. New York: McGraw Hill Book Co., Inc., 1945.

Stewart, Ian, "The Paper That Spreads the Cult of Mao," *New York Times Magazine*, December 18, 1966, 66.

Stranahan, Patricia. "Labor Heroines of Yan'an," *Modern China* 9, 2 (April 1983): 228–52.

————. *Yan'an Women and the Communist Party*. Berkeley: Center for Chinese Studies, Research Monograph no. 26, 1983.

Sullivan, Lawrence R. "Communist Party in the Shanghai Underground: 1931–34," *China Quarterly* 101 (1985): 78–97.

Teiwes, Frederick C. *Politics and Purges in China*. White Plains: M. E. Sharpe, Inc., 1979.

Thomas, S. Bernard. *Labor and the Chinese Revolution*. Ann Arbor: University of Michigan Press, 1983.

Ting, Lee-hsia Hsu. *Government Control of the Press in Modern China, 1900–*

*1949*. Cambridge: Harvard University East Asia Monograph Series, 1974.

Tuchman, Gaye. *Making News: A Study in the Construction of Reality.* New York: The Free Press, 1978.

Wang Ming. *Mao's Betrayal.* Moscow: Progress Publishers, 1979.

Watson, Andrew, ed. *Mao Zedong and the Political Economy of the Border Region.* Cambridge: Cambridge University Press, 1980.

White, Lynn T., III. "Local Newspapers and Community Change, 1949–1969." In *Moving a Mountain: Cultural Change in China*, edited by Godwin C. Chu and Francis L. K. Hsu. Honolulu: University Press of Hawaii, 1979.

White, Theodore and Annalee Jacoby. *Thunder Out of China.* New York: Da Capo Press, 1984.

Womack, Brantley, ed. *Media and the Chinese Public.* Armonk: M. E. Sharpe, 1986.

Wylie, Raymond F. *The Emergence of Maoism.* Stanford: Stanford University Press, 1980.

Yu, Frederick T. C. "China's Mass Communication in Historial Perspective." In *Moving a Mountain: Cultural Change in China*, edited by Godwin C. Chu and Francis L. K. Hsu. Honolulu: University Press of Hawaii, 1979.

———. *Mass Persuasion in Communist China.* New York: Frederick A. Praeger, 1964.

**Patricia Stranahan** received her Ph.D. in oriental studies from the University of Pennsylvania. At present she is an associate professor of history at Texas A&M University.

For Product Safety Concerns and Information please contact our
EU representative GPSR@taylorandfrancis.com Taylor & Francis
Verlag GmbH, Kaufingerstraße 24, 80331 München, Germany